14. 00

**NEW EDITION**

# Business Basics

## Student's Book

**OXFORD**
UNIVERSITY PRESS

# Unit 1 | You and your company

## 1.1 People in business

| Grammar | Present simple |
| --- | --- |
| | The verb *be* |
| Vocabulary | Daily activities |
| Communication skills | Introductions |
| Pronunciation | Alphabet |

### A Listening

Lorella Braglia

Lorella Braglia is a designer. She lives in the North of Italy between Milan and Bologna. Her company makes clothes, which sell all over the world.

**1** Two journalists are talking about Lorella. Listen and write down the information.

Name ............ *Lorella Braglia* ............................................................

Nationality ......... *Italian* .....................................................................

Home ................................................................................................

Age ...................................................................................................

Company ...........................................................................................

Job ....................................................................................................

Languages ........................................................................................

**2** Listen again. Complete these sentences.

1  Her name ............. Lorella Braglia.

2  She ............. in Reggio Emilia.

3  She ............. a designer.

4  She ............. for Dielle.

5  Her husband ............. the Marketing Director.

6  They ............. Italian.

7  They ............. English and Italian.

8  They ............. together.

### B Speaking

**1** Ask a partner these three questions. Write down the answers. Then ask other people.

Name ......................................................

Nationality ......................................................

Job ......................................................

**2** Now tell the class about the people you talked to.

e.g. *Her name is Gabrielle. She is French. She is a teacher.*

**The verb *be***

1 The verb *be* is irregular and is often contracted. We use it to talk about age, nationality, job, and status.

*I'm (I am) Italian.*          *She's (she is) married.*
*You're (you are) my line manager.*   *They're (they are) German.*
*He's (he is) thirty.*         *We're (we are) both engineers.*

2 To make a question with the verb *be* we invert the subject and the verb.

*Are you married?*          *Yes, I am.*
*Is she American?*          *No, she isn't.*
*What is his job and where is he from?*   *He is a designer. He's from Greece.*

## C Reading

1 Look at the article about Lorella Braglia. Complete the article using the verbs in the box. The first letter of each verb is given.

| | | | | | | |
|---|---|---|---|---|---|---|
| makes | designs | employs | eat | live | works | do |
| produces | travel | presents | plays | uses | are | play | is |

# Dielle

Lorella Braglia .i.................... ¹ the founder of Dielle, and also the main designer. Her husband, Danilo, .w.................... ² for the company as Marketing Director. Lorella .d.................... ³ two collections every year and .p.................... ⁴ them at fashion shows in London, Paris, and New York.

Dielle .m.................... ⁵ everything in Italy, and .u.................... ⁶ very modern equipment in its workshops. The company .e.................... ⁷ the services of seventy workshops in and around Reggio Emilia. It .p.................... ⁸ 100,000 units per year. Lorella and her husband .l.................... ⁹ in a house in the centre of Reggio Emilia, not far from the office. They .a.................... ¹⁰ not often there, because they both .t.................... ¹¹ a lot. How do they relax? 'I .d.................... ¹² yoga and Danilo .p.................... ¹³ golf,' says Lorella. At the weekends they .p.................... ¹⁴ golf together and .e.................... ¹⁵ out at local restaurants with their children.

2 Listen to the first part of the passage (up to 8). How is the final *s* of the verbs pronounced – /s/, /z/, or /ɪz/?

/s/ as in *likes* ..................................................................................................

/z/ as in *plays* ..................................................................................................

/ɪz/ as in *uses* ..................................................................................................

3 Listen again and check. Read the passage aloud, paying particular attention to the pronunciation of the verb endings.

## The present simple

1 When we talk about regular actions or permanent states we use the present simple tense.

*I work for Dielle.*          *We speak English and French.*
*You live in London.*          *They travel a lot.*

2 We add *s* to the end of the verb in the third person singular (*he, she,* or *it*).

*He plays golf.*          *It takes two hours to get to work.*
*She works at home.*          *She knows a lot about computers.*

**D Pronunciation**

**1** Listen to the alphabet in English. Write the letters in the correct sound groups, as in the examples.

| /eɪ/ | /iː/ | /e/ | /əʊ/ | /aɪ/ | /uː/ | /ɑː/ |
|------|------|-----|------|------|------|------|
| A | B | F | O | I | Q | R |
| H | C | L | | | | |
| | | | | | | |
| | | | | | | |
| | | | | | | |

**2** Listen again and check your answers. Practise saying the letters aloud.

**3** Work with a partner. Spell your company's or school's name, your town, and your address.

**4** Now say the following. What do the letters stand for?

**E Listening**

Listen to the following dialogues and write the letters you hear.

1 ...*BA*...          3 ............          5 ............          7 ............

2 ............          4 ............          6 ............          8 ............

**F Speaking**

**1** Listen to this interview and complete the notes below.

Name ......................................................

Company ......................................................

Job ......................................................

Nationality ......................................................

Home ......................................................

**2** Listen to the following questions and reply.

e.g. What is your job?          *I'm a …*

## LANGUAGE NOTE

**Meeting someone for the first time**

**1  Introducing yourself**

*Let me introduce myself. My name's ...*
*Hello. I'm ...*

*How do you do? Pleased to meet you.*
*Nice to meet you.*

**2  Introducing another person**

*Let me introduce you to ...*
*This is my colleague ...*
*Nice to meet you.*

*How do you do?* or *Nice / Pleased to meet you.*
*Nice to meet you too.*

**3  Other questions**

*Where are you from?*
*What do you do?*
*Who do you work for?*

*I'm from ... (but I work in ...)*
*I'm a ... What about you?*
*I work for ... And you?*

## G  Listening

**Sally Kent**

**Simon Hastings**

**Alessandra Boni**

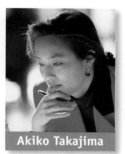
**Akiko Takajima**

**1** Sally Kent is the editor of *Business Monthly* magazine. She introduces Simon Hastings to two other people. Listen and fill in the gaps in the table below.

| A | B | C | D |
|---|---|---|---|
| Sally Kent | Simon Hastings | Alessandra Boni | Akiko Takajima |
| American | British | *Italian* .................. 3 | .................. 6 |
| editor | .................. 1 | .................. 4 | .................. 7 |
| *Business Monthly* | .................. 2 | *SAP* .................. 5 | .................. 8 |

**2** What expressions do A, B, C, D use to make introductions? Listen again and fill in the gaps.

A: Alessandra, ............. ............. ............. [1] you to my colleague, Simon Hastings.

B: How ............. ............. ............. ?[2] Pleased to ............. [3] you.

C: How ............. ............. ............. ?[4]

B: Do you work here, Alessandra?

C: No, I work for SAP. I'm a consultant. ............. ............. [5] my colleague Akiko Takajima.

D: Nice ............. ............. ............. .[6]

B: Nice ............. ............. ............. ............. [7] , Akiko. Where are you from?

D: I'm from Osaka, in Japan.

B: Where do you work?

D: I work for SAP in Frankfurt. I'm a ............. ............. .[8] And you?

B: I'm ............. ............. . ............. ............. [9] here at *Business Monthly*. Sally's my boss.

# 1.2 Talking about your company

| Grammar | Present simple question forms |
| --- | --- |
| | Present simple negative forms |
| **Vocabulary** | Nationalities |
| | Word families |
| **Pronunciation** | Word stress |

**Nokia across the Globe**

- factories in 10 countries
- employs 50,000 worldwide
- customers in 130 countries

## A Vocabulary

Here is some information about Nokia, the Finnish telecommunications company. Complete the sentences with the words below. Use the pictures to help you.

| | | | |
| --- | --- | --- | --- |
| competitors | product | employees | factories |
| markets | customers | sales | head office |

1 The ........................ of Nokia is in Helsinki.
2 Europe is one of the company's major ........................ .
3 ........................ in China are very high.
4 Ericsson is one of the main ........................ .
5 They have ........................ in ten different countries.
6 The company has more than 50,000 ........................ in the world.
7 The Nokia 9100 is a very successful ........................ .
8 Nokia has ........................ in at least 130 countries.

## B Listening

  **1** Simon Hastings has an interview with a senior manager at Nokia. Listen and complete the information below.

Company ..*Nokia* ...........................................................
Activity ..................................................................
Head office ..............................................................
Research centre ..*Tampere* ...............................................
Employees ...............................................................
Languages ...............................................................
Major markets ...........................................................
Main competitors ........................................................
Advertising .............................................................

**2** Listen to the interview again. Complete the questions below.

1 What ............. ............. ............. ............. ?
It produces and sells mobile telephones.

2 Where ............. ............. ............. ?
The head office is in Helsinki.

3 ............. ............. your biggest markets?
China.

4 ............. many ............. ............. ............. ............. ?
About 53,000.

5 What ............. ............. ............. ............. in the company?
Finnish. And English, of course.

6 ............. do you ............. ?
On TV, in magazines, and on buses.

**LANGUAGE NOTE**

## Present simple questions and negatives

1 To make questions and negative sentences we use the auxilary *do / does*.

| | |
|---|---|
| *Where do you live?* | *I live in Paris. I don't (do not) live in Milan.* |
| *When do they finish work?* | *They finish work at 12.00.* |
| | *They don't (do not) work in the afternoon.* |
| *Do you live here?* | *No, I don't.* |
| *Do you speak English?* | *Yes, I do.* |

2 We use *does* for the third person (*he*, *she*, or *it*).

| | |
|---|---|
| *What languages does she speak?* | *She speaks Finnish and English.* |
| | *She doesn't (does not) speak Spanish.* |
| *Does he smoke?* | *Yes, he does.* |
| *Does she work with them?* | *No, she doesn't.* |

## C Speaking

**1** Work in pairs. Student A, look at File I on page 151. Student B, turn to File O on page 152. Ask your partner questions and complete the table below. Guess the name of your partner's company.

| Activity | ................................................................................ |
|---|---|
| Employees | ................................................................................ |
| Location | ................................................................................ |
| Products | ................................................................................ |

**2** Ask your partner the same questions about the company where he or she works. Write a short description of this company. Then report back to the rest of the class.

## D Vocabulary

**1** Here are some facts about Nokia. Complete the sentences with the correct words.

1 Nokia ..................... on buses in China.    *advertisements / advertises*
  Nokia has ..................... on buses in China.

2 Nokia ..................... the 9100.    *products / produces*
  The 9100 is one of Nokia's ..................... .

3 Nokia ..................... a lot of telephones in China.    *sales / sells*
  Nokia has large ..................... in China.

4 There are 53,000 ..................... .    *employees / employs*
  The company ..................... 53,000 people.

5 Ericsson is one of Nokia's ..................... .    *competitors / competes*
  Nokia ..................... with Ericsson in the mobile
  phone market.

6 Texas Instruments is one of Nokia's ..................... .    *suppliers / supplies*
  Texas Instruments ..................... Nokia with parts
  for mobile phones.

**2** Write similar sentences about a company you know using the words in **1**.

**3** Complete the table of word families.

| Verb | Noun | Person | Expressions |
|---|---|---|---|
| sell | sales | .....................¹ | sales figures |
| compete | .....................² | competitor | competitive prices |
| .....................³ | advertising advertisement | advertiser | advertising campaign |
| employ | employment .....................⁴ | .....................⁵ employer | self-employed |
| produce | product .....................⁶ productivity | producer | productivity bonus |

## E Pronunciation

**1** Look at the table below. The items in the first column are typical of a particular country. Complete the table with the correct countries and nationalities, as in the example.

| | Country | Nationality |
|---|---|---|
| 1 Champagne | *France* ..................... | *French* ..................... |
| 2 Carnival | ..................... | *Brazilian* ..................... |
| 3 Pasta | ..................... | ..................... |
| 4 The Great Wall | ..................... | ..................... |
| 5 Port | ..................... | ..................... |
| 6 Kangaroos | ..................... | ..................... |
| 7 BMW car | ..................... | ..................... |
| 8 Sony | ..................... | ..................... |
| 9 Paella | ..................... | ..................... |
| 10 Tequila | ..................... | ..................... |

**2** Now listen and check your answers. Pay attention to the pronunciation. Listen again and put the words in the correct column according to the stress pattern.

| ● | ●○ | ○● | ●○○ | ○○● | ○●○○ |
|---|---|---|---|---|---|
| France | ............ | Brazil | Italy | ............ | Brazilian |
| French | ............ | ............ | ............ | ............ | ............ |
| ............ | ............ | ............ | ............ | ............ | ............ |
| ............ | ............ | ............ | ............ | ............ | ............ |

## F Listening

9

**1** Later on in his interview, the manager talks about his spare time. Listen and complete questions 1–5 below.

**2** Listen again and write down the answers.

1  What / weekends?

   I often ......................................................................... near Lake Pukkala.

2  What / there?

   I ......................................................... or ......................................................... .

3  Who / with?

   My ......................................................................................................................... .

4  Where / swim?

   In ......................................................................................................................... .

5  What / evenings?

   I ......................................................... or ......................................................... .

**3** Ask a partner similar questions using the words below and the question words *What? Where? Who? Why? When?*

1  weekends ...............................................................................................................

2  evenings ...............................................................................................................

3  on holiday ...............................................................................................................

## G Speaking

**1** Work with a partner. Take it in turns to talk for 60 seconds. Talk about your name, your town, your job, your company, your hobbies. Use the expressions below to help you.

My name is ........................................... .

I am ........................................... .

I live in ........................................... .

It's a ........................................... town / city in the north / south / east / west of .... 

I am a ........................................... .

I work for ........................................... .

In the evenings / at weekends I ........................................... .

**2** Now tell the class what you know about your partner.

e.g. *His / her name is …*

   *He / she's …*

# 1.3 Company facts and figures

| Grammar | Present simple – all forms |
|---|---|
| Vocabulary | Large numbers |
| Communication skills | Presentations 1 |
| Pronunciation | Weak forms of *do* and *does* |

## A Vocabulary

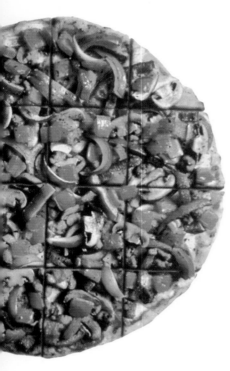

**1** Say these numbers. Then try to match them with items 1–5 below.

432

26,836,000     805,602

1,280     75,000,000

1 the price in dollars of *The Portrait of Dr Gachet* by Vincent Van Gogh
2 the average daily sales of *The Times* (UK newspaper)
3 the length in metres of the Golden Gate Bridge in San Francisco
4 the population of Tokyo in 1998
5 the number of Metro stations in Paris

**2** Here are some facts about Pizza Hut (UK). Use the words in the box to complete the sentences.

| turnover | employs | market share | located |
|---|---|---|---|
| products | subsidiary | competitors | outlets |

1 The headquarters of Pizza Hut (UK) is ........................ in London.
2 Their range of ........................ includes pizza, pasta, salads, and desserts.
3 The company ........................ 16,000 people.
4 Pizza Hut (UK)'s ........................ is over £300m.
5 Their main ........................ are Pizza Express and Ask.
6 They have ........................ in most large towns in Britain.
7 Pizza Hut (UK) is a ........................ of Tricon Global Restaurants.
8 Their ........................ at the moment is 6%.

## B Listening 10a

**1** Listen to the short presentation on Pizza Hut (UK). Are these statements true (T) or false (F)?

1 The talk is in four parts. .......
2 Tricon Global Restaurants is a subsidiary of Pizza Hut. .......
3 Jon Prinsell is the President of Pizza Hut (UK). .......
4 British people do not eat many pizzas. .......
5 Pizza Hut wants to expand. .......

**2** In the talk what do these numbers refer to? Listen again and match the numbers with the correct information on the right.

| | | | |
|---|---|---|---|
| 1 | 300,000,000 | a | number of pizzas the company delivers |
| 2 | 400 | b | number of employees |
| 3 | 16,000 | c | future market share |
| 4 | 80% | d | present market share |
| 5 | 75,000,000 | e | total sales |
| 6 | 6% | f | number of outlets |
| 7 | 10% | g | percentage of the population who eat at Pizza Hut at least once a year |

`10b`

**3** Listen to these extracts from the presentation again and fill in the gaps.

1 My name is Sarah James and I'm ........................ to give a ........................ presentation on the ........................ .

2 The ........................ ........................ of my presentation is about the company structure of Pizza Hut (UK). The second part ........................ ........................ the present activity of the company in the UK and in the ........................ ........................ I want to ........................ ........................ our future plans.

3 ........................ , the structure. ........................ ........................ with the parent company.

4 Now, ........................ ........................ ........................ our present activity.

5 Do you ........................ any ........................ ?

**LANGUAGE NOTE**

### Giving a talk

1 Presenting the structure of a talk

*I am here to talk about / give a presentation on ...*
*The subject of my talk is ...*
*The talk is in three parts.*

The first ⎫
second ⎬ part looks at / is about ...
last ⎭

2 Introducing each point

*Right / first / now / finally ...*
*Let's start with / let's look at / let's talk about ...*

3 Ending

*Do you have any questions?*
*Thank you.*

**1** Look at these notes on Swiss watch manufacturers the Swatch Group.

1  Swatch Group - group of 16 watch companies
2  Swatch - quartz mechanism - only 51 parts (most other watches more than 150)
3  The chairman and founder - Nicolas G Hayek Senior
4  New collection with more than 150 watches in four ranges twice a year.
5  50 production centres - in Europe: France, Switzerland, Italy, Germany - in Asia: Thailand, China, Malaysia
6  Most famous product - Swatch watch
7  Plans - components for telecommunications industry in future
8  The group - sell - 25% of the world's watches
9  Swatch - cheap, from $35
10  Companies in group include Omega, Tissot, Calvin Klein, Swatch, and Flik Flak - watches and watch components
11  Headquarters - Biel, Switzerland
12  Future plans - components for entire Swiss watch industry and companies outside Switzerland
13  Annual sales - 118 000 000 watches
14  Omega - luxury watches, Tissot and Calvin Klein - middle of the range, Swatch and Flik Flak - basic watches

**2** Now organize the information under the appropriate headings, as in the examples.

| Organization / Structure | Location / Distribution | Products | Sales | Future plans |
|---|---|---|---|---|
| 1 Swatch Group - group of 16 watch companies | | 4 New Collection of 150 watches in 4 ranges twice a year | | |

**3** Put your notes into complete sentences. Use the verbs in the box to help you.

e.g. *The Swatch Group is a group of sixteen watch companies.*
*The Swatch has a quartz mechanism with only fifty-one parts. Most other watches have more than one hundred and fifty.*

| be | plan | produce | manufacture |
|---|---|---|---|
| sell | present | make | have |

④ Make a short presentation on the Swatch Group using this information and the language from the Language Note below.

LANGUAGE NOTE

## Presenting a company

1 Structure and location

*The company / group is called …*
*It is a (French) company, based in (Paris).*
*It has factories / production centres / subsidiaries in …*
*The Chairman / CEO / founder / owner is …*
*It employs (200) people / It has (200) employees.*

2 Products and customers

*Their main activity is …*
*The main products / customers are … and …*

3 Results and future plans

*The annual turnover is ($30 million) with profits of ($2 million).*
*The company is successful because …*
*We plan to …*

## D Pronunciation ⌐11⌐

① In spoken English, the most important words in a sentence are stressed more than the others. In sentences 1–3 below, the stressed words are underlined. Listen, then underline the stressed words in sentences 4–6.

1  <u>Where</u> do you <u>work</u>?
2  How <u>much</u> does he <u>earn</u>?
3  <u>What</u> does she <u>do</u>?

4  He doesn't speak English.
5  Does she work here now? Yes, she does.
6  Do you use a PC? Yes, I do.

② Listen again and check. Notice how the pronunciation of *do* and *does* changes when they are unstressed: – *do* /duː/ becomes /də/, and *does* /dʌz/ becomes /dəz/.

③ Listen and repeat. Pay attention to stress and to the sound of *do* and *does*.

## E Speaking ⌐12⌐

① Listen to the questions about your company and reply. If you don't work, choose a company you know well. If you are not sure of the answer, say *Sorry, I don't know.*
e.g. *What's the company called?    It's called …*

② Now prepare a short presentation on your company or a company you know. Use the expressions in the Language Note and the headings below to help you.

Name ...............................................................................................................

Activity ...........................................................................................................

Location ..........................................................................................................

Employees .......................................................................................................

Products ..........................................................................................................

Production .......................................................................................................

Future plans ....................................................................................................

...............................................................................................................

...............................................................................................................

...............................................................................................................

# Unit 2 | Preparing a trip

## 2.1 Choosing a hotel

| Grammar | *There is / there are* |
|---|---|
| Vocabulary | Hotel facilities and services |
| Communication skills | Booking a hotel |
| | Making requests |
| Pronunciation | The sound *th* |

### A Vocabulary

| A | B |
|---|---|
| shuttle | safe |
| car | pool |
| swimming | centre |
| business | rooms |
| electronic | bus |
| conference | park |

**1** Can you identify these hotel services? Match a word from A with a word from B. Then label the pictures below, as in the example.

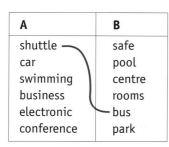

1 *shuttle bus*  2 .......................  3 .......................

4 .......................  5 .......................  6 .......................

**2** What other hotel services can you think of?
Read this fax and Sylvie Dutertre's note to her secretary. Then answer the questions below.

To:                                          Date: 5 September
Subject: HOTEL INFORMATION

Dear Sir or Madam,
I would be grateful if you could send me some
information about your hotel facilities. Could you
also let me know the price for a single room with
a bath for four nights at the beginning of November.
I look forward to hearing from you.

Yours faithfully

Sylvie Dutertre

Nathalie – for my trip to Bangkok
Please send copies of this to:

CENTURY PARK
(fax: 00 61 23445566)

ROYAL PRINCESS
(fax: 00 61 67894719)

### B Reading

1 Who does Sylvie Dutertre want her secretary to send this fax to?
2 Why is she sending the fax? What does she want?
    a to ask for information   b to reserve a room   c to change a reservation
3 What type of room does she want?

## C Speaking

**1** You need information about a hotel. What questions can you ask about the following? Use the Language Note below to help you.

1 business centre     2 conference rooms     3 shuttle bus to the airport

**LANGUAGE NOTE**

### *There is* and *there are*

1 Singular

| | |
|---|---|
| *Is there a swimming pool in the hotel?* | *Yes, there is.* |
| *Is there a health club?* | *No, there isn't.* |

2 Plural

| | |
|---|---|
| *Are there any restaurants?* | *Yes, there are.* |
| *Are there any conference rooms?* | *No, there aren't.* |
| *How many rooms are there?* | *(There are) 200.* |

**2** Work in pairs. Student A, look at the information below about the Century Park hotel. Student B, turn to File C on page 150 and read about the Royal Princess hotel. Take it in turns to ask and answer questions about your hotels. Use the Language Note to help you.

e.g. *How many rooms are there? There are 170.*
*Is there a TV in every room? Yes, there is.*

# Century Park Hotel

**Guestrooms**
*338 rooms all with:*
- refrigerator and mini bar
- radio
- television with satellite channels
- IDD (International Direct Dial) telephone
- safe
- separate bath / shower

- hairdryer
- shaver outlet 110/220 V

**Other facilities**
- two restaurants and a coffee shop
- 24-hour room service
- health club
- outdoor swimming pool

- fitness centre
- sauna
- beauty salon
- florist shop
- business centre
- internet and email service
- conference rooms
- shuttle bus to airport

## D Listening

**1** Somebody phones the Royal Princess Hotel to reserve a room. Listen, and complete the information about the caller.

| | | | |
|---|---|---|---|
| Name | .................... | Date of arrival | .................... |
| Company | .................... | Date of departure | .................... |
| Type of room | .................... | Confirmation by | .................... |

**2** Who asks these questions, the hotel receptionist (R) or the caller (C)?

1 Could I reserve a room for next week? .......

2 May I have your name, please? .......

3 Can you confirm your reservation in writing? .......

4 Can I fax you tomorrow? .......

5 Could you tell me your fax number? .......

**3** Listen again. How does the other person respond to the questions in 1, 3, and 4?

## Polite requests

1 If you want to ask to do something, use *could I?* or *may I?* (more formal), or *can I?* (less formal).

*Excuse me* ... (to get someone's attention)
*Could I have a room for two nights?*          *Certainly, sir.*
*May I open the window?*                       *Yes, of course.*
*Can I leave the meeting early?*               *I'm sorry, but ...*

2 If you want another person to do something, use *could you?* (more formal) or *can you?* (less formal).

*Could you confirm this in writing?*           *Yes, of course.*
*Can you do that by tomorrow?*                 *I'm afraid I can't, because ...*

## E Speaking

1 Look at these two conversations between Chris Sutton (S) and a receptionist (R) Use the expressions in the Language Note above to help you fill in the gaps. Use only one word for each space.

1   S: ............ ............ [1] . Is this Mr Maleta's office?

   R: Yes, it is. ............ ............ [2] help you?

   S: Yes, I'm Chris Sutton. I have an appointment to see Mr Maleta.

   R: ............ ............ [3] he's in another meeting at the moment, Mr Sutton.

    ......... ............ [4] wait a few minutes?

   S: Yes, ............ ............ [5] .

2   S: Hello ......... ......... [6] speak to Mario Maleta, please? It's Chris Sutton here.

   R: Hello, Mr Sutton. ............ ............ [7] , but Mr Maleta isn't here today.

   S: OK, it doesn't matter ............ ............ [8] ask him to call me back?

   R: Yes, ..................... [9] . Can I have your number?

2 Which conversation is on the telephone? And which one is face-to-face? Listen and check your answers.

3 In pairs, practise asking and answering questions. Use the verb in brackets.
e.g. In a restaurant, you want the menu. *(bring)*

A: *Could you bring me the menu, please?*
B: *Yes, of course, here you are.*

1 It's very hot and all the windows are closed. *(open)*
2 You want a cigarette. *(smoke)*
3 You want to know the time. *(tell)*
4 You're in a taxi with a colleague. You don't have your mobile phone. *(use)*
5 In a restaurant, you want a glass of water. *(have)*
6 Ask someone to phone you tomorrow morning. *(call)*
7 You want to read a colleague's newspaper. *(look at)*
8 You want a coffee. Ask your colleague. *(bring)*

## F Pronunciation 15a

**1** The letters *th* can be pronounced in two different ways θ (as in <u>think</u>), and ð (as in <u>the</u>). Listen to these words and put them in the correct row.

| think | the | bath | thank | this | theatre |
|-------|-----|------|-------|------|---------|
| that  | other | month | three | there | thirty |

| θ | *think* |
|---|---------|
| ð | *the*   |

15b

**2** Listen to these sentences and repeat.
1  Is that the theatre?
2  It's not this month, it's the other month.
3  I think there are three rooms with a bath.

## G Writing

**1** Look again at Sylvie Dutertre's fax in **B** and answer the following questions.
1  When we know the name of the person we are writing to, we start a letter with *Dear Mr …* or *Ms …* plus name, and finish with *Yours sincerely.* How does Sylvie Dutertre start and finish the fax? Why?

2  To make a request, Sylvie says *Could you also …?* What other expression does she use to make a request?

3  Which expression means 'I hope to receive your answer soon?'

**2** You have an appointment at the Compaq Computer Corporation in Houston on Friday 13 June. Write a fax to Mrs Martina Glens at Compaq and ask her for:
1  A road map of Houston (you want to come by car)
2  Confirmation of the exact time of the meeting

## H Vocabulary

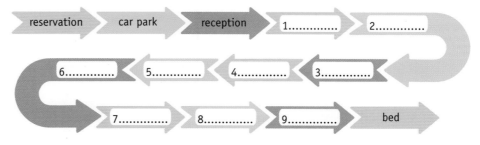

The word chain above shows what you do when you stay in a hotel.
e.g. You make a *reservation*, you arrive at the hotel and park in the *car park*, then you check in at *reception*, etc.

**1** What happens after you check in and before you go to bed? Use the words in the box to complete the chain.

| shower | restaurant | lift | phone call | key |
|--------|-----------|------|-----------|-----|
| room | satellite TV | suitcase | fitness room | |

**2** Match the nouns in your completed chain with a verb from the list below. You can use some of the verbs more than once.

| use | collect | take | watch | unpack |
|-----|---------|------|-------|--------|
| make | eat in | go to | park in | check in at |

# 2.2 Flying out

| | |
|---|---|
| **Grammar** | Saying the time |
| | Distance and frequency |
| **Vocabulary** | Plane travel |
| **Communication skills** | Reserving a flight |
| **Pronunciation** | Cardinal numbers |

**A Speaking**

Odil Tunali is at London Heathrow airport. Her plane to Budapest leaves in less than two hours. Look at the pictures and answer the questions below.

| London Heathrow Terminal 1 to Budapest | | | |
|---|---|---|---|
| Dates | Dep.Time | Arr.Time | Flight |
| Mon Tue Wed Thur Fri Sat Sun | 10.20 | 13.45 | BA 868 |
| Sat Sun | 18.00 | 21.25 | BA 870 |
| Mon Tue Wed Thur Fri | 19.35 | 23.00 | BA 870 |

NB Times given are local times. Budapest is one hour ahead of London

**Trading Hours**

| Opening | | Closing |
|---|---|---|
| 05 00 | Monday | 22 00 |
| 05 00 | Tuesday | 22 00 |
| 05 00 | Wednesday | 21 00 |
| 05 00 | Thursday | 22 00 |
| 05 00 | Friday | 22 00 |
| 05 00 | Saturday | 22 00 |
| 05 00 | Sunday | 22 30 |

1 Look at Odil's watch. What time is it now? And what day?
2 Look at the flight timetable. Which is her flight?
3 How long does the flight take? (Be careful, there's a time difference.)
4 Odil wants to go shopping. Are the shops open?
5 Where can you see the following times?
   a quarter to five in the afternoon
   b nine twenty-five p.m.
   c nineteen thirty-five

## Telling the time

There are three different ways of saying the time:

1 In conversation, we use *past* (or in American English *after*) and *to* (or in American English *of*).

*five past seven*    *quarter past seven*    *twenty past seven*    *half past seven*

*twenty to six*    *quarter to six*    *ten to six*    *six o'clock*

2 Sometimes we use the figures only. Say the figures in the order you see them.

| 5.05 | *five oh five* | 5.35 | *five thirty-five* | 5.30 | *five thirty* |
| 5.15 | *five fifteen* | 5.45 | *five forty-five* | 5.55 | *five fifty-five* |
| 5.20 | *five twenty* | 5.50 | *five fifty* | | |

With this form, we often say *a.m.* for the morning and *p.m.* for the afternoon and evening.

*The office closes at 5.30 p.m.*    *Breakfast is served between 7.00 and 9.00 a.m.*

3 In Britain and the USA, we usually use the 24-hour clock only to talk about travel timetables.

*17.20 seventeen twenty*    *22.45 twenty-two forty-five*

## B Listening

**16**

1 How can you say the times in the box below? Use the Language Note to help you.

2 Now listen to three short extracts, and circle the times you hear.

| 10.00 | 04.15 | 09.20 | 09.30 | 03.45 | 09.50 |
| 19.00 | 15.15 | 19.20 | 17.30 | 14.45 | 22.50 |

3 What time do you do these things? Complete the table for yourself, then ask a partner.

| | **You** | **Your partner** |
|---|---|---|
| get up (on work days) | ............................ | ............................ |
| get up (on Sundays) | ............................ | ............................ |
| have lunch | ............................ | ............................ |
| have dinner | ............................ | ............................ |
| finish work | ............................ | ............................ |
| watch the news | ............................ | ............................ |
| go to bed | ............................ | ............................ |

## C Speaking

Work in pairs. Student A, you want to fly to Warsaw. You want to arrive in Budapest in the early afternoon or late evening. Go to your travel agent (Student B) to reserve a flight. Begin like this:

*Good morning. Can I have some information about flights?*

Student B, you are the travel agent. Turn to File P on page 152.

## D Listening

17  1  Listen to this conversation between two colleagues about travel and shopping in Warsaw. Complete the notes.

- City centre to airport: ..........¹ km

- Airport shuttle bus – takes ..........² minutes to get to city centre.

- It leaves every ..........³ (at weekends) from ..........⁴ a.m. to ..........⁵ p.m.

- Banks open at ..........⁶

- Shops are usually open from ..........⁷ to ..........⁸

  N.B. Some specialist boutiques open at ..........⁹

  N.B. On Saturday shops close at ..........¹⁰

2  Match the questions on the left with the answers on the right. Then listen again to check.

1  How long does it take to get there?
2  How often does the bus go?
3  When are the shops open?
4  What time do the banks open?
5  How far is the city centre from the airport?

a  usually from eight to six
b  every half hour
c  about ten kilometres
d  about twenty-five minutes
e  at eight or nine in the morning

**LANGUAGE NOTE**

### Time, distance, and frequency

| | |
|---|---|
| *How far is it?* | *It's fifty miles away.* |
| *How long does it take?* | *It takes about two hours by plane / train, etc.* |
| *How often does it … (go)?* | *Every hour / week / month, etc.* |
| | *Once / twice / three times a day / week, etc.* |
| *When is it open?* (adjective) | *It's open from ten to six.* |
| *When does it open?* (verb) | *It opens at 8.00 a.m.* |

## E Speaking

Ask your partner questions about his or her company and work schedule (or school and study schedule) and complete the form below. Use the question words in the box to help you.

| When ...?   How often ...?   How far ...?   What time ...?   How long ...? |

### Questionnaire

| | |
|---|---|
| **Distance from your home to your company** | |
| **Time from your home to your company** | |
| **Reception hours** | from ................. to ................. |
| **Closed for holidays** | from ................. to ................. |
| **Your usual working hours** | from ...................................... to ...................................... |
| **Work after 6 pm** | every day / once or twice a week / three or four times a week |
| **Work at weekends** | always / sometimes / never |

## F Pronunciation

1  These numbers are often confused. How do you pronounce them?

17 70   15 50   14 40   16 60
18 80   13 30   19 90

**18**  2  Now listen and answer these questions. There is a number or time in each answer.

1  How many rooms are there? .............
2  How far is it from the airport? .............
3  What time is the plane? .............
4  How many companies are there? .............
5  How long does it take by road? .............
6  How many people are there? .............
7  How often does the bus come? .............

## G Speaking

Work with a partner. An American colleague wants to visit your company or school from Saturday evening to Wednesday evening. S/he will have meetings all day on Monday and Tuesday – but is free the rest of the time. What can you tell your colleague about the following?

– nearest international airport
– travel from airport to your home town or company
– shopping hours
– tourist attractions and opening hours
– banks – opening and closing times, cashpoints?
– transport in the town / city
– places to eat
– any other points of interest

# 2.3 Arriving

| Grammar | Countable and uncountable nouns 1 |
| --- | --- |
| | *Much* and *many* |
| | *Have* and *have got* |
| **Vocabulary** | Airport procedures |
| | Mind maps |

## A Vocabulary

**1** Here is a list of things you do when you travel by plane to another country. Match each phrase with one of the pictures above.

a  land .......
b  go to the arrivals hall .......
c  go to the baggage claim .......
d  get on / board the plane .......
e  take off .......

f  buy duty-free .......
g  wait in the departure lounge .......
h  go through customs .......
i  check in .......
j  go through passport control .......

**2** Now cover the phrases in **1**, and look only at the pictures. Can you remember the phrases?

## B Listening  `19`

**1** Olivier Miras is on a business trip. Listen to two conversations at the airport. Where exactly in the airport is he in each conversation?

1  ......................

2  ......................

**2** Now listen again, and complete these questions.

1 How ............. days are you here for?
2 How ............. money do you have with you?
3 How ............. luggage do you have?
4 How ............. bottles do you have?

**3** When do we use *how much* and when do we use *how many*?

## C Reading

**1** Customs regulations around the world are very different. Complete the questions below, using *much* or *many*.

1 How ............. bottles of perfume can you take into Japan?

2 How ............. beer can you import into Bahrain?

3 How ............. duty-free gifts or souvenirs can you take into Argentina?

4 How ............. butter can you import into Andorra?

5 How ............. fishing rods can you take with you to Iceland?

6 How ............. potatoes can you take into Great Britain?

7 How ............. jewellery can you carry with you into Algeria?

8 How ............. wine can you import into France?

**2** Now turn to File D on page 150 and match the answers with the questions.

## LANGUAGE NOTE

### Countable and uncountable

1 Countable [C] nouns have a singular and a plural form. They are usually physical objects which you can count, e.g. camera(s), gift(s), cigarette(s).

| Question | Affirmative / negative |
|---|---|
| Singular: *Do you have a book?* | *Yes, I do (have a book).* |
| | *No, I don't (have a book) but I have a travel magazine.* |
| Plural: *Do you have any cigars?* | *Yes, I do (have some cigars).* |
| | *No I don't have any cigars – or any cigarettes.* |
| *How many suitcases are there?* | *Three.* |

2 Uncountable [U] nouns only have one (singular) form. They refer to things which are difficult to count because they are in a mass – e.g. wine, perfume, sugar. They also refer to more abstract things which are not physical objects – e.g. information, advice.

| Question | Affirmative / negative |
|---|---|
| *Do you have any wine or spirits?* | *Yes I do. I have some whisky.* |
| | *No, I don't have any wine or spirits.* |
| *Do you have any advice for me?* | *I can give you some advice about travelling.* |
| *How much whisky do you have?* | *Two litres.* |

## D Vocabulary

**1** Are these words countable [C] or uncountable [U]?

 1 shop ...C...

 2 suitcase .......

 3 luggage .......

 4 information .......

 5 souvenir .......

 6 bottle .......

 7 money .......

 8 room .......

 9 news .......

 10 milk .......

**2** Now complete the spaces with *some*, *any*, or *a*.

1 I'm sorry, but we don't have ............. rooms free tonight.
2 Do you have ............. information about trains to Stockholm?
3 I have ............. good news – our sales are up by 20% this month.
4 I have ............. suitcase here, and ............. other luggage in the taxi
5 I haven't got ............. money. When do the banks open?
6 Do you have ............. bottle of 1996 *Château Margaux*?
7 We don't have ............. milk for our coffee. Is there ............. shop open near here?
8 I want to buy ............. souvenirs before I go home.

## E Listening

`20`

**1** Olivier Miras arrives at a hotel. Listen and answer the following questions.

1 Does he have a reservation?
2 What type of room does he take?

**2** Listen again and complete these extracts from the conversation.

A: ............. you ............. a reservation, sir?
B: No, I ............. .
B: ............. it ............. a shower?
A: Yes, it ............. , sir. It's ............. a shower and a bath.

**LANGUAGE NOTE**

> ### Have and have got
>
> In British English, we often use the construction *have got* as an alternative to *have* in the present tense. In this construction, *have* changes in form. *Got* stays the same.
>
> | | |
> |---|---|
> | *I have a car.* | *I've got a Harley Davidson.* |
> | *He has a new job.* | *She's (she has) got a new laptop.* |
> | *You don't have much time.* | *You haven't (have not) got much money.* |
> | *Do they have any money?* | *Have they got any information?* |
> | *Does she have a company car?* | *Has he got a computer?* |

## H Speaking

You are at an international business conference. On the first night you go to the hotel bar for a drink. You start talking to a colleague. Look at the examples:

A: *Have you got any customers in England?*
B: *Yes, we have. We've got two or three big customers.*
A: *How many employees does your company have?*
B: *It has 300.*

Now expand the notes below to make questions with *have* or *have got*. Then take it in turns to ask and answer the questions with a partner. Talk about yourself and your own company, or a company you know well.

1   any customers in the USA? ................................................................................
2   how many employees / your company? ..............................................................
3   any staff in other countries? ............................................................................
4   your company / factories abroad? .....................................................................
5   how many staff / the head office? .....................................................................
6   many competitors? ...........................................................................................
7   your company / a big market share? .................................................................
8   research department? .......................................................................................

## G Vocabulary

1   The diagram below shows some of the words you have learnt in Unit 2, organized in logical groups. Where in the diagram would you put the following words?

| department stores | departure lounge | confirm | land |
|---|---|---|---|
| sightseeing | conference room | car park | shower |

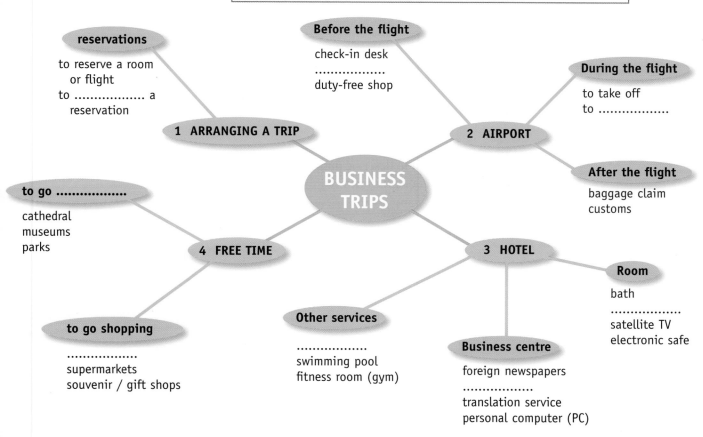

2   What other words from Unit 2 can you add in each category? Make a similar diagram for the words you learnt in Unit 1.

## H Speaking

Work with a partner. Choose a word or phrase from the mind map, e.g. *bath*. Make a sentence with the word in it. Say the sentence to your partner, but don't say the word, say 'fizz'. Your partner has to guess what the word is.

e.g.   A: *Can I have a room with a fizz, not with a shower?*
         B: *A room with a bath?*
         A: *That's right.*

## 3.1 Finding your way

| | |
|---|---|
| **Grammar** | Uses of the imperative |
| **Vocabulary** | Prepositions |
| **Communication skills** | Giving directions |
| **Writing** | Formal and informal letters |

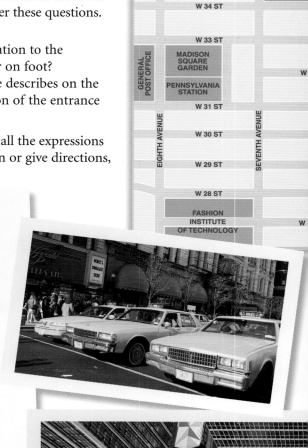

### A Reading

**1** Vernon Linkblatter has a meeting at Glick and Warburg in New York. Look at this letter from his contact Leanne Sands and answer these questions.

1 When is the meeting?
2 How is he going from the station to the company – by car, by taxi, or on foot?
3 Follow the route that Leanne describes on the map above. Mark the position of the entrance to Glick and Warburg.

**2** Read the letter again. Underline all the expressions that are used to describe position or give directions, e.g. *come out of*, *turn left*, etc.

---

## GLICK AND WARBURG

### Realtors • 5th Ave and 34th St, New York

FAX MESSAGE

Date: 9th June

To: Vernon Linkblatter
From: Leanne Sands

Dear Vernon,

As you requested, here are instructions on how to get to us on Friday 13th June.

When you come out of Penn station, walk up West 31st Street. Turn left and walk up Seventh Avenue. Take the third right onto West 34th Street. You'll see Macy's department store on your left when you turn. Go straight on down the street, past Macy's. At Herald Square, cross Broadway and then the Avenue of the Americas. Continue straight on down East 34th Street, and our building is on the next corner on the left, just across from the Empire State Building. The main entrance is on Fifth Avenue.

Give me a call if you have any problems on the way. Have a safe journey, and we look forward to seeing you again on the 13th.

Best regards,

*Leanne*

## B Vocabulary

**1** Study the Language Note below about describing position. Use the information to answer these questions.

1 Where is the office? Is it in building A, B, or C? Describe the position of the other two.

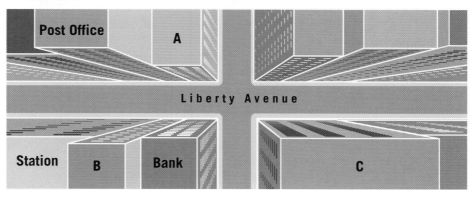

2 Which diagram shows the correct position of the restaurant? Describe the other two diagrams.

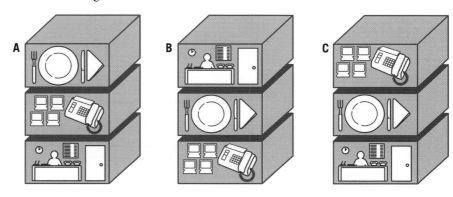

3 Which diagram shows the correct position of the car? Describe the other two diagrams.

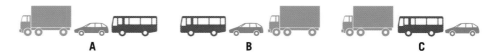

## LANGUAGE NOTE

### Prepositions

1 Describing position
   The office is *near* the station. (It's only two minutes on foot.)
   - It's *in / on* Liberty Avenue, *on* the corner, *on* the left.
   - It's *next* to the post office. (They are side by side.)
   - And it's *opposite / across* from the bank. (On the other side of the road.)

   The restaurant is *on* the second floor.
   - The business centre is *above* the restaurant, on the third floor.
   - Reception is *below* the restaurant, on the first floor.

   I can't move my car, because it's *between* two other vehicles.
   - There's a lorry parked *in front* of me, so I can't go forward.
   - And there's a bus *behind* me, so I can't go back.

## Prepositions

2 Giving directions
Come *out of* the General Post Office on Eighth Avenue,
- turn left *into / onto* Eighth Avenue,
- go *along / up / down* Eighth Avenue,
- and take the first right onto West 33rd Street.
Walk *past* Madison Square Garden and Penn Station,
- go *across* Seventh Avenue, Avenue of the Americas, and Broadway,
- go *into* the last building on the left,
- and take the lift (US elevator) *to* the 102nd floor.

**2** Now look at Part Two of the Language Note above. Trace the route on the map in **A**. Where are you at the end?

**3** Work with a partner. Cover the Language Note, but look at the map. Take it in turns to describe the route you took in **2**. Then describe how to get back to the General Post Office from where you are.

## C Listening   21

**1** Vernon Linkblatter is in New York, but he can't find Glick and Warburg. He calls Leanne on his mobile. Listen and answer these questions.

1 Where is Vernon exactly?
2 Which floor is Glick and Warburg on?
3 Mark the position of Glick and Warburg on this floor plan.

| Cyber Café | 1401 | Leisure and Fitness Center | 1402 | 1403 | 1404 | | |
|---|---|---|---|---|---|---|---|
| | | | | | | 1405 | 1406 |
| 1415 | | A → | 1416 | ← C | Library | Burger Bar | 1407 |
| 1414 | | B → | | ← D | | | |
| | | | | | | 1409 | 1408 |
| Business Center | 1413 | 1412 | Conference Center | 1411 | 1410 | | |

**2** You work in an office on the fourteenth floor. Decide where it is on the floor plan above, but don't tell your partner. Give your partner directions from one of the four lifts / elevators. Your partner must say which office it is.

## D Writing

**1** Look again at the letter in **A**. Leanne knows Vernon quite well, so she uses an informal style of language. Look at the formal phrases below, and find the corresponding informal expressions in the letter in A, as in the example.

| Formal | Informal |
|---|---|
| 1 Dear Mr Linkblatter | *Dear Vernon* ................... |
| 2 I am writing to give you instructions | ................................. |
| 3 Please do not hesitate to call me | ................................. |
| 4 We hope you have a safe journey | ................................. |
| 5 Yours sincerely | ................................. |

**2** Now write a letter to a client or colleague to give directions on how to get to your company or school on foot from the nearest station or bus stop. Draw a map if necessary. You can use a formal or an informal style.

**1** The short /ɪ/ and the long /iː/ sound are often confused. Listen and repeat.

| /ɪ/ | thirty | it | live | sit | this |
|-----|--------|-----|------|-----|------|
| /iː/ | thirteen | eat | leave | seat | these |

**2** Now say these sentences.
1 There are thirty names, but only thirteen people are here.
2 It's time to eat.
3 He lives in London, and he leaves home at eight.
4 A: Can I sit down?
   B: Yes. Please take a seat.
5 This is my book, and these are yours.

**LANGUAGE NOTE**

### The imperative

1 The imperative form of the verb is like the infinitive. It is used for:
   **Instructions and directions**
   *Turn left, then take the first right.*          *Sit down and listen carefully.*

   **Advice**
   *Wear comfortable clothes.*          *Buy a good road map.*

   **Offers**
   *Have another biscuit.*          *(Please) help yourself to coffee.*

2 To form the negative, use *don't (do not)*.
   *Don't turn left, turn right.*          *Don't drink any alcohol before you drive.*

**F** **Reading**

Travelling long distances by air can be stressful and very tiring. Here are some ideas for making long-distance air travel easier. Circle the appropriate form of each verb, as in the example.

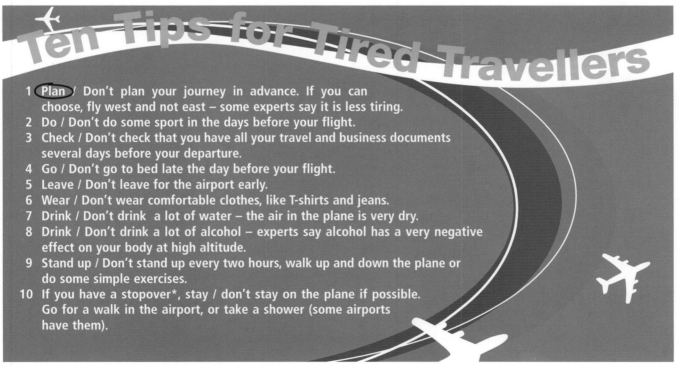

## Ten Tips for Tired Travellers

1 (Plan) / Don't plan your journey in advance. If you can choose, fly west and not east – some experts say it is less tiring.
2 Do / Don't do some sport in the days before your flight.
3 Check / Don't check that you have all your travel and business documents several days before your departure.
4 Go / Don't go to bed late the day before your flight.
5 Leave / Don't leave for the airport early.
6 Wear / Don't wear comfortable clothes, like T-shirts and jeans.
7 Drink / Don't drink a lot of water – the air in the plane is very dry.
8 Drink / Don't drink a lot of alcohol – experts say alcohol has a very negative effect on your body at high altitude.
9 Stand up / Don't stand up every two hours, walk up and down the plane or do some simple exercises.
10 If you have a stopover*, stay / don't stay on the plane if possible. Go for a walk in the airport, or take a shower (some airports have them).

\* when your plane stops to refuel or to take on more passengers

# 3.2 Going out

| Grammar | *Like* and *would like* |
|---|---|
| Vocabulary | Free-time activities |
| Communication skills | Telephoning: getting through |
| | Inviting |
| Pronunciation | Linking sounds |

## A Vocabulary

1 Which verbs do we use with the activities below? Put the words in the correct column, as in the examples.

| tennis | golf | the cinema | cycling | squash | a meal in a restaurant |
|---|---|---|---|---|---|
| skiing | DIY | sightseeing | football | shopping | a drink after work |
| sailing | karate | the theatre | jogging | the gym | the opera |

| play | go | have | go to | do |
|---|---|---|---|---|
| *tennis* | *skiing* | | | |

2 Which verb do we generally use for:
1 eating or drinking?
2 activities with *-ing*?
3 sports with a ball?
4 places where we do activities?

3 Ask some other people in the class what they like doing in their free time. Try and find out as much information as you can.

e.g. A: *What do you like doing in your free time?*
B: *I like skiing.*
A: *Where / When do you go? / Who do you go skiing with?*

### Like and would like

1 To talk about your interests in general, use *like + ing*.

> *I like going to the cinema.*  *He likes watching sport on TV.*
> *Do you like playing squash?*  *Does she like walking?*

2 To talk about what you want to do at a specific time, and to make invitations, use *would like to + verb*.

> *I'd like (I would like) to go to the cinema this weekend.*
> *They'd like to come to the football match on Saturday.*
> *Would you like to play squash this evening?*
> *Would your colleague like to come with us?*

## B Speaking

1 Look at this dialogue. Which question asks about general interests? And which question is an invitation?

A: Do you like volleyball?
B: Yes, I do.
A: Would you like to play this evening?
B: That would be very nice. / Thank you, but I'm afraid I'm not free.

2 Now have similar conversations with a partner. You can accept or refuse your partner's invitations. Use these prompts: *opera, films, football, sightseeing.*

## C Listening

1 Monique Dumont works for Execo in France. She wants to speak to David Payton, a customer in Sydney. Listen and complete the message below.

> Monique Dumont called
>
> re* ........................................................................
>
> Can you ........................................................................
>
> on 33-2 ........................................................................

\* re = 'regarding' or 'about'

2 Match the sentences in column A with the correct response from column B.

| A | B |
|---|---|
| 1 Could I speak to David Payton, please? | a Thank you for your help. Goodbye. |
| 2 Who's calling, please? | b Certainly. Hold on one moment, please. |
| 3 Can I take a message? | c This is Monique Dumont from Execo. |
| 4 Could you tell me your number? | d Yes, could you ask him to call me back? |
| 5 I'll give him the message. | e It's 33 – that's the code for France – then 2 51 25 89 74. |

3 Now listen again to check.

## Telephone language 1

C = Caller   R = Receiver of the call

**Identifying the caller**
R: *Who's calling, please?*   C: *This is Monique Dumont.*
C: *Is that David?*   C: *Yes, speaking.*

**Giving a reason for the call**
C: *I'm calling about my visit.*   C: *It's about your trip next week.*

**Asking the caller to wait**
R: *Hold on a moment, please.*   R: *One moment, please*

**Giving reasons for absence**
R: *I'm afraid he's in a meeting / at lunch / on holiday.*

**Leaving a message**
R: *Can I take a message?*   C: *Could you ask him / her to call me back?*
C: *Could you tell him / her that …*   R: *I'll give him / her the message.*

**Closing**
C: *Thank you for your help.*   R: *Thank you for calling.*

**D Speaking**

**1** David Payton returns Monique's call. He speaks to her assistant. Work with a partner and use the prompts below to help you have the conversation.

| David Payton | Assistant |
|---|---|
| 1  Ask to speak to Monique Dumont. | 2  Ask who the caller is. |
| 3  Give your name. | 4  Ask caller to wait. Say sorry – Monique is absent. Give a reason. |
| 5  Ask if Monique can call you back. Give a reason for the call (trip to France). | 6  Ask for the caller's phone number. |
| 7  Give your number. | 8  Repeat the number. Ask the caller to spell his / her name. |
| 9  Spell your name. | 10  Repeat the spelling. Say you will give Monique the message. |
| 11  Say thank you and goodbye. | 12  Say thank you and goodbye. |

**2** Now change roles. Repeat the same dialogue, but use your own names.

**E Pronunciation** [24]

In spoken English, a word beginning with a vowel sound is usually linked in pronunciation with a word ending in a consonant before it.
e.g. *an‿opera     Look‿at this.*

Mark the linked words in these sentences. Then listen and check.

1  Could I have your name?
2  Can I leave a message?
3  Hold on a moment.
4  Could you ask Ellen to call me back?
5  I'm afraid she's not in the office at the moment.

# Four exciting things to do with your clients on a trip to the Loire Valley

Visit the Renaissance Château du Clos-Lucé. This castle was the home of Leonardo da Vinci in his final years. See an exhibition of models of da Vinci's machines, reproduced by IBM from his original drawings. Enjoy a Renaissance dinner with traditional music and menu.

Visit the wine-tasting school at Saumur. Learn the secrets of sparkling 'champagne method' winemaking, and taste it for yourself.

Fly in a hot air balloon over magnificent châteaux and sleepy villages. After your 1½ hour flight, drink champagne and take time to enjoy the beauty of the French countryside.

Do our classic car rally. Visit châteaux, vineyards, and other places of interest in a classic Cadillac (with chauffeur), and ask questions as you go. Have fun and learn about the region at the same time.

## F Reading

1 Monique Dumont wants to invite David Payton to the Loire valley in France. Read the text above and discuss with a partner the different activities that you can do there.
e.g. *You can go wine-tasting; you can have dinner in a château.*

2 You are going to the Loire Valley this weekend. Which of the activities listed above would / wouldn't you like to do and why? Ask some other students.
e.g. *What would you like to do?*
*I'd like to learn about winemaking; I'm very interested in wine.*
*I wouldn't like to visit the château because I don't like museums.*

## G Listening

 `25`

1 Monique calls David again. Listen, and answer these questions.

1 Does she want to invite him:
   a to dinner in a restaurant?
   b to a conference?
   c for a weekend of sightseeing?
2 Why does David refuse the first time?
3 What activities from the text in F does she mention?

2 Listen again and complete David's three responses to Monique's invitations.

1 Well, that's ....................................................... , but I'm ......................... I have a flight back to England.

2 That ......................... be very ......................... .

3 Well, yes, ....................................................... .

## H Speaking

Work in pairs. An important client is visiting you. Make a list of things to do and places to visit in your town or area. Then phone his / her hotel, and suggest things to do this weekend. Give explanations where necessary. Your partner can accept or refuse your invitations.
e.g. *Would you like to visit the Schönbrunn? It's a beautiful castle in Vienna.*
    *That would be very nice / That's very kind of you, but …*

# 3.3 Eating out

| Grammar | Countable and uncountable nouns 2 |
|---|---|
| Vocabulary | Food and restaurants |
| Communication skills | Ordering in a restaurant |
| | Recommending and suggesting |

## A Reading

1 Look at the menu below. Can you identify the nine countries?
   e.g. *Nachos with guacamole is a Mexican dish. It comes from Mexico.*

# GLOBAL VILLAGE RESTAURANT

Nine dishes from nine countries. Our menu changes every day. We welcome your suggestions.

### STARTERS

**Nachos with guacamole**
Tortilla chips served with a spicy sauce made with avocado, tomato, lemon juice, and onion

**Sushi roll**
A rice roll filled with raw fish, seaweed, and cucumber, served with soy sauce

**Onion soup**
Onions cooked in white wine, topped with slices of bread and grated cheese

### MAIN COURSES

**Paella**
Rice cooked with fish, shellfish, chicken, and vegetables

**Lasagne al forno**
Strips of pasta cooked in beef and tomato and creamy béchamel sauce

**Green curry**
Chicken cooked in a fish and coconut sauce with oriental spices. Served with rice

### DESSERTS

**Apple Strudel**
Pastry filled with slices of apple and raisins

**Kulfi**
Ice cream made with almonds and pistachios

**Strawberries and cream**
The traditional fruit of Wimbledon, topped with thick Devonshire cream

After your meal, why not try our delicious Turkish, Brazilian, or Irish coffees?

**2** Here are some words from the menu. Add some words to each group. Use words from the menu and any other words that you know.

1  tomato, lettuce ...................................................................................................

2  lemon, strawberry  ............................................................................................

3  rice, pasta ..........................................................................................................

4  cheese, cream ....................................................................................................

5  chicken, beef ......................................................................................................

**3** For each sentence, circle the ending which isn't possible, as in the example.

1  The dish is made with …     onions / chicken / (menu) / rice.
2  The tomato is filled with …   cream / coconuts / sauce / spices.
3  The pastry is topped with …  cheese / red wine / cream / chocolate sauce.
4  It's cooked …                in wine / under the grill / in the oven / in lettuce.
5  It's served …                in the oven / with a salad / raw / with bread.

**4** Think of three typical dishes from your country or region. You are in a restaurant with a client who doesn't know these dishes. Describe them, using these phrases.

*It's made with …*
*It's filled with …*
*It's topped with …*
*It's cooked in / under …*
*It's served in / with …*

## B Listening

**1** Listen to two people discussing the menu at the Global Village restaurant. What do they decide to order?

**2** Look at the Language Note below, then listen again. Which expressions do you hear?

**LANGUAGE NOTE**

### Restaurant language

1  Recommending and suggesting
*What do you recommend?*          *I recommend the sushi.*
*What do you suggest?*            *I suggest you try the lasagne.*

2  Ordering
*What would you like?*            *I'd like the onion soup.*
*What will you have …*
  *– as a starter / to start?*      *I'll have the guacamole.*
  *– as a main course / to follow?*  *I'd like the paella.*
  *– for dessert / to finish?*      *I think I'll have strawberries and cream.*

3  Asking for things
*Could you bring me / Could I have some water / another glass / the bill, please?*

**3** Now you are in the Global Village restaurant with two of your colleagues. Have a conversation about what you want to order.

## C Vocabulary

**1** Look at the picture. What can you see? Identify the items, and indicate if they are countable [C] or uncountable [U]. Sometimes there is more than one possibility, e.g. *water* [U], or *jug* [C] of *water*.

**2** You're in a restaurant and you don't have some of these things. Ask the waiter for them.

e.g. *Could you bring me some water, please?*
    *Could I have a jug of water, please?*

## D Listening

**1** It's the end of the meal. Match a sentence on the left with the response on the right. Then, write who you think is speaking in each case – the waiter (W), the host (H), or the guest (G)?

1  Would you like some more coffee? ....... .......
2  Could I have a receipt? ....... .......
3  Do you accept credit cards? ....... .......
4  Please, let me get this. ....... .......
5  Thank you for inviting me. ....... .......
6  Could you bring me the bill, please? ....... .......
7  It's an excellent restaurant ....... .......

a  Yes, we do.
b  I'm pleased you like it.
c  You're very welcome.
d  Yes, certainly.
e  No, thanks.
f  Yes, of course.
g  No, you're my guest. This is on me.

**27** **2** Now listen to the complete dialogue and check your answers.

## E Speaking

Work in threes. You are inviting a customer to a restaurant. Toss a coin to move. Heads: move one square. Tails: move two squares. Follow the instructions on each square and start a conversation. The first person to finish is the winner.

## START
### The Blue Room

## START
### Greens

Invite your customer for dinner after your meeting.

HAVE ANOTHER TURN.

Phone the restaurant and ask when they open.

Phone your customer. Invite him / her for dinner.

Phone the restaurant. Reserve a table.

MOVE BACK ONE SPACE.

You're in the restaurant. Ask for the menu.

MOVE BACK ONE SPACE.

## START
### The Rose Garden

Offer your guest a drink before dinner.

You're in the restaurant. You only have one copy of the menu.

A friend invites you for dinner. Refuse the invitation.

What would your guest like to drink with the meal?

HAVE ANOTHER TURN.

Ask your guest what type of food he / she likes.

MOVE FORWARD TWO SPACES.

You're in the restaurant. Offer to take your guest's coat.

MOVE BACK ONE SPACE.

Phone your customer. Tell him / her where the restaurant is.

Your guest doesn't have a serviette.

Ask your guest what he / she would like to eat.

Recommend a starter. Describe it.

Recommend a main course. Describe it.

TIME TO GO HOME

Your guest loved his / her meal.

HAVE ANOTHER TURN.

There's a mistake in the bill.

MOVE FORWARD TWO SPACES.

TIME TO GO HOME

Ask your guest about his / her home town.

Your guest asks if you come here often.

MOVE FORWARD ONE SPACE.

MOVE FORWARD ONE SPACE.

Your guest thanks you.

MISS A TURN.

MOVE FORWARD ONE SPACE.

Ask for the bill.

Ask for the toilets.

Your guest wants to pay.

Order the food for yourself and your guest.

Recommend a dessert. Describe it.

Offer your guest some more wine.

MISS A TURN.

Ask your guest if he / she likes sport.

MOVE FORWARD TWO SPACES.

You don't have enough cash to pay the bill.

Ask for a receipt.

MISS A TURN.

TIME TO GO HOME

# Unit 4 | Visiting a company

## 4.1 Meeting people

| | |
|---|---|
| **Grammar** | Past simple: regular forms |
| | Past simple of *be* |
| **Vocabulary** | Time expressions |
| **Communication skills** | Welcoming visitors |
| **Pronunciation** | Weak forms |
| | Final *-ed* |

**A Listening**  `28`

Martin Kellermann has just returned from Argentina, where he was on a course. He phones his colleague, Thomas Hart. Listen and answer these questions.

1 Where was Thomas yesterday evening?

........................................................................................

2 Where was his wife Angela?

........................................................................................

3 Where were their children?

........................................................................................

**B Speaking**

① Put these time expressions in chronological order.

| yesterday morning | last week | at 9 o'clock last night |
|---|---|---|
| on Tuesday | in 1984 | at 6 o'clock this morning |

② Ask a partner questions using *Where …?* and the time expressions in ① above.

e.g. *Where were you last night?*     *I was at the cinema.*
     *Where were you in 1984?*     *I was at university in Seattle.*

**C Pronunciation**  `29`

Listen to these conversations. Underline the stressed words. How does the pronunciation of *was* and *were* change when they are not stressed?

1 A: Where were you? I called but there was
      no answer on this number.
   B: I was in Paris from Thursday to Saturday.
   A: Were you?

2 C: There were three of us at the conference.
   D: Was Christian there?
   C: Yes, he was.

3 E: How was the conference?
   F: It was interesting, but by eight we were all very tired.
   E: I'm sure you were.

**LANGUAGE NOTE**

## Simple past of *be* and regular verbs

**1** *Be*

| | |
|---|---|
| *Where were you last week?* | *I was in Paris, and Jan and Bob were on holiday.* |
| *Where was Rosa?* | *She was in New York.* |
| *Was he here yesterday?* | *No, he wasn't (was not).* |
| *Were you at the meeting?* | *No, we weren't (were not).* |

**2** Regular verbs

To form the simple past of a regular verb, add *ed*.
To make a question, use the auxiliary *did* + infinitive.

| | |
|---|---|
| *What did you do?* | *I visited Milan last week, but Nick stayed here.* |
| *When did she phone?* | *She phoned me last Monday.* |
| *Where did you live before?* | *We lived in Beirut for a few years.* |
| *Where did they move to?* | *They moved to Rio de Janeiro.* |

## D Listening

 ❶ Martin Kellerman is talking about his management course at the University of Buenos Aires. Listen to these questions and answers. If the answer is positive, put a tick (✔) in the space provided. If it is negative, put a cross (✗). Listen to the example.

*Did you enjoy the course?*

✔ *Yes, I did. It was really interesting.*

1 Did you improve your English?

.....................................................................

.....................................................................

2 Did you attend any Spanish classes?

.....................................................................

.....................................................................

3 Did you do any sport?

.....................................................................

.....................................................................

4 Did you live on the university campus?

.....................................................................

.....................................................................

5 Did you like the city?

.....................................................................

.....................................................................

6 Did you pass all your exams?

.....................................................................

.....................................................................

❷ Now listen again and check your answers. Write down the full answers in the space provided under the questions.

❸ Now work in pairs. Think about a course you did. Take it in turns to ask and answer questions. Use the questions in ❶ for ideas, and add some more questions of your own.

**4** The regular past simple ending *-ed* has three possible pronunciations, /ɪd/, /t/, or /d/. Listen to the sentences in **1** again and put the verbs in the answers in the correct column. Then add two verbs to each column.

| /t/ | /d/ | /ɪd/ |
|-----|-----|------|
|     | improved |   |
|     |          |   |

## E Speaking

Work in pairs. Student A, you work at the head office of a large company in London. Student B is one of your salesmen. You are checking the expenses for last week. Look at the notes below and ask questions to find out more information. Student B, turn to File H on page 151.

| | | |
|---|---|---|
| MONDAY | Travel. Birmingham to Manchester cost — £200 | How? (travel) |
| TUESDAY | Hotel — Liverpool cost — £150 | Where? (stay) |
| | Telephone — £50 | Who? (telephone) |
| WEDNESDAY | No information | Where? (be) |
| THURSDAY | Visits — £250 | Who? (visit) |
| FRIDAY | Golf £85 — (Important customer) | Who? (play) |

## F Reading

**1** Yuji Ishiguro visits Paco Reverte in Madrid. Paco meets him at his hotel. Put the conversation in the right order, as in the example.

a Yes, that's right. You must be Paco Reverte. Thanks for coming. .......

b By car. I parked just outside the hotel. This way. .......

c Yes it is. .......

d Oh I'm sorry to hear that. Did you sleep well? .......

e About midnight. My plane was late. .......

f Yes, thanks, I did. What time is our meeting? .......

g That would be nice. Do we get to the centre by car or on foot? .......

h What time did you arrive? .......

i Excuse me. Are you Yuji Ishiguro? .......

j At 10.00. Shall we go? We can have a coffee in the city centre. .......

k No problem. Is this your first visit here? .......

[31] **2** Listen to the dialogue and check your answers.

**3** Yuji Ishiguro is visiting you in your town. Practise the dialogue in pairs.

## G Listening

[32] **1** You are visiting one of your customers in Rome. Listen and reply to his questions.

**2** Now listen again and match each question with one of the responses below, as in the example.

**a** Yes, please. Black with 2 sugars.

**b** It's a pleasure. Thank you for inviting us.

**c** Yes, thanks. It was fine.

**g** Thanks very much.

**d** Yes, it's my first time in Rome.

**e** No, thank you. I don't.

**f** That would be nice.

**h** That's a pity.

**i** Thank you. I'm pleased to hear that.

**j** Fine, very comfortable.

## H Speaking

**1** Work in pairs. Student A, you are meeting a visitor at your office. Student B, you are the visitor. Have a conversation using the prompts below.

| A | B |
|---|---|
| Welcome. | Respond. |
| Introduce yourself. | Respond. |
| Ask about journey. | Respond (negative reply). |
| Say you're sorry. Ask about hotel. | Respond. |
| Respond, then offer drink. | Respond (positive reply). |
| Ask if this is B's first visit. | Respond. |

**2** Now change roles and repeat. This time try and continue the conversation.

# 4.2 Reporting on a trip

| | |
|---|---|
| **Grammar** | Past simple: irregular forms |
| | Questions and answers |
| **Vocabulary** | Verb and noun collocations |
| **Communication skills** | Writing an e-mail of thanks |

## A Vocabulary

Work in pairs. Take it in turns to ask and answer these questions.

1 What is the day today?
2 What is the time?
3 What was the day before yesterday?
4 What is the day tomorrow?
5 When was your last lesson?
6 What time was it?
7 Were you busy last week?
8 Every day?
9 What did you do?
10 What did you do at the weekend?

## B Reading

1 Piera Macaluso works for Credito Reggio, an Italian bank. Below is her diary for one week last year. Use the information in the documents to help you fill in the blanks in the diary.

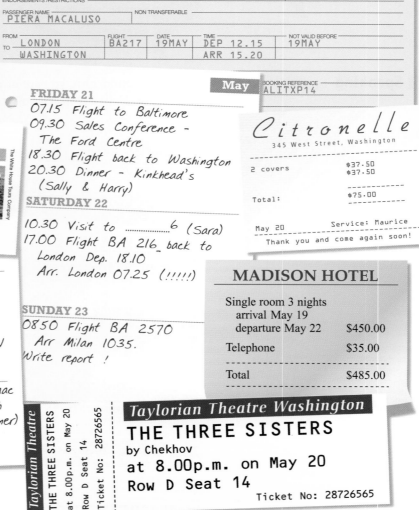

Receipt No: 938124     MAY 19
TAXI FROM DULLES
AIRPORT TO MADISON
HOTEL

TOTAL: $60

---

ISSUED BY **BRITISH AIRWAYS**     DATE OF ISSUE 11MAY     ORIGIN/DESTINATION
ENDORSEMENTS /RESTRICTIONS
PASSENGER NAME **PIERA MACALUSO**     NON TRANSFERABLE
FROM     FLIGHT     DATE     TIME     NOT VALID BEFORE
**LONDON**     BA217     19MAY     DEP 12.15     19MAY
TO **WASHINGTON**     ARR 15.20
BOOKING REFERENCE ALITXP14

---

**THE WHITE HOUSE**
Nº 2836664
**Admit One Adult**
You are requested to preserve your ticket until you leave the site
The White House Tours Company

---

**May**

**FRIDAY 21**
07.15 Flight to Baltimore
09.30 Sales Conference -
  The Ford Centre
18.30 Flight back to Washington
20.30 Dinner - Kinkhead's
  (Sally & Harry)

**SATURDAY 22**
10.30 Visit to ..............6 (Sara)
17.00 Flight BA 216 back to
  London Dep. 18.10
  Arr. London 07.25 (!!!!!)

**SUNDAY 23**
0850 Flight BA 2570
  Arr Milan 1035.
  Write report !

---

$\mathcal{C}itronelle$
345 West Street, Washington
----------------------------
2 covers     $37.50
             $37.50
----------------------------
Total:       $75.00
----------------------------
May 20     Service: Maurice
Thank you and come again soon!

---

**MADISON HOTEL**
Single room 3 nights
arrival May 19
departure May 22     $450.00
Telephone            $35.00
----------------------------
Total                $485.00

---

**WEDNESDAY 19**
Fly to Washington
Flight: BA ..............1
Dep. 12.15 - Arr. ..............2
Taxi booked - ..............3 Hotel
19.00   Meet Isaac Cady at Hotel

**THURSDAY 20**
09.00 Visit Training Centre - Isaac
12.30 Lunch at ..............4 with
  Training Manager (Priscilla Weiner)
14.30 Meeting at Citibank
20.00 ..............5

---

**Taylorian Theatre Washington**
THE THREE SISTERS
at 8.00p.m. on May 20
Row D Seat 14
Ticket No: 28726565

Taylorian Theatre
THE THREE SISTERS
at 8.00p.m. on May 20
Row D Seat 14
Ticket No: 28726565

**THE THREE SISTERS**
by Chekhov
**at 8.00p.m. on May 20**
**Row D Seat 14**
Ticket No: 28726565

**②** Answer the questions below using the verbs indicated.

**Regular verbs**
The Past simple ends in -*ed*.

**Irregular verbs**
Look at page 157 for irregular forms.

1 What did she do on Wednesday morning?    fly
   *She flew to Washington.*...............

2 What time did she leave London?    leave  .........................................

3 How did she get to her hotel?    take  .........................................

4 Where did she stay?    stay  .........................................

5 What did she visit on Thursday?    visit  .........................................

6 Where did she have lunch on Thursday?    have  .........................................

7 Where did she go on Friday morning?    go  .........................................

8 How did she get to Baltimore?    fly  .........................................

9 What did she do on Sunday morning?    return  .........................................

10 When did she write her report?    write  .........................................

**③** Now make questions for the answers 1–8 below, as in the example. Use the words in the box to help you. Use each word or phrase at least once.

| | | | | |
|---|---|---|---|---|
| Where | | | have dinner | with? |
| Who | | | meet | on Wednesday evening? |
| Why | | | visit | on Wednesday morning? |
| What | | | go | with Sally and Harry? |
| Which airline | did | she | fly | to Baltimore? |
| When | | | do | with Priscilla Weiner? |
| What time | | | have lunch | the White House? |

1 She flew to Washington.
   *What did she do on Wednesday morning?*...............

2 British Airways.
   .........................................

3 Isaac Cady.
   .........................................

4 At 12.30 on Thursday.
   .........................................

5 On Friday morning.
   .........................................

6 For a sales conference.
   .........................................

7 At Kinkheads.
   .........................................

8 Yes, she did – on Saturday morning.
   .........................................

## C Listening

**1** A colleague phones Piera on the Monday after her trip. He asks her about it. Look at her answers, and suggest the questions he asks, as in the example.

1 Fine thanks.
   *How are you?*
   .................................................................................

2 I got home on Sunday morning.
   .................................................................................

3 It was very long. We didn't finish until six, but it was a good meeting.
   .................................................................................

4 Yes, I went out on Thursday evening – to the theatre.
   .................................................................................

5 I stayed at the Madison.
   .................................................................................

6 Yes, I bought some perfume and some shoes.
   .................................................................................

7 In the afternoon I wrote my report, and in the evening I answered my e-mail.
   .................................................................................

`33` **2** Now listen and check your answers.

## LANGUAGE NOTE

### Simple past irregular verbs

Many of the most common verbs in English are irregular. Some of the irregular verbs from this unit are given below. For a full list, see page 157.

| buy | bought | | leave | left |
|-----|--------|---|-------|------|
| fly | flew | | meet | met |
| go | went | | take | took |
| have | had | | write | wrote |

## D Writing

**1** On Sunday, Piera writes an e-mail to Isaac Cady. Put the sentences in the correct order, as in the example.

To: Isaac Cady   Date: 23 May
From: Piera Macaluso   Subject: Thanks

Piera
I also enjoyed the meals and the trip to the theatre.
Dear Isaac,[1]
When you come to Italy next month do not hesitate to contact me.
I had a very good three days and I think the meetings were useful.
Kindest regards
Thanks again.
Many thanks for your warm welcome in Washington.[2]

**2** Now write a similar e-mail. Use the information below.

You went to the USA for a conference. It took place in Los Angeles. You had a day-trip to San Francisco. Your host was Lorraine Zimmermann. On the last night she invited you to a barbecue at her house. Her next trip to your country is in August.

## E Vocabulary

**1** The two lists below contain words that are often used together. Match a verb from column A with a noun from column B to make seven common expressions, as in the example.

| A | B |
|---|---|
| send | a report |
| take | a meeting |
| write | a customer |
| make | a trip |
| go on | an e-mail |
| meet | a phone-call |
| attend | a train |

**2** Make one sentence for each collocation using the simple past tense.

e.g. *This morning I sent an e-mail to my boss in Hong Kong.*

## F Speaking

**1** Work in pairs. You are going to compare what you did last week. Student A, turn to File K on page 151 to find out what you did. Student B, turn to File W on page 153. Ask your partner questions to complete the diary below with his / her information.

e.g. *Where did you go on Monday? Where did you travel from? How did you travel?*

**2** When and where did you nearly meet? You can ask up to ten questions.

**February**                    Week 6

**5** Monday

...................... *from* ......................
*to* ......................
*Hotel* ......................
*Dinner at* ......................

**6** Tuesday

*Visit* ......................
*Plane to* ......................
*Dinner at* ......................

**7** Wednesday

*Visit* ......................

**8** Thursday

*Interview* .......... *o'clock*
*Mr.* ......................
(...................... ......................)

**February**
Friday **9**

Visiting a company   49

# 4.3 Describing company structure

| Vocabulary | Jobs |
| --- | --- |
| | Company structure |
| Communication skills | Presentations 2 |

## A Listening

34

**1** Isaac Cady is on a visit to Milan. Piera Macaluso introduces him to some colleagues. Listen to the dialogues and write down what jobs they do.

**a** William Bernstein

..........................

**b** Marianna Tardelli

..........................

**c** Carla Dendena

..........................

**d** Gianni Baresi

..........................

**e** Daniel Jones

..........................

**f** Erika Chang

..........................

**g** Frank Jensch

..........................

**2** Work in pairs. Introduce yourself to the person sitting on your right. Then, together, introduce yourselves to other pairs.

## B Vocabulary

Match the jobs in the box with the descriptions below.

| | | | |
| --- | --- | --- | --- |
| managing director | personal assistant | sales representative | training officer |
| purchasing manager | laboratory technician | quality control manager | |

1 I organize training courses for members of staff – languages, computers, etc.
2 I set up the equipment and do experiments and tests.
3 I am the senior executive.
4 I check that products are made to the right standards.
5 I visit customers and try and increase business.
6 I work with the Managing Director. I am responsible for his diary, organize his travel, and take calls for him.
7 I buy everything the company needs, from raw material to stationery.

## C Reading

**1** Read the text below about the French company Perrier Vittel and fill in the gaps. Use the words in the box.

| | | | | | |
|---|---|---|---|---|---|
| product | takeover | subsidiary | market leader | research centre | turnover |
| division | brands | customers | market share | production sites | acquisition |

# Perrier Vittel

Perrier Vittel is a ..s............[1] of the Nestlé Group. It has millions of ..c............[2] all over the world.
It is the water ..d............[3] of the group and has many famous ..b............[4] such as San Pellegrino, Contrex, Panna and Aquarel. There are sixty-seven ..p............ s............[5] producing billions of litres of bottled water. The main ..r............ c............[6] of the Nestlé Group is in Lausanne and there is a network of seventeen other centres on four continents employing 2,500 staff. This research helps produce safe and affordable water for everybody.
A recent new ..p............[7] is Nestlé Pure Life.

The company bottles this water locally in developing countries such as Pakistan and Brazil. Nestlé's interest in water began in 1969 with the ..a............[8] of 30% of Vittel. After the ..t............[9] of Perrier in 1992 the new company Perrier-Vittel became a major part of the Nestlé Group. Today water sales represent 8.8% of the group's ..t............[10]. The group is the international ..m............ l............[11] for bottled water with a 15% ..m............ s............[12].
A new CEO, Frits van Dijk took over in 2000 and he aims to keep Perrier-Vittel at the front of the bottled water market in both sales and technology.

**2** Look at this organization chart. Use the information from the text above to complete the missing information. The first is done for you.

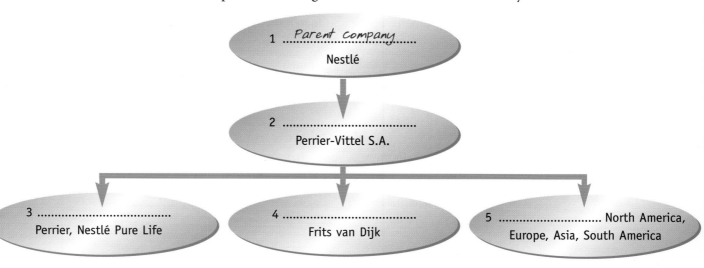

1 *Parent company*
Nestlé

2 ............................
Perrier-Vittel S.A.

3 ............................
Perrier, Nestlé Pure Life

4 ............................
Frits van Dijk

5 ............................ North America, Europe, Asia, South America

**3** Try and draw a similar chart for your company or a company you know. Describe it to a partner.

working in this field for 12 years at present a... challenge that it involves.

I look forward to meeting you and discussing further the post that you are advertising.

Please find enclosed my CV and application form.

Yours sincerely

*Jennifer Plater*

**a**

## Newlands laboratories

**Initial test results @ 31/07/00**

| Age | Weight (Kg) | | | Time (mins) | | | Dosage (mg) |
|-----|-----|-----|-----|-----|-----|-----|-----|
| 65 | 90 | 80 | 70 | 35 | 30 | 25 | 20 |
| 55 | 90 | 80 | 70 | 25 | 20 | 15 | 20 |
| 45 | 90 | 80 | 70 | 22 | 18 | 12 | 20 |
| 35 | 90 | 80 | 70 | 20 | 17 | 10 | 20 |
| 25 | 90 | 80 | 70 | 15 | 15 | 15 | 20 |

**e**

### Telephone Message **b**

Perry Wright called.
(journalist from Economic News)
Wants to interview the chairman
about our results.
Call back on 08145 0168975

## Contract

THIS AGREEMENT is made the sixteenth day of January two thousand

BETWEEN
**Carter Powell Management Services** of Frith Road Lancaster Lancashire *(hereinafter called 'CPMS')* of the one part

... Penrith Cumbria *(hereinafter called ... as follows:*

**INVOICE/CREDIT NOTE APPROVAL FORM**
(ONLY ONE INVOICE/CREDIT NOTE PER APPROVAL SLIP)

- Finance use only
- Input required for balance sheet
- Accounts

**Vendor number**
25960 – 28

**Currency**
€

**Document number**
154

**Discount**
20%

**Supplier invoice date**
25/10/2000

**Gross amount**
€ 459

**Invoice number**
023

**VAT**
17.5%

Is the payee a member of staff? If yes please forward to salaries.

**c**

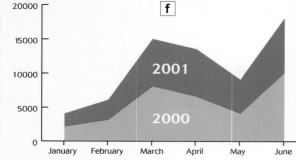

**f**

**D Vocabulary**

1. Most large companies have different departments. Look at the extracts from the documents above and match them with the appropriate department. There is one for each department.

   1 Research and Development .......
   2 Sales and Marketing .......
   3 Financial .......
   4 Legal .......
   5 Human Resources .......
   6 Communications .......

2. Can you think of any other departments?

3. Where do these people usually work?

   1 Accountants work in the ........................ department.
   2 Scientists often work ........................................ .
   3 Sales people ........................................ .
   4 Lawyers ........................................ .
   5 PR people ........................................ .
   6 Training Managers ........................................ .

35a  **1**  At a budget meeting four managers talk about their departments. Listen and complete the grid below.

|  | **1** | **2** | **3** | **4** |
|---|---|---|---|---|
| Department |  |  | Human Resources |  |
| Staff |  | 12 (5+7) |  |  |
| Office |  |  |  | large, open-plan office-ground floor |
| Activity | software research |  |  |  |
| Other information |  |  |  |  |

35b  **2**  Listen again and complete these sentences.

1  We ........................ a ........................ with ........................ companies in the USA, so we ........................ a lot of our ........................ on ........................ .

2  We are ........................ for ........................ purchases, raw material, components, and other ........................ .

3  ........................ ........................ six ........................ ........................ in the department, plus the Director.

4  We are ........................ ........................ ........................ internal and external communications and public relations.

**LANGUAGE NOTE**

### Describing your department

1  Describing the activity of a department

*My department deals with / is responsible for marketing / administration, etc.*
*We organize tests / studies / research.*
*We work with customers / suppliers / subsidiaries / other companies in the group.*

2  Describing the staffing of a department

*There are ... people in the department.*
*Pierre Ducros is in charge of the department.*
*I am one of the managers / technicians / secretaries / engineers.*

3  Describing the equipment / premises of a department

*We have a large office / three laboratories / a small building.*
*We use computers / fax / e-mail a lot.*
*We have a well-equipped laboratory / a lot of technical equipment.*

**F** Speaking

Think about your department or a department you would like to work in. Draw an organization chart for it like the one in **C** on page 51. Use the language from the Language Note above to give a short presentation about your department.

## 5.1 Current activities

| | |
|---|---|
| **Grammar** | Present continuous |
| | Present simple vs continuous |
| **Vocabulary** | Company activities |
| **Communication skills** | Describing company projects |
| **Pronunciation** | Weak forms |

### A Speaking

a ........

c / ........

e ........

d ........

b ........

1. What are the people in the photos doing? Complete the sentences with these verbs and match them to the pictures, as in the example.

| train | design | assemble | build | do |
|---|---|---|---|---|

1 They ...*are building*... a house.

2 They ........................................ market research.

3 She ........................................ new employees.

4 He ........................................ a new product.

5 They ........................... cars.

**2** Where are you now? What are you doing? What is your teacher doing?

**3** Talk about your job or your studies. What are you working on at the moment? What are your projects for this month?

> e.g. *We are working on a European project, so I'm travelling a lot. I'm preparing the budget.*

**LANGUAGE NOTE**

### The present continuous

1 The present continuous tense is formed using the verb *be* and the main verb with an *-ing* ending.

> *He's (he is) working at home today.*
>
> *I'm (I am) learning to play the piano.*

> *They aren't (are not) designing any new products this year.*
>
> *Are you leaving now, or are you staying for lunch?*

2 We use the present continuous to talk about:
   – actions happening now, at this moment

> *I'm reading this sentence.*     *The teacher's writing on the board.*

   – actions happening over a longer period of time, including now

> *My company's building a factory in Venezuela.*
>
> *We aren't working on any new projects just now.*

> *She's travelling a lot at the moment.*
>
> *I'm reading a good book.*

## B Vocabulary

**1** 1 Match the verbs in A with the phrases in B, as in the example.

| A | B |
|---|---|
| 1 to design / to manufacture | a a system or service |
| 2 to open / to reorganize | b staff |
| 3 to introduce / to improve | c a new market |
| 4 to recruit / to lay off | d a new product |
| 5 to look for / to enter | e a factory or office |

2 Which verb in A means:
   1 to bring something into use?
   2 to make something better?
   3 to find new employees?
   4 to make people unemployed?
   5 to try to find?

**2** Work with a partner. Ask and answer questions about your company's present projects. Use the phrases in **1** to help you.

> e.g. A: *Are you recruiting any staff at the moment?*
>    B: *No, we aren't.*
>    A: *And are you introducing any new systems?*
>    B: *Yes, we are. We're introducing the ISO 9002 quality standard.*

## Present simple or present continuous?

1 The present simple is used for permanent or regular actions.
*She often calls the USA.*
*We don't have lessons on Saturdays.*
*Does Microsoft sell software?*

2 The present continuous is used for temporary, present actions.
*At the moment she's calling a client in Lima.*
*This week we're not having any lessons.*
*Are you selling a lot of products in Asia this year?*

## C Listening

Alicia Gonzalez of Repsol YPF, the Spanish oil company, meets Jan Petersen at a conference. He asks her about her job.

**1** Listen and answer these questions.

1 What are her company's main products?
2 Which department does she work in?
3 What is the company doing in Spain?
4 In which country is the company's South American headquarters?
5 Why is the company introducing a specialized training programme?

**2** Here is a shorter version of Alicia's and Jan's conversation.

1 Expand the notes to make complete sentences, using the present simple or present continuous tense.
2 Practise the conversation in pairs. Then listen again to check.

| Jan | Alicia |
|---|---|
| Which company / you / with? | I / work / Repsol YPF<br>The company / also / manufacture / distribute / gas / electricity |
| What job / you / do? | I / train / new employees<br>We / invest / a lot / money / training / at the moment |
| The company / expand / very quickly? | Yes / Repsol YPF / develop / activity / Latin America |
|  | In Spain / we / build / new technology centre |
| Where in Latin America / Repsol / operate? | Company / have / new headquarters / Buenos Aires |
| What / you / work on / at the moment? | We / organize / specialized training programmes<br>Company / introduce / a lot of new technology |

## D Reading

**1** Complete the text opposite with an appropriate form of the verbs below – present simple or present continuous.

| own | expand | sponsor | specialize | research | |
|---|---|---|---|---|---|
| help | have | produce | grow | sell | be |

# Repsol: A growing presence in Latin America

Repsol ...............[1] its operations in Latin America at the moment.

Following a takeover in 1999, Repsol now ...............[2] YPF, the biggest industrial company in Argentina. YPF ...............[3] and sells oil and gas in seven South American countries, Indonesia and the USA. Repsol also has a 67.86% share in the Argentinian oil company Astra C.A.P.S.A., which ...............[4] in oil exploration and production.

The new Repsol YPF company ...............[5] a worldwide production capacity of 1.2 million barrels of oil per day, of which 364,000 barrels are produced in Argentina. As for distribution, Repsol

YPF ...............[6] its petrol in a network of about 3,300 service stations in Argentina, compared with 800 before. Sales ...............[7] usually very high in these stations, and the Argentinian petrol market ...............[8] very quickly, so the prospects for further expansion are very good.

Currently, Repsol YPF ...............[9] Latin America to discover its cultural history. It ...............[10] a special community programme which ...............[11] the traditional music of Latin America from the 16th to the 19th century.

**②** What big foreign companies operate in your country?
What do these companies do? What are they doing at the moment?

## E Pronunciation

It can be difficult to hear small words in a sentence – such as prepositions (*for, of, to*), conjunctions (*and, but*), and auxiliaries (*do, does, are*) – because they are usually unstressed.
When unstressed, the vowel sound in these words is normally pronounced /ə/.

37  **①** Listen to the dialogue below and complete the missing words, as in the example.

A: So, what company ....*are*.... you with?

B: I work ............ a company called ATC.

A: And what ............ ATC do?

B: We sell perfumes ............ beauty products.

A: And where ............ you work?

B: In our head office, in the centre ............ Stockholm.

A: So where ............ you travelling today?

B: I'm flying ............ Brussels.

A: Oh really. My mother comes ............ Belgium, so I know the country well.

B: Really? Please excuse me. I have to go. My flight's ............ two o'clock.

**②** Listen again and repeat each sentence. Make sure you stress the correct words.

# 5.2 Company developments

| | |
|---|---|
| **Grammar** | Present continuous vs past simple |
| **Vocabulary** | Describing trends |
| **Communication skills** | Presentations 3: referring to visual aids |
| **Pronunciation** | Word stress |

## A Vocabulary

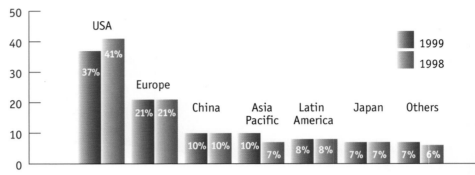

**1** Look at the information about the American company Motorola. Are these sentences true (T) or false (F)? If they are false, correct them. Use the Language Note below to help you.

1 Between 1998 and 1999, the percentage of sales went down in three sales regions. .......

2 Sales rose in two regions. .......

3 In three regions, sales remained stable. .......

4 Sales in other regions fell by 1%. .......

5 Sales to Asia Pacific went up by 3%. .......

6 Total sales outside the USA decreased by 4%. .......

**2** Now look again at the Motorola figures and complete these sentences with an appropriate verb.

1 Sales in the USA ............... by 4%, but they didn't ............... in any other region.

2 Sales in Europe ...............  ............... at 21%.

3 The percentage of sales to all Asian countries ...............  ............... , except for Asia Pacific, where sales ............... by 3%.

4 Sales to other countries ............... from 6% to 7%.

**LANGUAGE NOTE**

### Describing trends

1 to rise / to go up / to increase
*Sales rose / went up / increased from March to September last year.*
*Prices are rising / going up / increasing this year.*

2 To fall / to go down / to decrease
*Sales fell / went down / decreased between 1998 and 2000.*
*Exports are falling / going down / decreasing at the moment.*

3 To remain stable
*Sales remained stable last month.*

4 By, from, and to
*Our market share rose by 2%, from 7% to 9%.*

## B Reading

**1** Find these numbers in the text below and write them in words.

1 1984 ...............................................................................................................................

2 2.59 ...............................................................................................................................

3 12% ...............................................................................................................................

4 725,800 ..........................................................................................................................

**2** Now work with a partner. How do you say the other numbers in the text?

**3** Complete the text with:

1 the correct form of the verb in brackets: past simple or present continuous
2 the correct preposition: *by*, *from*, or *to*.

# Social trends in the UK

### Marriage and divorce

Between 1984 and 1996, the number of new marriages (fall) ...............[1] by 19.78%, from / by 395,800 to 317,500. In the same period, the number of divorces (go up) ...............[2] by / from 16.88% to 168,900.

### Living alone

Now more and more people (decide) ...............[3] to live alone. The percentage of one-person homes (rise) ...............[4] from 10% in 1984 to / by 12% in 1995. The average household size (also / fall) ...............[5] at the moment. In 1984 it was 2.59 people per household, but now it is less than 2.4.

### An ageing population

Currently, the number of retired people (increase) ...............[6]. In 1994, life expectancy (go up) ...............[7] from / to 73.9 years for men, and 79.2 years for women. Between 1984 and 1997, the number of people over 75 years of age (increase) ...............[8] by / from 14.3%, and this number (continue) ...............[9] to rise now.

### A fall in births

Currently, the number of children (also / fall) ...............[10]. From 1984 to 1997, the number of new births (go down) ...............[11] by / from 3.8% to 725,800.

Source: Office for National Statistics

**4** Now talk about present trends in your country. If you can, give figures and / or suggest reasons for the trend.

– the number of marriages / divorces
– the birth rate (the number of children born)
– the number of people living in towns and cities
– the number of foreign tourists
– the cost of living (food, clothes, housing)
– the price of computers and telecommunications

## C Speaking

Work in pairs. Student A, use the information below. Student B, turn to File M on page 152.

**1** You work for a small company in England which sells skis. Describe your sales figures for last year, then ask your partner to guess what kind of products you sell. Start like this:

*In January we had sales of £50,000. In February they rose by £5,000 to £55,000.*

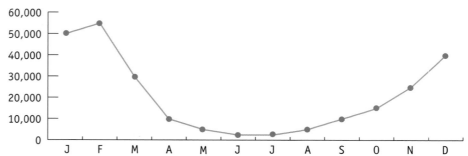

**2** Now listen to your partner's description of a company in the USA. Mark the sales results on this graph.

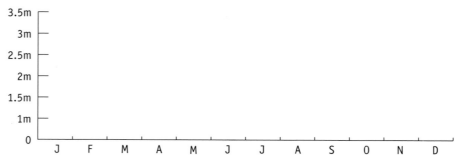

What do you think your partner sells? Is it:

– sun cream
– children's toys
– Christmas decorations?

## D Listening

**1** Look at the two diagrams opposite. Which one is a table and which one is a pie chart?

On which diagram(s) can you see:
1  segments
2  columns
3  figures?

**2** A business consultant is speaking to a group of export managers about e-commerce in Asia-Pacific. Listen and complete the missing information on the table and pie charts.

**3** Listen again and complete these extracts from the presentation.

1  Let's ............ ............ ............ at this first slide. Can everybody ............ ?

2  On the third line, you have the figures for Asia-Pacific. ............ ............ the number of Internet users is rising rapidly.

3  I'd like to ............ ............ ............ to the white and green segments.

4  So ............ ............ ............ ............ , consumption is increasing dramatically in all Asia-Pacific countries.

**World market Internet users and E-Commerce**

| | Internet users (in millions) | | Increase | E-commerce sales (in billions) |
|---|---|---|---|---|
| | **1997** | **2002** | | **2002** |
| USA | 38.7 | 135.9 | 251% | $ 268.8 |
| Western Europe | 16.8 | 82.0 | 389% | $ 55.5 |
| Asia-Pacific (not Japan) | 3.8 | 36.8 | .......[1] | $ .......[2] |
| Japan | 4.9 | 22.1 | 352% | $ .......[3] |
| Rest of world | 4.5 | 43.0 | 852% | $ 40.8 |

Source: International Data Corporation

**Estimated number of families with Internet connection in Asia-Pacific market**

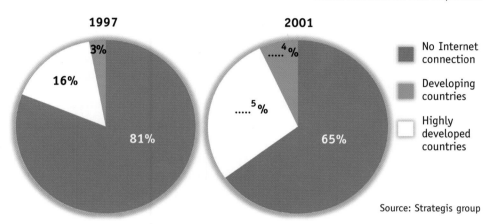

**1997**   **2001**

- No Internet connection
- Developing countries
- Highly developed countries

Source: Strategis group

**LANGUAGE NOTE**

## Referring to visual aids

1 Introducing visual aids
*Let's have a look at the first slide / this pie chart / the next diagram.*
*This pie chart / table / graph / slide / diagram shows ...*
*Can everybody see that?*

2 Indicating important details
*Notice that the number of users is rising.*
*I'd like to draw your attention to the figures for Asia-Pacific.*
*As you can see, consumption is increasing.*

**E Pronunciation** 39

1 Where is the stress in these words? Listen and put them into the correct column, as in the example.

| recruitment | India | figures | remain | period | diagram |
|---|---|---|---|---|---|
| Japan | compare | consumer | segment | percentage | column |

●○        ○●        ●○○        ○●○

........................  ........................  *India*        *recruitment*

........................  ........................  ........................  ........................

........................  ........................  ........................  ........................

........................  ........................  ........................  ........................

2 Now listen again and check. Practise saying the words. Do you have three words in each column? If not, listen again.

# 5.3 Personal developments

| **Vocabulary** | Descriptive adjectives |
| **Communication skills** | Exchanging personal news |
| | Talking about a trip |

## A Listening

**1** Match the questions on the left with the responses on the right.

| | | | |
|---|---|---|---|
| 1 | How do you do? | a | Fine, thanks. |
| 2 | How are you? | b | I'm looking for a new job. |
| 3 | How's the family? | c | How do you do? |
| 4 | What do you do? | d | They're all fine. |
| 5 | What are you doing at the moment? | e | I work for Pinel. |

**2** Which questions above do you ask when you meet someone for the first time? Which questions do you ask when you already know the other person?

**3** Listen to these two conversations in a lift, and match them to the photos below.

1 What do you think is the relationship between the speakers in each case?
2 In which conversation, A or B, do the speakers:
   a use first names?
   b use surnames?
   c talk about the weather?
   d talk about families?
   e give short answers?
   f give more detailed answers?

A

B

**④** Look at the Language Note below. Which expressions did you hear in the two dialogues? Listen again to check.

**LANGUAGE NOTE**

### Meeting People

**1 Meeting someone for the first time**

*How do you do?*      *How do you do?*
*Pleased to meet you.*      *Nice to meet you too.*

**2 Meeting someone you know**

*How's your wife / family etc. ?*    *Very well / Fine, thank you.*
*How are things?*      *Not so bad / Pretty good.*
*How's business / the job?*      *Not very good, I'm afraid*

**3 Responding to news**

Good news      *I'm (very) pleased / glad / happy to hear that.*
     *That's great news!*

Bad news      *I'm (very) sorry to hear that.*
Surprising news      *That's incredible! Really?*

## B Speaking

**①** Choose two possible responses for each remark.

1 How's your family?
   a They're all well.
   b Fine, thanks.
   c She's well, thank you.

2 How are you?
   a Pleased to meet you.
   b Not so bad.
   c Fine, thanks.

3 How's business?
   a So-so.
   b Pretty good, thanks.
   c Yes, it is.

4 I really like my new job.
   a I'm sorry to hear that.
   b That's great news.
   c I'm glad to hear that.

5 She isn't very well, I'm afraid.
   a I'm sorry to hear that.
   b Really? I am sorry.
   c I'm happy to hear that.

6 What about you?
   a I'm fine, too.
   b I'm very well, too.
   c I'm sorry to hear that.

**②** Here are some answers. What are the questions?

e.g. *Not very well. I was ill for several days last week.*
Question: *How are you?*

1 He's fine, thanks, and the children are well too.
2 We're having an excellent year – lots of new contracts.
3 She's very well – she's studying at business school now.
4 Fine, thank you. I really like my new boss.
5 Not so bad.

**③** You meet your partner for the first time in three months. Ask and answer questions about the following:

– your companies
– your jobs
– your families
– your English course

You can tell the truth or invent your answers. Start like this:
*(Peter), great to see you again. What a surprise! How are you?*

## C Listening

[41]

1 Danuta is speaking to a colleague about a trip to New York. Listen to the conversation. Was Danuta's trip generally a positive or negative experience?

2 Listen again, and complete the questions in column A.

| A | B |
|---|---|
| .................................. New York | .................................................. |
| .................................. ? | .................................................. |
| .................................. your hotel | .................................................. |
| .................................. ? | .................................................. |
| .................................. the conference? | *Friendly people. She made two or three useful contacts.* |
| .................................. presentations | .................................................. |
| .................................. ? | .................................................. |

3 Can you remember Danuta's answers to the questions in A? Write them in column B above. Listen again if necessary.

## LANGUAGE NOTE

### What is / was it like?

We use the construction *What...like?* to ask for a general description.

1 Present
*What's (what is) the weather like today?*    It's sunny / cloudy, etc.
*What are the teachers like?*    They are very friendly / interesting, etc.

2 Past
*What was the food like at the conference?*    It was very good / fantastic.
*What were the presentations like?*    They were very long / boring, etc.

## D Vocabulary

1 Match the adjectives in A with their opposites in B, as in the example. Which adjectives are generally positive and which ones are negative?

| A Adjectives | | | |
|---|---|---|---|
| 1 (noisy) | | 6 | friendly |
| 2 cheap | | 7 | fantastic |
| 3 small | | 8 | useful |
| 4 boring | | 9 | clean |
| 5 convenient | | 10 | long |

| B Opposites | | | |
|---|---|---|---|
| a | dirty | f | expensive |
| b | short | g | interesting |
| c | large | h | unfriendly |
| d | useless | i | (quiet) |
| e | inconvenient | j | terrible |

2 For each category in A below, circle the adjective in B which can't be used. Add two or three adjectives in C which are possible, as in the example.

| A | B | C |
|---|---|---|
| Towns | noisy / (easy) / beautiful / small | *large / quiet / modern* |
| The weather | tiring / changeable / hot / friendly | .................................. |
| People | friendly / inconvenient / boring / quiet | .................................. |
| Hotels | convenient / dirty / old-fashioned / difficult | .................................. |
| Business meetings and trips | long / difficult / clean / dull | .................................. |
| Presentations | terrible / large / short / useful | .................................. |

## E Speaking

You and your partner have just returned from business trips. Ask questions about each other's trip e.g. *What was your trip like? Which airline did you fly with? Where did you stay? What was the hotel like?* etc. You can invent as many extra details about your trip as you like.

Student A, your information is below. Student B, turn to File BB on page 154.

- You went to visit a new supplier in Portugal. Your experience was very positive.
- You flew to Lisbon – the flight was short and you arrived early.
- The weather was hot and sunny. Your hotel was luxurious.
- You visited the factory, and had meetings with a number of the staff. It was very interesting.
- You attended three technical presentations. They were very informative.
- The Managing Director showed you Lisbon by night.
- You ate out in an excellent restaurant. The seafood was delicious.

## F Reading

**1** Match the sentences with the cartoons below.

1 Did you have a good weekend?
2 Cheers!
3 See you on Monday.
4 Good luck!
5 Have a safe journey.
6 Speak to you soon.

**2** What alternatives can you think of for the expressions in **1**?

e.g. *See you on Monday.*
*See you later / tomorrow / on the 20th / soon.*

# 6.1 Dates and schedules

| Grammar | Present continuous for future |
|---|---|
| Vocabulary | Dates |
| Pronunciation | Ordinal numbers |

## A Listening 42

José Bordas and Isabella Romero are organizing a conference in Rio de Janeiro. The programme is not finished. Listen to the conversation and complete the missing information.

International Future of Transport Conference

**Wednesday 27th July**

| 8.00 p.m. | Welcome Dinner |
| *arriving from? Time? Hotel? Nights? single/Double?* | Guest Speaker: *Who?* |

**Thursday 28th July**

| 9.00 a.m. | Professor Timothy Railton Airport Design |
| 1.00 p.m. | Lunch – Garden Room |
| *Time?* p.m. | Professor Patricia Lingwood *Subject?* |
| 4.00 p.m. | Poster Presentations |
| 7.00 p.m. | Cocktail Party |
| 8.30 p.m. | Gala Dinner |

**Friday 29th July**

| 9.00 a.m. | Round Table Discussions *Prof Denier?* |
| 10.00 a.m. | Jaime Gallado Underground train systems in the 21st century |

## LANGUAGE NOTE

### The present continuous for future

When we have a fixed plan for the future we use the present continuous. Usually there is a date or a time in the sentence, or the date or time is understood.

*What are you doing this evening?*    *I'm going to a concert.*
*When is she arriving?*    *She's coming on Wednesday.*
*Where is he staying tonight?*    *He isn't (is not) staying here.*

## B Reading

Look at the conference programme in **A** again. Use the words in the boxes below to make questions for the answers provided. Take one word or phrase from each box, as in the example.

| When | | she | staying? |
|---|---|---|---|
| Where | is | they | arriving? |
| Who | are | Elizabeth Cortes | coming with? |
| How long | | Patricia Lingwood | speaking about? |
| What | | | arriving from? |
| What time | | | |

1  *When is Elizabeth Cortes arriving?*  On Wednesday.
2  ...........................................................  From Boston.
3  ...........................................................  At midday.
4  ...........................................................  Her husband.
5  ...........................................................  At the Ramada.
6  ...........................................................  One night.
7  ...........................................................  Trans-European road networks.

## C Speaking

Work in pairs. You are arranging the arrivals and transfers of the guests coming to the conference. You do not have all the information. Ask questions to complete your table.
Student A, turn to File E on page 151.
Student B, turn to File Q on page 153.

## D Listening

**1** Jaime Gallado is attending the conference next week. Read this fax from his personal assistant, Andrea Kraler.

```
To:        Jaime Gallado
From:      Andrea Kraler
-----------------------------------------------------------------------
Re:        FUTURE OF TRANSPORT CONFERENCE
-----------------------------------------------------------------------
Dear Jaime,

Best of luck at the conference. Just to confirm the details. Your travel
arrangements are as follows:

26th July — Vienna-Rio — Flight number: OS121 Dep: 07.25
30th July — Rio-Vienna — Flight number: LH507 Dep: 14.30
Hotel: Sheraton — 4 nights.

You are speaking on Friday 29th at 10.00 a.m. The title of your talk is
'Underground Train Systems in the 21st century'. Don't forget your
appointment with Thérèse Blanc on Thursday 28th at 7.30 p.m. at your hotel.
You are not booked for the cocktail party.

    Best wishes
    Andrea
```

**43a**  **2** You are Jaime. A colleague calls you with some questions. Listen and use the information in the fax to help you answer his questions.

43b  **3**  Listen again and check your answers.

## E Pronunciation

44a  **1**  Listen and circle the number you hear.

| 16th / 60th | 18th / 80th | 12th / 20th | 13th / 30th |
|---|---|---|---|
| 10th / 12th | 1st / 3rd | 31st / 33rd | 15th / 50th |

**2**  Listen again and check your answers. Practise saying the pairs of numbers aloud.

44b  **3**  Complete these sentences. Listen to check your answers, then read aloud.

1  May is the ............. month of the year.

2  12.5% is one ............. .

3  The last day of April is the ............. .

4  The person who finishes ............. gets a gold medal.

5  October–December is the ............. quarter of the year.

## LANGUAGE NOTE

### Dates

1  In spoken British English we use ordinal numbers for dates. We usually say and write the day, then the month, then the year. We also usually say *the* before the day and *of* before the month.
e.g.

| We say: | *the eleventh of February, two thousand and one* |
|---|---|
| We write: | *11 (or 11th) February 2001 or 11/02/01* |
| We say: | *the thirtieth of August, two thousand and five* |
| We write: | *30 (or 30th) August 2005 or 30/08/05* |

2  In American English, we usually say and write the month, then the day, then the year. We don't use *of* and *the*.
e.g.

| We say: | *January tenth, nineteen ninety-seven* |
|---|---|
| We write: | *January 10 (or 10th) 1997 or 01/10/97* |
| We say: | *October twenty-first, two thousand three* |
| We write: | *October 21 (or 21st) 2003 or 10/21/03* |

## F Speaking

**1**  Put these dates in chronological order, as in the examples.

☐ 11/09/99 (UK)

| *1* | 11/23/89 (USA) |

☐ September 22nd 1998

| 2 | twenty-first of September nineteen ninety-eight |

☐ 09/08/00 (USA)

☐ Christmas Day 2000

☐ 21/12/99 (UK)

☐ 23 September 1999

☐ 01/01/01

☐ 10/10/00

**2** Read the dates aloud.

**3** Work in pairs. Ask your partner for the following information.

1 his or her birthday
2 a date on an official document in his or her wallet
3 start date with present employer or school
4 expiry date on bank card
5 the date of the next lesson
6 a famous date in history

**G Listening**

**1** Here are some more famous dates. Do you know why are they famous? Discuss with a partner.

| | | |
|---|---|---|
| 15th April 1912 | 1st January 2000 | 1st June 1953 |
| 11th November 1918 | 21st May 1932 | 12th July 1998 |

**45** **2** Now match the dates with the appropriate headlines below. Then listen to check your answers.

# Dawn of the New Millennium

**d**
# GREAT WAR ENDS

**e**
# Mount Everest conquered for the first time

**b**
# TITANIC SINKS

# AMELIA EARHART CROSSES THE ATLANTIC

**f**
# FRANCE WIN WORLD CUP

**3** Which months of the year are missing from the box in **1**? Can you think of an important date for each of them?

# 6.2 Getting connected

| | |
|---|---|
| **Vocabulary** | Telephone expressions |
| **Communication Skills** | Telephoning: taking messages |
| **Pronunciation** | Contractions |

## A Listening

 **①** Jordi Marrero wants to visit Diana Wong in Hong Kong. He telephones her four times. Listen to the four conversations. What is the problem each time?

Dialogue 1 ............................................................................................................

Dialogue 2 ............................................................................................................

Dialogue 3 ............................................................................................................

Dialogue 4 ............................................................................................................

**②** Listen again and answer the following questions.

1 Who does Diana work for?
2 What is her mobile number?
3 Which department is she in?
4 When is she due back in the office?
5 When does Jordi want to meet?
6 What is his direct line?

**③** Listen again. Which dialogues do these lines come from?

a Speaking. ...4...

b How can I help? .......

c I'm sorry, sir, but there is no reply from her office. .......

d You've got the wrong extension. .......

e No thanks. I'll call later. .......

f Hold the line. I'll transfer you. .......

g Thanks for calling. .......

h Would you like to hold? .......

i I'll put you through. .......

j Can I take a message? .......

k Could you transfer me to her? .......

l Is that Diana? .......

## B Reading

Match sentences 1–9 with responses a–i.

1 Could I speak to Diana Wong, please?    a   G-I-N-S.
2 Can I take a message?    b   My name is Phillip Nevill.
3 I'm afraid you've got the wrong number.    c   Yes I'm here all day.
4 Can she call you back?    d   About 4 o'clock.
5 Could you spell that, please?    e   No thanks. I'll call back.
6 Would you like to hold the line?    f   Speaking.
7 When are you expecting her back?    g   Yes, please. Tell her Tom called.
8 Who's calling?    h   That's OK. I'll hold.
9 I'm sorry, the line is busy.    i   Oh, no. Sorry.

## C Speaking

Work in pairs. Make up a dialogue using these prompts. Take one route through the flow chart. Then change roles and choose another route.

**Route 1**
- Answer the phone for Patricia Lopez.
- Ask to speak to Patricia.
- Ask who is calling.
- Give your name.
- Offer to transfer the call.
- Say thank you.
- Patricia answers.
- Carry on the conversation.

**Route 2**
- Ask the caller to wait. Say that the line is busy. Ask the caller if he / she wants to wait.
- Agree to wait.
- Say that the line is still busy. Ask the caller if he / she would like Patricia to ring her back.
- Say no politely and ask for Patricia's mobile number.
- Give her mobile number to the caller.
- Say thank you and end the call.

**Route 3**
- Ask the caller to wait. Apologize and say that she is not there. Say why.
- Ask about her return.
- Say when. Offer to take a message.
- Agree and leave a message / phone number.
- Repeat the message / number back to the caller.
- Say that the message is correct. End the call.

## D Pronunciation

**1** In spoken English many words are contracted. Look at the sentences below and decide which words to contract.

1 I am arriving in Hong Kong on Friday.
   *I'm arriving in Hong Kong on Friday.*

2 Where is he staying?
   ......................................................................................................................

3 When is she due back?
   ......................................................................................................................

4 You are welcome.
   ......................................................................................................................

5 No thanks. I will call back later.
   ......................................................................................................................

6 I am afraid she is out this afternoon.
   ......................................................................................................................

7 He is in a meeting this morning.
   ......................................................................................................................

8 He has got a meeting this morning.
   ......................................................................................................................

**2** 47 Listen and check your answers. Repeat the sentences.

## E Writing

48 Diana Wong receives a lot of messages. Listen to her voice mail and write down as much information as you can for each message. Use the message pads below.

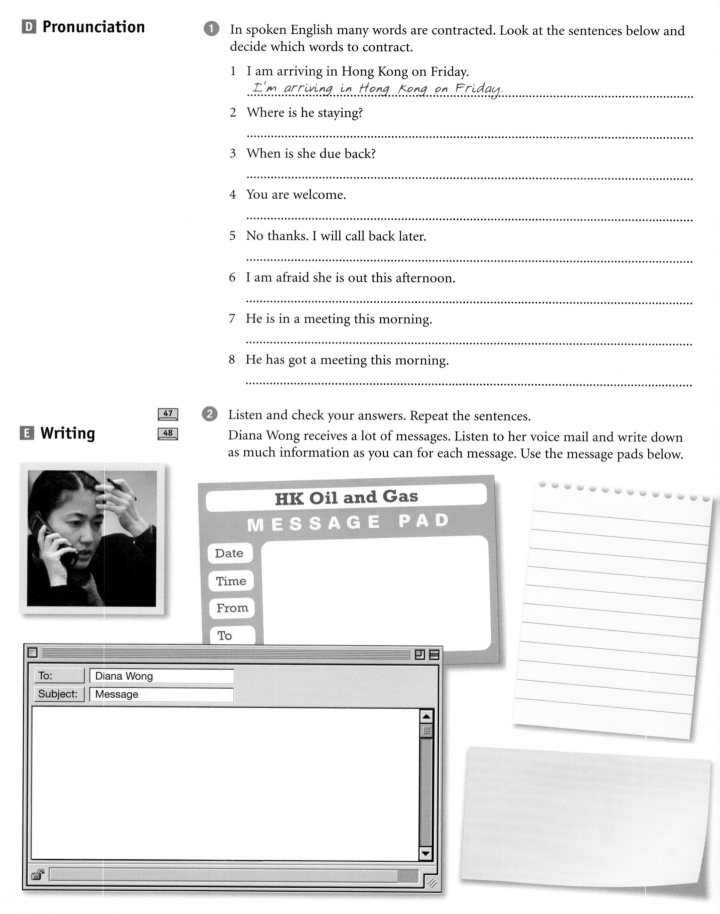

**HK Oil and Gas**

**M E S S A G E   P A D**

Date

Time

From

To

To: Diana Wong

Subject: Message

## F Speaking

1 Diana calls Jordi back at the Royal Garden Hotel. Work in groups of three. Make the conversation between the receptionist (R), Diana (D), and Jordi (J), by choosing one expression from each row, as in the example.

**R** 1 Royal Garden Hotel. How can I help? | Good morning, Royal Garden Hotel. | Good morning. Reception.

**D** 2 Hello. Could I speak to Mr Marrero please? | Jordi Marrero, please. | Is Mr Marrero there, please?

**R** 3 Do you have the room number? | Hold the line, please. | Could you spell that, please?

**D** 4 M-A-R-R-E-R-O. | OK. | 1081.

**R** 5 The line is busy. Will you hold? | M-A double R did you say? | Ten eighty-one?

**D** 6 Yes. | Yes, thank you. | Yes, that's right.

**R** 7 I'm putting you through now. | I'm connecting you. | It's ringing.

**D** 8 Thank you. | Thanks. | Thanks very much.

**J** 9 Hello? | Hello, Jordi Marrero speaking. | Yes?

**D** 10 Is that you Jordi? This is Diana. | Hi there. It's Diana. | Hello Jordi. This is Diana. I got your message.

**J** 11 Diana! At last! | Hello, Diana. Nice to hear from you. | Good evening, Diana.

**D** 12 Sorry, I was out yesterday. | Nice to hear from you too. | Good evening, Jordi.

**J** 13 Are you free this evening? | That doesn't matter. | Are you doing anything later?

2 Finish the conversation. Confirm the time and the place for dinner.

# 6.3 Arranging to meet

| Vocabulary | Time expressions |
| --- | --- |
| | Appointments and meetings |
| Communication Skills | Making and changing appointments |

## A Reading

**1** Natasha Hall works for a pharmaceutical company. It is 7.30 p.m. on Monday the third of April. Answer the following questions.

1   What was the time half an hour ago?
2   What was the date a week ago?
3   What is the date tomorrow?
4   What day was it yesterday?
5   What is the day after tomorrow?
6   What was the date the day before yesterday?
7   What was the date last Thursday?
8   What day is it in four days' time?

| | | | | | | |
| --- | --- | --- | --- | --- | --- | --- |
| Monday | 27 | 3 | 10 | 17 | 24 | 1 |
| Tuesday | 28 | 4 | 11 | 18 | 25 | 2 |
| Wednesday | 29 | 5 | 12 | 19 | 26 | 3 |
| Thursday | 30 | 6 | 13 | 20 | 27 | 4 |
| Friday | 31 | 7 | 14 | 21 | 28 | 5 |
| Saturday | 1 | 8 | 15 | 22 | 29 | 6 |
| Sunday | 2 | 9 | 16 | 23 | 30 | 7 |

**2** Now complete this table.

| | |
| --- | --- |
| −3 | ................................................... |
| −2 | ................................................... |
| −1 | *yesterday* |
| 0 | *today* |
| +1 | ................................................... |
| +2 | ................................................... |
| +3 | ................................................... |

**3** Read this information and complete the diary opposite.

1   On Friday she is flying to Washington.
2   Last Friday she attended a trade fair in Boston.
3   Tomorrow morning she's going to a sales meeting.
4   She flew to New Orleans yesterday.
5   She's spending the weekend with friends in Baltimore.
6   On Wednesday afternoon she's meeting Jack Rogers at 4.00 p.m. and Yuki Aoki two hours later.
7   She spent the day before yesterday in New York.
8   She was on holiday from Monday to Thursday.

**B Listening**

Natasha is at the HTO conference. She wants to meet a number of people. Listen to her four telephone calls and write down the appointments in her diary. Remember that it's now 7.30 p.m. on Monday the third of April.

| MARCH | | APRIL |
|---|---|---|

**Monday March 27**

..........................

**Tuesday March 28**

..........................

**Wednesday March 29**

..........................

**Thursday March 30**

..........................

**Friday March 31**

..........................

| **Saturday April 1** | **Sunday April 2** |
|---|---|
| .................... | *Fly to* .................... |

**Monday April 3**

........  HTO Conference starts
.................................

**Tuesday April 4**

9.00 – 12.00  ............ *Meeting*   8.00   *Dinner*
2.00   *Presentation*         ........  ..................
       *of JC432*                      ..................

**Wednesday April 5**

9.00 – 12.00  *IT Training 1*   6.00   *Yuki Aoki*
2.00   *Presentation of*        ........  ..................
       *new organization*                ..................
4.00   *Jack Rogers*   8.00   *Dinner*
                       10.00  *Jazz concert*

**Thursday April 6**

........  .................................
          .................................
9.00 – 12.00  *IT Training 2*
12.30   *Lunch* ..............................

**Friday April 7**

9.00 –11.00   *Tour of New Orleans*
.................................

| **Saturday April 8** | **Sunday April 9** |
|---|---|
| ............................ | |
| ............................ | |

**LANGUAGE NOTE**

## Making arrangements

More formal expressions

**1 Asking about availability**
*Would it be possible to meet?*
*When would be convenient?*

**2 Suggesting dates / times / places**
*Would Friday after dinner suit you?*
*Shall we meet in the lobby at 7.00?*
*Shall we say 8.30?*
*Are you doing anything on Tuesday?*

**3 Accepting and refusing**
*That suits me.*
*(I'm afraid) I'm not free.*
*(I'm afraid) I have another engagement.*

**4 Confirming**
*So that's 7 o'clock on Wednesday, then.*
*I look forward to meeting you.*

Less formal expressions

*Do you want to meet up?*
*When are you free?*

*How about Friday evening after dinner?*
*How about (meeting in) the lobby at 7.00?*
*Would 8.30 be OK?*

*That would be nice / fine (with me).*
*(I'm sorry) I can't make it then.*
*(I'm sorry) I've got something else on.*

*See you on Thursday, then.*
*Great. I look forward to it.*

## C Speaking

Work in pairs. You are at a conference in Spain and you want to meet an old friend for coffee. Look at your diary for tomorrow and call him or her to find a time when you are both free. You will need half an hour.

Student A, go to File F on page 151, Student B, go to File N on page 152.

## D Listening

**1** Natasha Hall telephones Mikael Stefansson again. Listen to the conversation and choose the best answer.

| | | | |
|---|---|---|---|
| 1 She wants to | a | confirm the appointment. | *Would* .......................... |
| | b | cancel the appointment. | .......................... |
| | c | change the appointment. | .......................... ? |
| 2 She suggests | a | the next day. | *Could* .......................... |
| | b | two hours earlier. | .......................... |
| | c | two days later. | .......................... ? |
| 3 He says | a | 5 o'clock is fine. | *5 o'clock? I'm* .......................... |
| | b | he is free. | .......................... |
| | c | he has another engagement. | .......................... |
| 4 She wants | a | to postpone it to Thursday. | *Could* .......................... |
| | b | to bring it forward to Friday. | .......................... |
| | c | to postpone it to Friday. | .......................... ? |
| 5 She suggests | a | Thursday. | *How about* .......................... |
| | b | Friday. | .......................... |
| | c | Saturday. | .......................... ? |
| 6 They agree to meet | a | at 6 on the 8th. | *So* .......................... |
| | b | at 8 on the 6th. | .......................... |
| | c | at 9 on the 6th. | .......................... |

**2** Now listen again and complete the expressions that are used.

## LANGUAGE NOTE

### Changing appointments

We can change an appointment in three ways.

We can *bring it forward* to an earlier date.  24 25 26 27 28

Or we can *postpone* it to a later date.  24 25 26 27 28

Or we can *cancel* it completely.  24 25 ✗ 27 28

**3** We had an appointment for Wednesday 16 January at 7.00 p.m. First we brought it forward an hour. Then we moved it to the same time the following day. Then we postponed it for a week. Finally we brought it forward again by two days. She telephoned me to suggest the following day and one hour later. I was an hour late and she arrived half an hour after me. What time and date did we finally meet?

4 Work with a partner. Look again at your information in File F on page 151 and File N on page 152.

Student A, phone Student B to change the time of your meeting. You can both change or cancel one other appointment in the day, if necessary.

## E Reading

Read these e-mails and put them in the order they were sent.

**a**
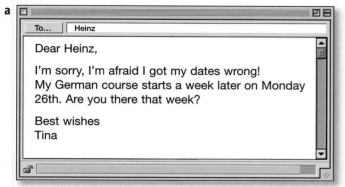

To... Heinz

Dear Heinz,

I'm sorry, I'm afraid I got my dates wrong! My German course starts a week later on Monday 26th. Are you there that week?

Best wishes
Tina

**b**
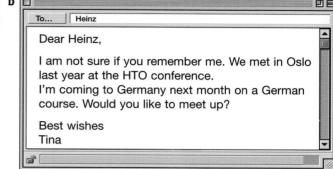

To... Heinz

Dear Heinz,

I am not sure if you remember me. We met in Oslo last year at the HTO conference.
I'm coming to Germany next month on a German course. Would you like to meet up?

Best wishes
Tina

**c**
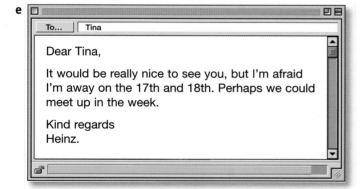

To... Tina

Dear Tina,

That's fine with me. It will be nice to see you again and to meet your colleague.

See you at the airport.
Heinz

**d**
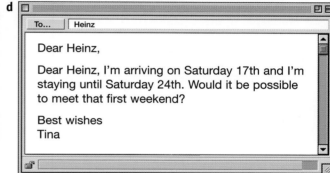

To... Heinz

Dear Heinz,

Dear Heinz, I'm arriving on Saturday 17th and I'm staying until Saturday 24th. Would it be possible to meet that first weekend?

Best wishes
Tina

**e**

To... Tina

Dear Tina,

It would be really nice to see you, but I'm afraid I'm away on the 17th and 18th. Perhaps we could meet up in the week.

Kind regards
Heinz.

**f**
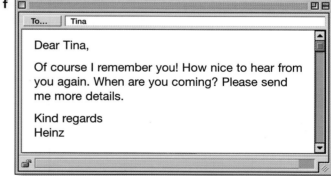

To... Tina

Dear Tina,

Of course I remember you! How nice to hear from you again. When are you coming? Please send me more details.

Kind regards
Heinz

**g**

To... Heinz

Dear Heinz,

Thanks for your kind offer. I'm now coming with a colleague. I hope that's OK. We're arriving on Saturday 24th at 17.30. Can we all go out for dinner that evening?

See you soon
Tina

**h**
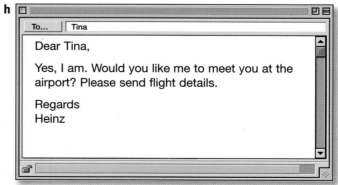

To... Tina

Dear Tina,

Yes, I am. Would you like me to meet you at the airport? Please send flight details.

Regards
Heinz

# Unit 7    Describing and comparing

## 7.1 Comparisons and contrasts

| | |
|---|---|
| **Grammar** | Comparative forms |
| | Superlative forms |
| **Vocabulary** | Descriptive adjectives |
| **Pronunciation** | Weak forms |

### A Reading

Richard: I drive to work every day. I leave at 5.30 a.m. to avoid the traffic. Parking in London is expensive, but I prefer going by car. It's more relaxing than taking the train because I always arrive on time. The train is often late, or sometimes doesn't come at all.

Virginia: I take the subway. I live near the end of the line, so I always have a seat on the train. The journey takes about thirty-five minutes. I read a newspaper or watch other passengers. It's cheaper and quicker than taking your car, and it's much safer too.

**1** Read what Richard and Virginia say about travelling to work. What reasons do they give for travelling this way?

**2** How do you travel to work or school?
   - How long does it take?
   - What do you do during the journey?
   - Why do you travel this way?

### B Vocabulary

**1** How many types of transport can you think of? Continue this list: *car, subway (British English = underground), bus ...*

**2** Complete the table with words which mean the opposite, as in the example.

| A | B |
|---|---|
| fast / quick | slow |
| cheap | ex |
| healthy | un |
| relaxing | str / ti |
| interesting | bo |
| easy | di |
| good for the environment / your health | b environment / your health |

**3** Which adjectives in **2** would you use to describe the following?
   a  travelling to work by car      b  learning English      c  smoking

## C Speaking

**1** Think about travelling to work in your own town or city. Make three sentences, using the language below.

> Travelling by car is
> - quicker / slower
> - more relaxing / more tiring than travelling by train because …
> - safer / more dangerous

**2** All the adjectives in **1** are in the *comparative* form.

We add *-er* to the end of the adjective, e.g. *quicker, slower*.
or   We put *more* before the adjective, e.g. *more relaxing, more tiring*.
Can you say what the rule is?

**3** How do you prefer to travel generally? Using the adjectives below, write sentences comparing different forms of transport.

cheap ..............................................................................................................................

fast ..................................................................................................................................

relaxing ...........................................................................................................................

comfortable ....................................................................................................................

Compare your sentences with a partner. Ask extra questions if necessary.
e.g. *Travelling by bus is more relaxing than travelling by car.*
    *Why do you think travelling by car is more stressful?*
    *Because it's very slow – it takes me 45 minutes to drive 5 kilometres.*

**LANGUAGE NOTE**

### Comparative forms

1  We use the comparative form to compare two things.
   e.g. *London is more expensive / cheaper than Tokyo.*

| Category | Example | Comparative |
|---|---|---|
| One-syllable adjectives | *cheap* | *cheaper* |
|  | *big* | *bigger* |
| Two syllables ending *-y* | *easy* | *easier* |
| Two or more syllables | *expensive* | *more (less) expensive* |
| Irregular adjectives | *good* | *better* |
|  | *bad* | *worse* |

2  When we want to talk about things being the same, we use *as … as.*
   *Paris is as expensive as London.*    *Madrid is not as big as Paris.*

## D Pronunciation  `51`

Words in a sentence sometimes sound different when they are unstressed. Vowel sounds are often replaced by the sound /ə/. Listen to a sentence and repeat. Now read sentences 2–5 aloud. Then listen and check.

　　　/ə/　　　　　/ə/ /ə/
1  The car's quicker than the bus.
2  The train's more tiring than the car.
3  The bus is slower than the train.
4  The train's more dangerous than the car.
5  The country isn't as stressful as the town.

**E Listening**

**1** Look at the photos of three different cities. In which do you think houses and apartments are:
– most expensive
– biggest?

Paris

Tokyo

New York

**52** **2** Now listen to three people talking about housing in the cities where they live. Complete the table below.

| Country | Average living area (in m²) per person | Average rent |
|---|---|---|
| 1 .................................. | .............................. | .......................... than New York / Paris |
| 2 .................................. | .............................. | .......................... than Tokyo / Paris |
| 3 .................................. | .............................. | ............. ........... than New York .......................... than Tokyo |

**3** Complete the sentences below, using the adjectives given in brackets, as in the example.

1 The USA has ......*the biggest*.......... living area per person. (big)
2 Japan has .................................... living area per person. (small)
3 New York is .................................... city to live in. (cheap)
4 Tokyo is .................................... city to live in. (expensive)

**4** In your country, which is:

1 the biggest city?
2 the highest building?
3 the most popular tourist attraction?

**LANGUAGE NOTE**

**Superlative forms**

We use the superlative form to compare three or more things.
*Munich is the most expensive / the cheapest of the six cities.*

| Category | Example | Superlative |
|---|---|---|
| One-syllable adjectives | cheap | (the) cheapest |
| | small | (the) smallest |
| Two syllables ending -y | easy | (the) easiest |
| Two or more syllables | expensive | (the) most expensive |
| Irregular adjectives | good | (the) best |
| | bad | (the) worst |

**1** Complete the questions with the superlative form of the adjective indicated, as in the example.

1 What's the _most important_ thing in your life? (important)
2 What's the ............................... thing in your life? (stressful)
3 What's the ............................... time you start work in the morning? (early)
4 What's the ............................... time you finish work in the evening? (late)
5 What is your ............................... meal of the day? (big)
6 When is the ..................... time of day to have a meeting with colleagues? (good)
7 What's the ............................... time to call you for business? (bad)
8 On holiday, what's the ............................... thing to take with you? (important)

**2** Match 1–8 in **1** with A–H below to complete the questionnaire, as in the example. Then choose your own answer to each question.

**3** Compare your answers with a partner. Now look at File S on Page 153 and calculate your score. Are you working too hard?

# Are You Working too Hard?

**A Question**
a After 6 p.m. when the telephone stops ringing.
b In the morning.
c In the afternoon.
d I don't have time for meetings.

**B Question**
a 6 a.m. or earlier.
b Between 7 and 8 a.m.
c Between 8 and 9 a.m.
d 9 a.m. or later.

**C Question** [ / ]
a My job.
b My company.
c My family and/or friends.
d My health.

**D Question**
a Family holidays.
b Not enough time to do my job well.
c Travelling to work.
d Learning English.

**E Question**
a At home in the evening.
b Phone me when you want. If it's important, I want to know.
c At weekends.
d When I'm on holiday.

**F Question**
a My computer.
b My mobile phone.
c Sun cream and sunglasses.
d Some paperwork from the office.

**G Question**
a 6 p.m. or earlier.
b Between 7 and 8 p.m.
c between 8 and 9 p.m.
d 9 p.m. or later.

**H Question**
a Lunch.
b Dinner.
c Breakfast.
d I don't have a big meal. I have little snacks when I have time.

**G** Listening    [53]    Listen to these sentences and say if you agree or disagree. If you disagree, say why.

# 7.2 Describing products and services

| Grammar | The present simple passive |
| --- | --- |
| | Sequence linkers |
| Vocabulary | Customer service |
| Communication skills | Describing technical processes |

## A Speaking

When there's a problem with your computer system at work or your washing machine at home, you probably call a customer service number to ask for help.

1 Look at this list of customer service promises. Which points are important to you as a customer? Give examples from your experience of really good (or bad) customer service.

**Service with a smile**

> **1** When you phone us, you speak to a real person, not a machine.
>
> **2** Our staff are polite and friendly at all times.
>
> **3** We send you a technician within 24 hours.
>
> **4** If we say we're coming on Tuesday morning, we come on Tuesday morning.
>
> **5** Our technicians explain the problem simply and resolve it in the quickest possible time.

2 Does your company have a customer service department? What services do you offer to your customers?

## B Reading

1 Read this text about customer service at North West Energy, and answer these questions:

1 Which words in the text mean:
  a to complete or do?     c changed or improved?
  b a plan or timetable of work?   d permits or makes it possible?

2 How many jobs do North West Energy technicians do every day, on average?

3 What are the advantages of the new improved system?

## Bringing Power to the People

Here at NorthWest Energy we carry out 12,500 maintenance jobs every day. We have developed an automated system, the Work Finder, which arranges work schedules for our 2,500 technicians. Our new updated process uses a process called 'power planning'. This allows us to send you the right person for the job in the quickest possible time. Now our schedules are arranged up to five days in advance.

**2** Look at this diagram which shows how the Work Finder works. Then read the description of the process below. Put the sentences in the correct order, as in the example.

.......... **A** This is the new intelligent part of the system. It monitors the work of the technicians.

.......... **B** The Work Finder gives the technicians their schedules by telephone or computer.

....*!*..... **C** The Customer Service Department receives a request for help.

.......... **D** The Work Finder passes the details of the call to the Power Planner.

.......... **E** It always knows where they are, what their speciality is, and when they will be free.

.......... **F** It sends the customer request to the Work Finder – that's the central part of the system.

.......... **G** The Power Planner arranges the work schedule, and sends the information back to the Work Finder.

**LANGUAGE NOTE**

### The present passive

1 We use the passive form when we don't know, or it is unimportant, who has performed an action. The passive is often used to describe technical processes, where we are more interested in the process itself than who or what is responsible for it.

2 The present simple passive is formed with the present of the verb *be* and the past participle. (For a list of irregular past participles, see page 157.)

| Active | Passive |
|---|---|
| *The company carries out 12,500 jobs every day.* | *12,500 jobs are carried out every day.* |
| *We use a system called 'power planning'.* | *A system called 'power planning' is used.* |
| *We arrange schedules up to 4 days in advance.* | *Schedules are arranged up to four days in advance.* |

3 If we want to mention who or what has done something, we use *by*.
*The maintenance work is carried out by our team of technicians.*
*Schedules are arranged by the Work Finder.*

## C Writing

Your boss has asked you to write a technical report on how the Work Finder system works. Expand these notes to make complete sentences. Use the present passive.

1 A request for help / receive / Customer Service department
*A request for help is received by the Customer Service department.*

2 This request / send / Work Finder

.................................................................................................

3 The details of the call / pass / Power Planner

.................................................................................................

4 The work of the technicians / monitor / Power Planner

.................................................................................................

5 The work schedule / arrange / and / the information / send back / Work Finder

.................................................................................................

6 The technicians / give / their schedules / Work Finder

.................................................................................................

## D Listening

1 You are going to hear a description of another new automated system called 'Veggie Vision', for identifying food items in supermarkets. Before you listen, check the meaning of these words. Use the pictures below to help you.

— a scanner
— a checkout
— a cashier
— size and shape
— a selection of items

**2** Listen to the first part and answer these questions.

1 What does Veggie Vision do?
2 Who is it used by?
3 What is the main advantage of the system?
4 How is it better than present supermarket scanners?

**3** Now listen to the second part. Using the pictures opposite, make notes on how Veggie Vision works. What happens when it can't identify the item correctly?

**4** Listen to part two again. Which phrases are used to introduce the different steps in the process?

1 *First of all ...*
2 ...................................
3 ...................................
4 ...................................
5 ...................................

**5** Now combine words and phases from A and B to describe how Veggie Vision works. Use the phrases you found in **4** to introduce the different steps.

e.g. *First of all the product is scanned by the cashier.*

| A | B |
|---|---|
| a photo | select |
| the cashier | compare with the database |
| information about size & shape | show a picture |
| the correct item | scan |
| the choice | take |
| the product | confirm |
| the product details | record |

## E Speaking

Work with a partner. Take it in turns to make true sentences, using words from each box. Use the passive form of the verb. For some sentences you can use more than one verb.

| A | B | C |
|---|---|---|
| Microsoft software | grow | rare, medium, or well done |
| Bordeaux wine | produce | on a Friday |
| rice | rob | at Flushing Meadow |
| Italian | eat | in the USA every day |
| 50% of banks | speak | in Atlanta |
| steak | use | in parts of Switzerland |
| the Coca-Cola company | play | in China |
| 38 million banknotes | base | in the south-west of France |
| the US Open tennis championships | print | in 85% of the world's computers |

# 7.3 Evaluating products

| Vocabulary | Dimensions and specifications |
|---|---|
| Communication skills | Exchanging opinions |

## A Vocabulary

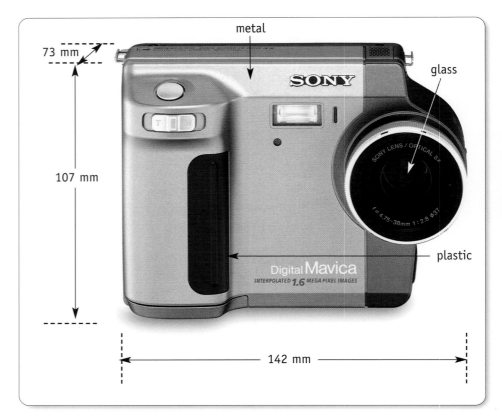

1. Look at the photo and complete these sentences with words from columns A, B, C, and D.

    1   It's 142 mm in ........................ , 107 mm in ........................ , and 73 mm in ........................ .

    2   It's about 670 grammes in ........................ .

    3   It's made of ........................ , ........................ , and ........................ .

    4   It's more or less ........................ in shape.

    5   It's black and ........................ .

| A | B | C | D |
|---|---|---|---|
| width | glass | square | green |
| height | plastic | rectangular | blue |
| length | metal | round | yellow |
| depth | wood | cylindrical | white |
| weight | leather | oval | grey |
| diameter | rubber | conical | red |
| thickness | | | multi-coloured |

**2** Now use the words in columns A-D to describe the following.

> a desk    a golf ball    a TV remote contol    a soft drink can

**3** Did you need any other words? Add them to the table in **1**.

LANGUAGE NOTE

### Product characteristics

**1 Size and dimension**

| **Noun** | | **Adjective** | |
|---|---|---|---|
| *What's the ... ?* | | *How ... is it?* | |
| *It's (50) cm in ...* | length | *It's (50)cm ...* | long |
| | height | | high |
| | width | | wide |
| | depth | | deep |
| | thickness | | thick |
| | diameter | | |

**2 Weight**

*How much does it weigh?*    *It weighs 50 kg.*

**3 Materials and function**

*It's made of ... + material.*    *It's made of glass, plastic, metal, etc.*
*It's used for ... + -ing.*    *It's used for changing channels on the TV.*

**4** Use the Language Note to complete these questions. You can't use the same word twice.

1 What's the ../....................... of the Great Wall of China?
2 How ..*h*...................... is the Empire State Building in New York?
3 How much does a human brain *w*......................?
4 What's the average ..*d*...................... of the Atlantic Ocean?
5 What's the maximum ..*w*...................... of the Grand Canyon?
6 What's the ..*d*...................... of the holes on a golf course?
7 How ..*t*...................... is a surfboard?

**5** Now match the questions with the answers below.

> | 432.3 metres | Between 7 and 10 cm | 3,926 metres | 1.4 kg |
> |---|---|---|---|
> | Over 6,400 km | About 29 km | 10.3 cm | |

You can check your answers in File B on page 150.

### B Listening    `55`

Listen to descriptions of three familiar products from the late twentieth century. Every time you hear a tone, try to guess what the product is. You will hear the answer at the end.

1 ............................................................
2 ............................................................
3 ............................................................

## C Speaking

Work in pairs to complete this crossword. Give your partner clues for the words you have. Student A, your word list is in File J on page 151. Student B, turn to File V on page 153.

e.g.  A: *What's 2 across?*
B: *It's cylindrical. It's made of metal. It's about 15 cm high. It's used for storing and preserving food.*
A: *Is it a can?*
B: *Yes, it is. What's 1 down?*

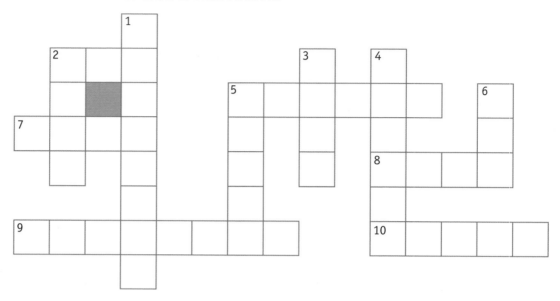

## D Listening

A breakfast cereal company is launching a new muesli product. It is intended for adults who want a healthy diet. To maximize sales, the company is considering three promotional gifts.

**1** Work with a partner. Look at the three gifts. Which one would you choose to promote the new cereal, and why?

**2** Three managers – Carmen, Anna, and Ned – are discussing the gifts. Listen. Which one do they choose?

**A pedometer**
For people who go running or jogging. Measures speed and distance.
*Free when you send the coupons from 12 packets of cereal.*

**The Calorie Counter**
A booklet of recipes (with calorie values) for people who want to lose weight.
*Free in every packet of cereal.*

**The 'Relax-Max CD'**
An audio CD with relaxing music and audio instructions for yoga exercises
*Free when you send the coupons from 6 packets of cereal.*

**3** What advantages and disadvantages do they mention for each gift? Listen again and check.

| Advantages | Disadvantages |
|---|---|
|  |  |

**4** Listen again. Which expressions from the Language Note below do you hear? Which words do the speakers stress?

### Giving opinions

1 Giving an opinion
*I think / I don't think ...*      *If you ask me ...*      *In my view ...*

2 Asking for an opinion
*What do you think?*      *What's your view on this?*      *How about you?*

3 Agreeing / disagreeing
*I think so too / I agree / You're right.*      *I'm not sure.*
*I don't agree / I disagree.*      *Yes, I do / No, I don't.*

## E Speaking

Work in threes. You all work for an American company which wants to launch a new low-calorie chocolate bar in your country or countries. Hold a meeting to discuss the points on the agenda below, and make a decision for each one.

# AGENDA
### Marketing planning meeting

**Low-calorie Chocolate bar**

1 Target customer?
  – Age
  – Sex

2 Dimensions?
  – 10 cm x 4 cm x 3 cm
  – 15cm x 3cm x 3 cm
  – 8 cm x 8 cm x 3 cm

3 Wrappings?
  – sporty
  – classic
  – young / sexy

4 Product name?
  – Choc'Lite
  – Athlete's Friend
  – Fantasy

5 Price?
  – same as other chocolate bars
  – higher than usual
  – lower then usual

6 Launch date?
  – June
  – November
  – January

7 Advertising?
  – A famous personality to promote it
  – A slogan for the advertising campaign

# Unit 8 | Life stories

## 8.1 Success stories

| Grammar | Past simple revision |
| --- | --- |
| | Time expressions |
| | Past passive |
| **Vocabulary** | Word families |
| **Communication skills** | Checking information |

**A Vocabulary**

**1** Think of words to do with travelling by air. Look at the definitions below and find the words. The first letter is given.

1 Heathrow, JFK, Charles de Gaulle     *airports*
2 KLM, Air France, United     *a*
3 Boeing 707, Jumbo, Concorde     *a*
4 Rome, Paris, New York, Moscow     *d*
5 the people who pay to take a plane     *p*
6 a two-way ticket     *r*
7 a journey by air     *f*
8 to reserve a seat     *b*
9 Economy, Business, First     *c*
10 to leave the ground in an aeroplane     *t*

**B Reading**

**2** Can you think of five more words associated with flying?
Look at this brief history of Juan Trippe, then answer the questions that follow.

Juan Trippe was one of the pioneers of modern air travel. His company – Pan American Airways – was one of the first to offer cheap air travel round the world. Trippe was born in New Jersey <u>in 1899</u>. After graduating from Yale in 1921, he worked first on Wall Street, and then as a flying taxi pilot. <u>From 1924 to 1926</u> he worked for Colonial Air Transport, and founded Pan American Airways <u>the following year</u>.

At first, Pan Am offered flights across the Caribbean and South America. This was so successful that Trippe started to offer flights to Asia <u>eight years later</u>. At the end of the thirties he introduced the first transatlantic flights. <u>Immediately after the Second World War</u>, Trippe decided to offer cheap transatlantic flights. Other airlines objected – they wanted to keep prices high, and earn maximum profits. <u>For several years</u>, many airports in Europe refused to accept Pan Am flights. The other airlines only finally agreed to offer economy flights in 1952.

Trippe started on his next project the same year – the development of the jet engine. This would make it possible for planes to fly longer distances at higher speeds. He commissioned Boeing to build passenger jet planes for Pan Am. The first Pan Am jet – a Boeing 707 – flew from New York to Paris <u>in 1958</u>.

<u>In the sixties</u>, Trippe commissioned Boeing to build an even bigger jet, which could carry more passengers. This was the 747, nicknamed the Jumbo jet. Unfortunately, Trippe ordered too many 747s and put Pan Am into financial difficulties. In 1968 he resigned from the company. <u>Thirteen years later</u> he died.

## Juan Trippe Pioneer of the Jet Age

**Departures**

1. In what ways was Trippe important in the history of flight?

2. Answer the following questions.
   1. Where did he do his studies?
   2. Where was his first job?
   3. When did he found his own airline?
   4. When did he offer the first passenger flights to Europe?
   5. Why did other airlines not want to offer economy flights?
   6. Why was the passenger jet a great invention?
   7. What was the advantage of the Boeing 747?
   8. Why did he resign?

3. Look at the article again and match the underlined expressions with the expressions below. Use each expression once only. The first is done for you.

   1. in 1981 ............*thirteen years later*............
   2. for three years ....................................................
   3. in 1945 ....................................................
   4. six years later ....................................................
   5. about forty years ago ....................................................
   6. in 1927 ....................................................
   7. for a number of years ....................................................
   8. over 100 years ago ....................................................
   9. in 1935 ....................................................

**LANGUAGE NOTE**

**Time expressions**

1. *Ago* is used with the simple past tense. It relates actions in the past to now.

   *He was born about one hundred years ago.*     *The flight left ten minutes ago.*

2. We use these expressions to talk about actions and events in the past.

   | | |
   |---|---|
   | in 1981 | He died in 1981. |
   | for two / three / four years | He studied at Yale for three years. |
   | two / three / four years later | He started a new job two years later. |
   | the following year | He founded his own company the following year. |
   | from (1924) to (1926) | From 1924 to 1926 he worked for Colonial Air Transport. |

## C Listening

`57`

**1** Go is another airline which tries to offer cheap travel. Listen to this news story about Go and put the events below in order.

a  Barbara Cassani announced the start of a new airline.    .............
b  The first flights started.    .............
c  Robert Ayling decided to create a low-cost airline.    .............
d  Go had thirteen aircraft in operation.    .............
e  She chose Stansted Airport as a base.    .............
f  She chose the name 'Go'.    .............
g  Barbara Cassani presented her business plan to the BA board.    .............

**2** Now match these time expressions with the correctly ordered events.

1  in December    .............
2  the following month    .............
3  in March 1997    .............
4  in November    .............
5  by 1999    .............
6  six months later    .............
7  in May 1998    .............

## D Listening

A journalist wants to interview Barbara Cassani. Before the interview she telephones Barbara's secretary to get some background information.

`58a`

**1** Listen to the conversation and complete the journalist's notes below.

- BIRTH  Where  ................................
         When  ................................
- EDUCATION  ................................
- HUSBAND  ................................
- 1981  First vacation job
  ................................
  ................................
- ........  First post abroad (with Coopers and Lybrand)
  1987  ................................
  1992  ................................
- ................................  General Manager of BA in New York
- ................................  CEO of Go

`58b`

**2** Listen to these sentences again and complete the gaps.

1  ................................................ here by Coopers and Lybrand in 1986.
2  ................................................ the job of General Manager in New York.
3  ................................................ CEO in 1997.

> ## The past passive
>
> 1 The past passive is formed with *was / were* (the simple past of the verb *be*) and the past participle.
>
> 2 We use the past passive when:
> We don't know, or it is unimportant, who performed an action.
> *When was she appointed?*                *She was appointed in April.*
>
> We are more interested in the result of the action than who did it.
> *The system wasn't properly installed.*        *The offices were painted bright red!*
>
> 3 If we want to say who performed the action, we use the preposition *by*.
> *The company was taken over by a large multinational last year.*
> *The accounts were audited by Coopers and Lybrand.*

## E Writing

Use the information in **D** to write a brief life-story of Barbara Cassani. Use the dates and verbs below to help you.

| 1960 | 1987 | be born | have a baby |
|------|------|---------|-------------|
| 1981 | 1992 | work | be appointed |
| 1984 | 1997 | be transferred | start working |
| 1986 |      | join |  |

## F Speaking

**1** Look at the table below. For each item make a question using a word from each column, as in the example. Use each verb only once.

| When | was | the telephone | built? |
|------|-----|---------------|--------|
|      | were | the Channel Tunnel | founded? |
|      |      | the Titanic | formed? |
|      |      | Sony | launched? |
|      |      | penicillin | discovered? |
|      |      | the Beatles | invented? |

**2** Work in pairs. Take it in turns to ask and answer the questions. Find the answers in the box below. Ask *where* each event happened, as well as *when*.

e.g. *When was the telephone invented?*        *The telephone was invented in ...*
     *Where was it invented?*                *It was invented in ...*

| 1946 | 1994 | Liverpool | 40 metres under the seabed |
|------|------|-----------|-----------------------------|
| 1912 | 1928 | the US | London |
| 1962 | 1875 | Tokyo | Belfast |

**3** Now think about who was responsible for these events. Work with a partner and take it in turns to ask and answer questions using *Who ... by?* Find the answers in the box below.

e.g. *Who was the telephone invented by?*  *The telephone was invented by ...*

| Alexander Fleming | Akio Morita | Alexander Graham Bell |
|-------------------|-------------|------------------------|
| Cammells Shipyard | Eurotunnel | John Lennon and Paul McCartney |

# 8.2 Making money

| Vocabulary | Financial vocabulary |
|---|---|
| | Deducing from context |
| | Collocations |
| **Communication skills** | Dealing with numbers |
| **Pronunciation** | Numbers |

## A Vocabulary

**1** Sometimes you can understand a new word by looking at the context (the other words in the sentence where it appears). Look at the sentences in the text below. Complete them using one of the words in the box. The first one is done for you.

| shares | shareholders | worth | invested | stake | spend | earn |
|---|---|---|---|---|---|---|
| owe | borrowed | save | dividend | lent | tax | pay |

# Me and my money

## In the latest in our series on tips for new investors, John Graham describes how he manages his investments

When I was eighteen I inherited £1000 from my grandmother. I _invested_ [1] half of the money on the Stock Market and the rest I put in the bank. I bought ................[2] in three different companies and each one pays me a ................[3] every year. I also have a 20% ................[4] in a small company started by a friend of mine. There are four other ................[5] in the company. I have a small house in London. It is probably ................[6] £250,000 now. I ................[7] £100,000 from the bank when I bought it. I work as an accountant and ................[8] a reasonable salary, but I have to pay a lot of ................[9]. My father ................[10] me quite a lot of money for my studies and I still ................[11] him about £5,000. I ................[12] him back about £100 a month. I ................[13] a lot of money on my favourite sport, skiing, but I also like to try and ................[14] for my old age.

**2** Read the article again. Are these statements true (T) or false (F)?

1 He owes his grandmother £1,000. .......

2 He sold his house in London. .......

3 He has shares in four companies. .......

4 He lent the bank money to buy the house. .......

5 He is a lawyer. .......

6 He pays a lot of tax. .......

7 His father gives him £100 a month. .......

8 He spends a lot of money on his hobby. .......

## B Reading

**1** Work in pairs. Read the first four sentences below and decide how many shares each person had in 1999. Then complete the pie chart.

**A** *600 shares*  **B** ..................  **C** ..................  **D** ..................  **E** ..................

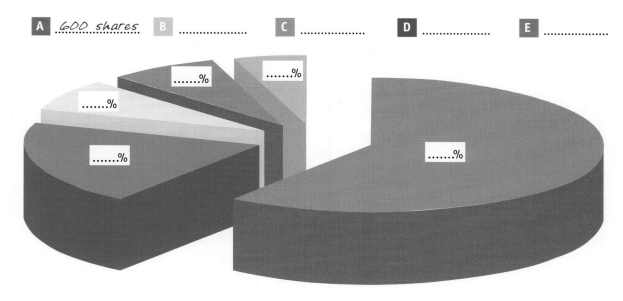

1 A founded the company in 1994. There were 1,000 shares.
2 In 1995 he sold 20% of the shares to B and C. B bought $^3/_4$ and C bought $^1/_4$ .
3 In 1996 D borrowed £10,000 from the bank to buy 25% of A's shares.
4 In 1998 E spent £15,000. She bought half of B's shares.
5 In 1999 the company made a profit of £50,000. The dividend was £20 per share.
6 In 2000 the accounts showed the company was worth £200,000.

**2** Now read the rest of the sentences in **1**, and calculate the answers to these questions. Check your answers in File A on page 150.

1 What was the dividend of each shareholder in 1999?
2 Did D make a good investment?
3 Who is the majority shareholder?
4 What is E's stake worth?

## C Pronunciation 59

**1** Listen to these sentences and write down the year you hear.

**2** Listen again and write down the amount.

**3** Listen again and check your answers.

1 In ............. Michael Jordan earned ............. .
2 In ............. a bottle of Coca-Cola cost ............. .
3 In ............. Russia sold Alaska to the USA for ............. .
4 The first American millionaire was Cornelius Vanderbuilt who left .............
   when he died in ............. .
5 In ............. the company secretary of Glaxo wrote a cheque for ............. .
6 In ............. Dr Ronald Dante earned ............. for a 2-day lecture course.

Look at this article and answer the questions below.

**P**rince Alwaleed is a member of the Saudi royal family. He is also Chairman of Kingdom Holdings. This company has investments all over the world, totalling over $15 billion. It is a major shareholder in Disneyland Paris, where it holds a 25% stake. It also owns the Four Seasons hotel group, has a 5% shareholding in Citicorp, owns 5% of Apple Computers, and in addition has stakes in many other companies such as TWA, Netscape, Daewoo, and Motorola. Prince Alwaleed is one of the most successful investors in the world. Chairman of his first company at the age of fourteen, Prince Alwaleed was brought up in Beirut before returning to Saudi Arabia to attend military school.

## Prince Alwaleed bin Talal

He studied at university in San Francisco and got his Masters from Syracuse University. He made his first fortune in the eighties investing in real estate in Saudi Arabia. He also worked as a local partner for Korean companies in the country. By 1988 he was worth over $1 billion. Luckily for him there is no income tax in Saudi Arabia!

In 1991 he made the best investment of his life. He bought shares for $890 million in Citicorp, America's largest bank at that time. That stake is now worth $5.5 billion. His latest project is to build the highest skyscraper in Riyadh. Riyadh is continuing to grow as the commercial capital of Saudi Arabia, and it looks as if the $350 m Kingdom Centre will be yet another profitable investment.

**1** Choose the correct answer to these questions.

1 Kingdom Holdings …
  a is a subsidiary of Citicorp.
  b has a stake in Citicorp.
  c borrows money at 5% from Citicorp.

2 When he was fourteen he …
  a studied in San Francisco.
  b ran his first company.
  c bought shares in Disneyland Paris.

3 In the eighties he …
  a invested in property in Saudi Arabia.
  b worked in Korea.
  c lost over $1 billion.

4 His stake in Citicorp …
  a is worth $890 million.
  b has increased by $890 million.
  c cost $890 million.

5 Kingdom Holdings …
  a owns a quarter of the shares in Disneyland Paris.
  b has a small stake in Disneyland Paris.
  c is the majority shareholder in Disneyland Paris.

**2** Find these numbers in the text. What do they refer to?

a five
b 14
c twenty-five
d nineteen ninety-one
e eight hundred and ninety million
f one billion
g five point five billion
h three hundred and fifty million

## E Listening

`60` **1** Look at these headlines from the financial press. Listen to the financial news stories and match them with the headlines.

**a**
### Shares fall as interest rates rise

**b**
### Italian investor takes 30% stake in hotel group

**c**
### German giant buys French insurance company

**d**
### STAFF RECEIVE DAY'S INCOME

**2** Listen again and answer the following questions.

1. How much did Mr Vieri pay for his stake?
2. What was the share price at the end of the day?
3. What nationality is the furniture company?
4. Why was the money given to the staff?
5. How much was the base rate increased by?
6. What was the effect on share prices?
7. Is AGF buying Allianz, or is Allianz buying AGF?
8. Where will the headquarters of the new company be?

## F Speaking

Work with a partner. Find ways of completing these sentences.

1. My company spends too much on ...
2. My company does not spend enough on ...
3. I owe money to ...
4. I am paid ...
5. It's best to borrow from ...
6. I spend a lot on ...
7. My best ever investment was ...
8. Money is ...
9. I can't afford ...
10. A new car costs ...

## G Vocabulary

A good way to remember vocabulary is by *collocations*, words which often appear together. Look back through the section and find words which can go with these key words, as in the examples.

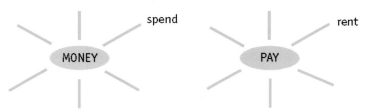

spend — MONEY

rent — PAY

# 8.3 Company history

| | |
|---|---|
| **Grammar** | Question making |
| **Vocabulary** | Word families |
| **Communication skills** | Presenting company history |

### A Speaking

**1** Look at these logos and answer the following questions.

1 Whose logos are they?
2 What products or services are they associated with?
3 Are they well-known in your country?
4 Which logos are the most famous in your country?
5 Why are logos important?

**2** McDonald's is one of the most famous brands in the world. Do this quiz with a partner to test how much you know about the company.

| | | A | B | C |
|---|---|---|---|---|
| 1 | The first McDonald's was opened in Illinois in ... | 1955 | 1965 | 1975 |
| 2 | The Big Mac™ was invented in ... | 1968 | 1978 | 1988 |
| 3 | The 25,000th McDonald's was opened in ... | 1959 | 1979 | 1999 |
| 4 | Ronald McDonald appeared on TV for the first time in ... | 1963 | 1983 | 1993 |
| 5 | At McDonald's a client is served in ... | 90 secs | 105 secs | 120 secs |
| 6 | The company was floated on Wall Street in ... | 1956 | 1965 | 1985 |
| 7 | A new McDonald's is opened every ... | 5 hours | 5 days | 5 weeks |
| 8 | The number of customers served daily is ... | 400,000 | 4,000,000 | 40,000,000 |
| 9 | The Happy Meal™ was introduced in ... | 1979 | 1990 | 1997 |
| 10 | By 1996 McDonald's had opened in ... countries | 50 | 75 | 100 |

## B Listening

**1** Listen to this talk about McDonald's and check your answers to the quiz in **A**.

**2** Listen again and complete the gaps below with the appropriate verb. Which verbs are in the passive form?

1955 Ray Kroc ....................... his first restaurant in Illinois. He .......................
the name from two brothers called McDonald.

1963 Ronald McDonald ....................... in the first television advertising for
McDonald's.

1965 The company ....................... on Wall Street. 100 shares .......................
$2,250. Today those shares are worth $2.5 million!

1967 Kroc ....................... his first restaurants outside the USA in Puerto Rico
and Canada.

1968 The Big Mac™ ....................... .

1979 The Happy Meal™ ....................... .

1984 Ray Kroc died.

1990 McDonald's Restaurants ....................... in Moscow and Beijing.

1995 Burghy, the Number 1 in Italian fast food ....................... . Within one
month the company's turnover ....................... by 50%.

1996 Belarus became the 100th country in the world with a McDonald's.

1999 The 25,000th McDonald's ....................... in Chicago.

**LANGUAGE NOTE**

### Active and passive questions

The past simple passive question form is different from the active form.

1 Active questions use *did* and infinitive of the verb (without *to*).

*When did Ray Croc buy the name?*
*Where did they open their restaurant?*

2 Passive questions use *was / were* and the past participle of the verb.

*When was the company founded?*
*Where were the first restaurants located?*

**3** Make questions for these answers. Sometimes you need the passive form of the
questions, and sometimes the active, as in the example.

1 When *did Ray Croc open his first restaurant?* 1955.

2 When ......................................................................... ? 1963.

3 When ......................................................................... ? 1965.

4 How much ................................................................. ? $2,250.

5 When ......................................................................... ? 1968.

6 When ......................................................................... ? 1979.

7 When ......................................................................... ? 1984.

8 Where ....................................................................... ? Moscow and Beijing.

9 When ......................................................................... ? 1995.

10 Where ...................................................................... ? Chicago.

## C Speaking

Work in pairs. Ask each other questions about two famous companies to fill in the grid below. Then try to guess the name of your partner's company. Student A, your information is in File G on page 151. Student B, turn to File T on page 153.

| | Company A | Company B |
|---|---|---|
| Founded<br>Founder<br>Location<br>Activity<br>Famous products<br>Key date<br>Company name | | |

## D Vocabulary

Complete this table.

| Verb | Noun(s) | Example |
|---|---|---|
| ..................... | founder /<br>foundation | Sony was ..................... by Akio Morita. |
| ..................... | acquisition | AOL ..................... Time Warner in 2000. |
| increase | ..................... | Inflation ..................... by 2% last year. |
| launch | ..................... | The official ..................... of the product took place in Rome. |
| create | ..................... | The company was ..................... in 1955. |
| ..................... | introduction | The iMac was ..................... onto the market in 1999. |
| open | ..................... | There are new ..................... in the Asian market – that's why we have a sales team there. |
| ..................... | expansion | The company has no plans for ..................... at the present time. |

1 Prepare a short presentation on Henry Ford and Ford Motors based on this file.

# Henry Ford

| | |
|---|---|
| 1863 | born in Michigan |
| 1879-1902 | worked in various workshops building cars and engines |
| 1903 | founds Ford Motors |
| 1908 | launches Model T-Ford |
| 1913 | introduces the car assembly line – makes it possible to produce more cars more quickly |
| 1918 | Candidate for US Senate – loses election |
| 1941 | allows unions at Ford for the first time |
| 1947 | dies |
| 1999 | William Clay Ford Junior (great grandson) becomes Chairman of Ford |

2 Choose a company you know and prepare a short presentation on its history. Use the grid on the opposite page.

3 Look at these other famous brands, buildings, and products. Work with a partner and try and guess when they were launched, built, or opened. Then match another piece of information from column B. Check your answers in File L on page 152.

| | A | B |
|---|---|---|
| Concorde | 1931 | It offers the best view of London. |
| Eiffel Tower | 1979 | There is now one in New York, Bilbao, Venice, and Berlin. |
| Walkman | 1891 | It was originally designed as a fairground attraction. |
| Guggenheim museum | 1890 | They were originally made for cowboys and gold prospectors. |
| London Eye | 1958 | It was originally called the Soundabout. |
| Empire State Building | 1969 | It was the original plastic money. |
| Escalator | 1999 | It was built to celebrate the 100th anniversary of the French Revolution. |
| American Express Card | 1889 | It was featured in *King Kong*. |
| Levis | 1959 | It was the first supersonic passenger plane. |

## 9.1 Making decisions

| | |
|---|---|
| **Grammar** | *Will* or present continuous |
| | *Shall I ....* ? |
| **Communication skills** | Arranging a schedule |
| **Pronunciation** | Future tense contractions |

### A Listening

**1** Rosalind Butcher is Personal Assistant to Tony Ralph. On Monday morning she opens this letter. Read the letter and answer the questions below.

**Autospark GmbH**
Autospark GmbH, Bahnhofstrasse 7, 52538 Gangelt, Deutschland

Mr Tony Ralph
Regional Director
Autospark Distribution UK
24 Binsey Lane
Manchester M18 23P          13 February 2001

Dear Mr Ralph

The President of Autospark group, Frau Astrid
Köhnen, is coming to London from .............[1] to
.............[2] March for a ............. .............[3] .

During her trip, she would also like to take the
opportunity to visit you and some of the key
.............[4] in Manchester, and meet one or two of our
English .............[5] .

I would be grateful if you could arrange a
schedule of visits and appointments for Frau
Köhnen on the afternoon of  .............[6] 7 March and
the morning of .............[7] 8 March. She is planning
to arrive in Manchester at about .............[8] p.m.

Please let me know if you require any further
information. I look forward to hearing from you.

Yours sincerely

*Katya Muster*

Assistant to Astrid Köhnen

1  Where is the head office of the company – in the UK or Germany?
2  Who is the letter from?
3  What does Tony Ralph have to do?

**2** Now listen to Rosalind and Tony discussing Frau Köhnen's visit. Complete the missing information in the letter.

**3** Listen again and complete these sentences from the conversation.

Rosalind: Astrid Köhnen ............ ............ to England next month.

Tony: How long ............ she ............ with us?

Tony: ............ she ............ the night here in Manchester?

Rosalind: All I know is that ............ ............ here at about one in the afternoon.

**4** In the second part of their conversation, Tony and Rosalind begin to plan the visit. Rosalind makes notes on the memo pad below. Listen, and complete her notes.

THINGS TO DO

Phone Katya Muster.
- Is it necessary to ............................ ?
- Ask about Frau Köhnen's ........................ .
- Offer to ........................ .
- What time ........................ ?

If necessary, call Palace Hotel to
........................ .

Ask Joseph to ........................ .

**5** Rosalind makes a lot of decisions. Which form of the verb does she use?

*I phone / I'll phone / I'm phoning Katya Muster in Germany.*
*I see / I'll see / I'm seeing if we need to reserve a hotel room.*

Listen again. What other examples of the same tense do you hear in the conversation?

**LANGUAGE NOTE**

### *Will* and present continuous

1 To talk about definite arrangements – meetings, appointments, visits, etc. – we use the present continuous.
*She's (She is) coming to England next month.*
*When's (When is) he arriving?*
*They aren't (are not) staying for the weekend.*

2 When we make a decision at the time of speaking, we use *I'll* (*I will*) or *we'll* (*we will*) + the infinitive of the verb without *to*.
*I don't know his travel arrangements. I'll phone him and ask.*
*It's 11 o' clock and I'm tired. I think I'll go to bed.*
*I'm not sure if we're free then. We'll let you know on Friday.*

## B Speaking

You are flying to England next Tuesday to visit Tony Ralph at Autospark. You have some problems. Make a decision in each case, using *I'll*, as in the example.

1 You want to stay at the Palace Hotel in Manchester, but it's fully booked. *I'll stay at the Hilton instead.*
2 There aren't any more Business class seats on your flight.
3 You remember that it's your wedding anniversary next Tuesday.
4 You hear that your airline is going on strike next Tuesday.
5 Now you hear that the taxi drivers in Manchester are going on strike.
6 It's Monday. Tony's assistant Rosalind calls to say that Tony is ill.
7 It's Tuesday. You wake up and look at your alarm clock. Your plane to Manchester left 15 minutes ago.

## C Pronunciation

**1** Listen to these sentences, and complete the missing words.

1 ........................ give her a call.
2 ........................ arriving on the 5.50 train.
3 ........................ coming to see us next week.
4 ........................ see you at 2.00 p.m. on Thursday.
5 ........................ staying at the Palace Hotel.
6 ........................ meeting her on the first day.
7 ........................ giving an answer?

**2** Now repeat the sentences. Pay particular attention to the pronunciation of contractions.

## D Vocabulary

**1** Here are some notes about things to do when planning a big conference. Complete the sentences using verbs from the box below. Use each verb once only.

| send | check | invite | ask | remind | make |
|------|-------|--------|-----|--------|------|
| hire | book | pick up | print | order | take |

### Time in months

| 8 | 7 | 6 | 5 | 4 | 3 | 2 | 1 | CONFERENCE |
|---|---|---|---|---|---|---|---|------------|
| 1 ............... hotel and conference rooms. 2 ............... guest speakers. | | 3 ............... guest speakers to send a summary of their talk. | | | 4 ............... guest speakers to send their summary! | 5 ............... students to work as conference officials.<br><br>6 Prepare and ............... conference programme.<br><br>7 ............... conference programme to all participants. | 8 ............... food for conference lunches and dinners. | 9 ............... that all audio-visual equipment (overhead projectors, microphones, etc.) is working.<br><br>10 ............... last-minute changes to the programme.<br><br>11 ............... guest speakers at the airport.<br><br>12 ............... guest speakers to their hotel. |

**2** Find three words or phrases that can follow each verb below, as in the example.

to check    *an invoice / a bill / that everything is OK* ..................................................

to order    ................................................................................................

to hire     ................................................................................................

to send     ................................................................................................

to invite   ................................................................................................

## E Listening

[64]

**1** Two people are planning a conference. Listen and complete the missing words.

A: So what about the hotel rooms? ............. you book them or ............. I?

B: ............. you do that? You're good at negotiating prices.

A: Sure. How about the guest speakers? ............. I invite them?

B: No, ............. do that. I have all their addresses.

A: Great. And ............. you ask them to send a summary of their talk?

B: Yes, of course.

**2** Which expression in **1** means *Do you want me to ... ?*
Now repeat the conversation with a partner.

**LANGUAGE NOTE**

> ### Shall I ...?
>
> We use *shall I* + infinitive (without *to*) when we offer to do something for somebody.
> *That looks heavy. Shall I carry it for you?*
> *You look busy. Shall I do the post?*
> *The phone's ringing. Shall I answer it ?*

**3** Now continue the conversation in **1** in the same way. Use the checklist of points in Exercise **D**. To decide who's going to be responsible for each point, read the following information.

**Person A**
– is good at negotiating prices
– has contacts at the university
– knows a cheap printing firm
– worked in catering before
– has a car

**Person B**
– has the addresses of all the guest speakers
– is good at planning
– understands how machines work
– is a quick thinker
– has a car

# 9.2 Thinking ahead

| | |
|---|---|
| **Grammar** | *Will* for predictions |
| | Conditional sentences |
| **Vocabulary** | Advertising and marketing |
| **Pronunciation** | Contractions of auxiliaries |

## A Vocabulary

**1** Put these terms into the correct column below, as in the example.

| | | |
|---|---|---|
| department stores | newspapers | hoardings (USA: billboards) |
| the general public | mail order | the 20–30 age group |
| direct mailing | companies | shopping centres (USA: shopping malls) |
| specialist shops | supermarkets | TV and radio adverts |
| business people | retired people | specialist magazines |

| Customers | Distribution / sales outlets | Advertising |
|---|---|---|
| ................................. | *department stores* | *hoardings* |
| ................................. | ................................. | ................................. |
| ................................. | ................................. | ................................. |
| ................................. | ................................. | ................................. |
| ................................. | ................................. | ................................. |

**2** What other words can you add to each list?

**3** Think about the companies which produce the clothes you are wearing or the objects you have with you – e.g. your briefcase, your mobile phone, your watch.

- What type of customers do they attract?
- How do they distribute or sell their products?
- Where do they advertise?

## B Listening

Look at the picture of the DBCV501 and read the product description below.

> **Product Features**
> - Voice record, playback
> - World time: 24 time zones
> - 50 pages of Telememo: 8 letters and 12 numerals per page
> - Calculator
> - Stopwatch
> - 5 multi-function alarms
> - Auto-calendar (pre-programmed until the year 2039)

**1** Here are some of the benefits of its special features. Which feature does each sentence describe?

1  You can see how long your international phone call lasted.  *a stopwatch*
2  You can see what the time is in Rome when you're in Tokyo.  ...........................
3  You can leave a message for yourself and listen to it later.  ...........................
4  You can check that the figures on an invoice are correct.  ...........................

Think about the other features. What are the possible benefits?

**2** Maria Jarvis exports electronic goods. She is in Madrid to present some new products to Juan Carlos Almirez, a Spanish distributor. Listen to them discussing sales strategy for the DBCV501, and make notes under these headings.

| Types of customer | Sales outlets | Advertising |
|---|---|---|
|  |  |  |

**3** Listen again, and complete these extracts from the conversation. Do you agree with their analysis?

M: Well, I think ....................... have more success with men in the twenty to thirty-five age group. The product has a younger high-tech image. Older men ....................... be interested.

J: How about sales outlets? ....................... supermarkets buy it?

M: No, they ....................... . It's too specialized.

J: But I'm sure ....................... have customers in airport shopping centres.

M: Yes, absolutely.

**4** Match the two halves of the sentences. Listen again to check if necessary.

1  You'll get a lot of sales            a  ... it'll be necessary to do some direct mailing.

2  If we want to sell by mail order,    b  ... you won't have another chance later.
3  If you don't decide now,             c  ... if you advertise in business magazines.

- Which tense do we use in the half of the sentence with *if*?
- Which tense do we use in the other part?
- When do we use a comma?

**Other uses of *will***

1 We use *will* when we want to make predictions about the future.
*I think we will sell a lot in Europe.*
*The product will be very popular with young children.*

2 *Will* often contracts to *'ll* after personal pronouns.
*Will not* abbreviates to *won't.*
*You'll / We'll / They'll have customers in shopping centres.*
*Older men won't be interested.*

3 Notice the construction in first conditional sentences with *if*:
*If + present simple + will / won't or Will / won't + if + present simple*
*If you don't buy it now, you'll have problems later.*
*You won't have enough time if you wait until tomorrow.*

## C Speaking

1 A big banking group is thinking of closing its smaller branches, and opening new branches in big shopping centres. What do you think will be the advantages of this?

2 The President of the bank has made some notes on the possible consequences of the new strategy. Work with a partner. How many sentences with *if* can you make? Look at the examples and continue.

e.g. *If we open new branches in shopping centres, we'll have more contact with customers. If we have more contact with customers, we ...*

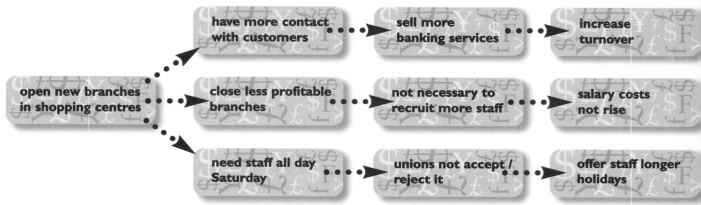

## D Pronunciation

1 Look at these phrases. Which ones can be contracted? Which ones have two different contracted forms? Write the contracted forms, then say them.
e.g. *I am not – I'm not*

| | A | B |
|---|---|---|
| 1 | I am not ............................. | I have not got ............................. |
| 2 | She is not thirty ..................... | She has got thirty ......................... |
| 3 | I want to sell ........................ | I will not sell ............................. |
| 4 | Who will work ........................ | Who is working ........................... |
| 5 | We will buy ........................... | We buy .................................... |
| 6 | I liked ................................ | I would like ............................... |
| 7 | Would you like ....................... | Do you like ............................... |
| 8 | They are not ......................... | There are not ............................. |

66  2 Now listen. Which phrase do you hear, A or B?

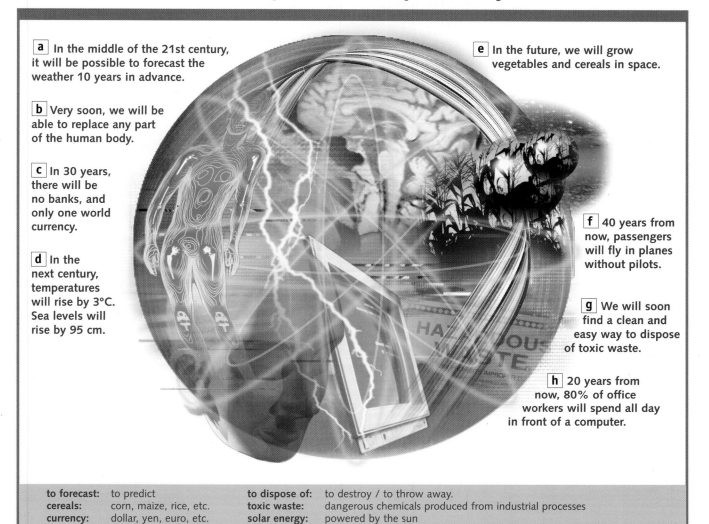

**a** In the middle of the 21st century, it will be possible to forecast the weather 10 years in advance.

**b** Very soon, we will be able to replace any part of the human body.

**c** In 30 years, there will be no banks, and only one world currency.

**d** In the next century, temperatures will rise by 3°C. Sea levels will rise by 95 cm.

**e** In the future, we will grow vegetables and cereals in space.

**f** 40 years from now, passengers will fly in planes without pilots.

**g** We will soon find a clean and easy way to dispose of toxic waste.

**h** 20 years from now, 80% of office workers will spend all day in front of a computer.

| | |
|---|---|
| **to forecast:** to predict | **to dispose of:** to destroy / to throw away. |
| **cereals:** corn, maize, rice, etc. | **toxic waste:** dangerous chemicals produced from industrial processes |
| **currency:** dollar, yen, euro, etc. | **solar energy:** powered by the sun |

1 Pilotless planes are already used in different countries for military purposes. There are also experiments with unmanned planes running on solar energy. None of these carry passengers, however, and it's difficult to imagine that this situation will change.

2 This is the most pessimistic estimate. The lowest figures given are 1.6°C and 15 cm.

3 The USA is already experimenting with this. With the support of NASA, scientists are developing equipment to enable plants to grow on the Space Shuttle and the International Space Station.

4 It's very possible that this will come true. At the moment, for example, the figure is already 48% for the UK, and 67% for the USA.

5 Yes, this is possible. Scientists have discovered a bacterium called *deinococcus radioducans*, which can be modified to 'eat' toxic waste; it can also absorb nuclear radiation.

6 This will almost certainly come true. Doctors can already transplant many internal organs from one person to another. There is also great potential for 'growing' parts of the body by genetic engineering.

7 More and more people are buying things by credit card in shops or on the Internet. We are using less and less cash. If we don't need cash, we won't need currencies. And if we don't need currencies, we won't need banks!

8 Yes and no. Research by scientists at Oxford University shows that it is possible to predict the weather by looking at the activity of the sea. However, this will only be useful for general weather trends. We might be able to predict that the summer of 2010 will be hot, but it's impossible to know if 6 June 2010 will be a good day for a barbecue!

# 9.3 Complaining and apologizing

| | |
|---|---|
| **Grammar** | *I'll...* and *Shall I..?* |
| **Vocabulary** | Customer problems and solutions |
| **Communication skills** | Complaints and apologies |
| | Spoken versus written complaints |

## A Vocabulary

Look at the eight people in this office.

1. Which person …
   1. has received a bill which is too high? .......
   2. is waiting for a delivery? .......
   3. has received the wrong quantity of goods? .......
   4. wants to buy something, but can't? .......
   5. would like to receive a cheque? .......
   6. has an IT problem? .......
   7. is waiting for a call? .......
   8. can't read a document? .......

2. Now match the responses below to the complaints in the picture.
   a. I'm sorry about that. I'll check with the transporter. .......
   b. I do apologize. I'll dispatch the missing items today. .......
   c. One moment, please. I'll connect you to the Accounts Department. .......
   d. Sorry about that. I'll send it again. .......
   e. Yes, I'm afraid there's only one person there today. Would you like to fax the details? .......
   f. I'm sorry to hear that. I'll inform the IT support department immediately. .......
   g. I do apologize. I'll send you a credit note for the difference. .......
   h. I'm sorry about that. I'll ask him to call you immediately. .......

**67a** **1** A customer calls Stephanie Rowe at Benn Distribution. Listen to the first part and complete the memo.

---

**BENN DISTRIBUTION LTD**
Customer Service department

*Complaint Form*

Caller .................................... Company ....................................
Order No. ...............................
Description of goods ..........................................................
Problem ..............................................................................
Action .................................................................................
.............................................................................................

---

**67b** **2** In the second part, Stephanie Rowe calls back. Listen. Where are the instruction manuals? What does she offer to do?

**3** Complete these extracts from the two dialogues. Who says each sentence: Stephanie (S), or the customer (C)? Listen again if necessary.

I'm .............. about my order.

1 .......

I'm very sorry .............. that.

2 .......

Can you .............. .............. the problem?

3 .......

.............. .............. send them by express mail?

6 .......

.............. call you .............. in ten to fifteen minutes.

4 .......

I'm .............. .............. we found them here in our factory.

5 .......

I do .............. once again.

7 .......

**LANGUAGE NOTE**

**Responding to complaints**

1 Giving bad news
*I'm sorry, but we found the missing items here in our factory.*
*I'm afraid we can't send them immediately.*

2 Saying sorry
*I'm very sorry about that.*
*I do apologize for the mistake.*

3 Promising to do something
*I'll look into the problem.*
*I'll dispatch the missing items today.*

4 Offering to do something
*Would you like me to send it by express mail?*
*Shall I send it today?*

## C Speaking

Discuss these problems on the telephone with a partner. Student A, use the information below. Student B, turn to File Y on page 154.

**1** You are Gloria Powell, Accounts Manager at SIMCO.

1 A client phones you about an invoice. Ask for the invoice number and date. Promise to look into the problem, and ask when you can call back.

2 Call back. Apologize – the invoice is for $800, not $900. Promise to send a new invoice.

**2** You are John Miller-Jones. You are still waiting for an order of 150 champagne glasses from Funglass Inc.

1 Call Angelica Geraldo, Sales Manager of Funglass Inc. Explain the problem. Offer to send a copy of your order form.

2 Ms Geraldo phones you back. Your address is 149 East River Drive, Trenton, New Jersey. Ask if it's possible to deliver tomorrow.

## D Reading

**1** Read this e-mail. What is the problem? What does Ms Shining want Ms Geraldo to do?

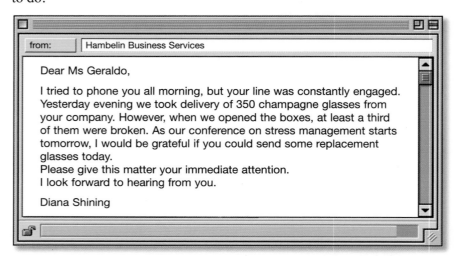

from: | Hambelin Business Services

Dear Ms Geraldo,

I tried to phone you all morning, but your line was constantly engaged. Yesterday evening we took delivery of 350 champagne glasses from your company. However, when we opened the boxes, at least a third of them were broken. As our conference on stress management starts tomorrow, I would be grateful if you could send some replacement glasses today.
Please give this matter your immediate attention.
I look forward to hearing from you.

Diana Shining

**2** Look at the phrases on the left from the telephone dialogue in **B** . Which phrases in the e-mail are used to say the same thing in more formal language?

| Telephone dialogue | E-mail |
|---|---|
| They arrived | ..................................................... |
| Can you send ...? | ..................................................... |
| Can you look into the problem? | ..................................................... |
| Speak to you soon. | ..................................................... |

**3** Now change these sentences from letters into more informal telephone language.

1 We would like to apologize for the delay.
Sorry ...........................................................................................................

2 I look forward to meeting you on 23 January.
See .............................................................................................................

3 I regret to inform you that your order will be three days late.
I'm .............................................................................................................

4 I will be pleased to send you some more information, if you require it.
Shall ....................................................................................................... ?

5 I hope you will have a pleasant trip to the USA.
Have ...........................................................................................................

**4** Ms Shining isn't answering her phone, and it is impossible to speak to her. Write an e-mail in reply to hers. Use the formal letter phrases in **3** to help you.

## E Speaking

Work in pairs. In this game, you have to try to complete a row of four squares – horizontal, vertical, or diagonal – before your partner does. To 'win' a square you have to make a sentence or question.

1 Take it in turns to choose a square. ✆ squares are telephone conversations.

⬚⬚ squares are face-to-face conversations.

2 If it is a ✆ square, look at the corresponding question in the ✆ list below.

If it is a ⬚⬚ square, look at the corresponding question in the ⬚⬚ list.

3 To answer the question, use one of these structures.
*Shall I … ?    Can you … ?    I'll …    Present continuous (I'm … -ing …)*
*Would you like me to … ?    Could you … ?*

4 If your answer is correct, you win the square. Write your initials in it.

---

### ✆ SQUARES

**1** You are calling someone. He's not in the office this morning. What do you say?

**2** You're calling a hotel. Ask if it's necessary to confirm your reservation by fax.

**3** A caller wants to speak to Mario. He's not there. Offer to do something.

**4** Someone suggests a meeting on Tuesday. It's not possible. Say why.

**5** The line's engaged. Ask if the caller can wait.

**6** A customer asks when you can send a brochure. What do you say?

**7** You're on a business trip. Ask a colleague to fax you this month's sales figures.

**8** You are arranging to meet a colleague in your town, but where? In his / her office, or in yours? Ask your colleague.

### ⬚⬚ SQUARES

**A** You or your colleague have to meet Mr Andros at the airport. Who's going to do it? Ask your colleague.

**B** You're meeting a friend at the airport. Her suitcase looks very heavy. What do you say?

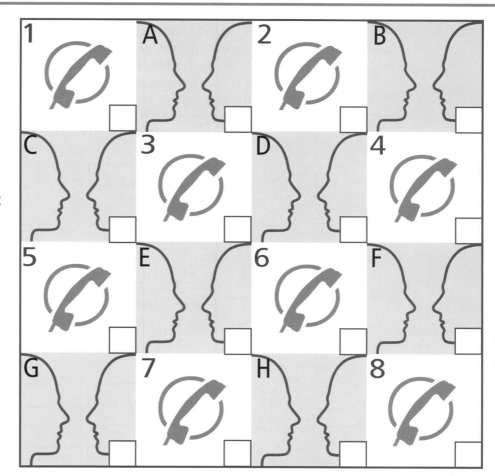

**C** You need to make 200 photocopies of a document. Ask a colleague to do it.

**D** Ask a friend about his plans for this weekend.

**E** Your visitor says it is hot in your office. Offer to do something.

**F** You're in a restaurant. Order your meal.

**G** Talk about three appointments or meetings you have next week.

**H** You need to wash your hands before dinner. Ask your visitor to excuse you for a minute.

# Unit 10 People at work

## 10.1 Suggesting and recommending

| **Vocabulary** | Managing a small business |
|---|---|
| **Communication skills** | Making suggestions |
| | Giving advice |

### A Vocabulary

Use the definitions below to complete the word square. The first letter of each word is given.

1　to send by post (often in large numbers)
2　a special reduced price offered to good customers
3　to change the location of your business (or home)
4　a regular payment for the use of a building
5　the total sales of a company
6　the people who work for a company
7　buildings and / or land used by a business
8　a contract to use a building and / or land for a fixed period of time
9　other companies who are trying to sell the same goods as you
10　to promote or publicize a company or product

### B Reading

1　Look at this extract from a business magazine. Owners of small businesses write to Dr Biz to ask for advice. Read the first two letters and answer the questions below.

1　What kind of small business does the writer of each letter have?
2　What decision does the writer of letter A have to make next month?
3　What does the writer of letter B want to do?

# Dear Dr Biz

**Dear Dr Biz**

I am the owner of a restaurant in Cambridge where I serve traditional English food. During the day we get a lot of business from coach parties of tourists. We are very busy, but our prices are low because there's a lot of competition for the lunchtime market. In the evening it's very quiet. The restaurant has a cellar downstairs which is not used. I pay a high rent because we are in the centre of town. Next month I have to decide if I want to renew my lease. Do you think we should move to cheaper premises further from the town centre?

**Francis Beaney**
**Cambridge, England**

A

**Dear Dr Biz**

My husband and I run a translation agency. We work from our home, which is outside Essen (Germany). We have a staff of three translators – one for English, French, and Russian. Some weeks we are very busy and other weeks we have little work. Our turnover goes up and down. When business is bad, we advertise in local newspapers, and we mail companies in Essen once a year. Unfortunately, the response to our advertising isn't good, and we can't afford to spend any more. How can we get more business?

**Astrid Heiner**
**Essen, Germany**

B

*Dear Mr Beaney,*
*I would advise you to introduce some changes to your menus. Then you can increase your prices. How about offering more European food and not just English dishes? I don't think you should move because town centres are always popular. Perhaps you should use your cellar for private parties and offer discounts to local firms. Why don't you mail some local companies and see what they say?*

*Dr Biz*

2 Now read Dr Biz's advice to Francis Beaney. Do you agree with what he says? Underline the structures that he uses to give advice, e.g. *How about?* Which ideas does he strongly recommend, and which are just suggestions?

3 Work with a partner. Use the same expressions to give advice to Astrid Heiner and her husband in Germany.

## C Listening

Dr Biz also has a radio phone-in programme, where he answers people who have written to him. He is speaking to Astrid Heiner, the writer of the second letter in **B** .

**[68]** **1** Dr Biz makes five suggestions. Listen, and complete the left-hand column below, as in the example.

| Suggestions | Responses |
|---|---|
| 1 ...*I think you should*... use your present customers more. | I ................. ................. that's the ................. . |
| 2 ................. ................. advertising your agency on the Internet? | I'm ................. ................. about that. |
| 3 ................. ................. ................. offer language training courses in their companies? | ................. , ................. out of the ................. . |
| 4 ................. ................. ................. ................. offer more unusual languages. | ................. , that's a ................. . |
| 5 ................. ................. looking for specialist translators on the Internet? | ................. , that's a ................. ................. . |

**2** Listen again, and complete Astrid Heiner's responses to each suggestion. What reasons does she give for each response?

**3** Number the responses in the right-hand column from the most positive (1) to the most negative (5).

**LANGUAGE NOTE**

### Making suggestions

1 For making strong recommendations we use these expressions.
*You should / you shouldn't recruit any more staff.*
*I think / don't think you should advertise on the Internet.*
*I would advise you to offer other languages.*

2 To suggest other possibilities we use these expressions.
*What about starting a language school?*
*How about looking on the Internet?*
*Why don't you mail some companies?*

3 To respond to suggestions we use these expressions.
*That's a good idea.*           *That's out of the question.*
*That's a possibility.*          *I don't think that's the answer.*
                                 *I'm not sure about that.*

## D Speaking

1 You and your partner are managers in the same company. You have a number of problems. One solution is suggested for each problem. Think of some more.

| Problem | Solution | Other ideas |
|---------|----------|-------------|
| Your best salesman has an interesting job offer from your competitor. | Offer him more money. | |
| You spend a lot on advertising without increasing sales. | Reduce your prices. | |
| If you introduce a no-smoking policy, your financial director will leave. | Let her leave. | |
| Your biggest customer wants a 5% discount, and your company has a no-discount policy. | Just say 'no'. | |
| The boss is seventy-two and has been in charge for too long. | Arrange a party to celebrate X number of years. | |

2 Now discuss each problem following these guidelines. Use the language from the Language Note.

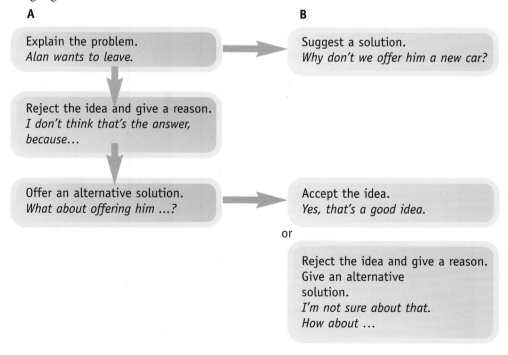

A

Explain the problem.
*Alan wants to leave.*

Reject the idea and give a reason.
*I don't think that's the answer, because...*

Offer an alternative solution.
*What about offering him ...?*

B

Suggest a solution.
*Why don't we offer him a new car?*

Accept the idea.
*Yes, that's a good idea.*

or

Reject the idea and give a reason. Give an alternative solution.
*I'm not sure about that. How about ...*

## E Speaking

Work in pairs. Both of you have some business problems. Take it in turns to tell each other about your problems and to offer advice. Use the expressions in the Language Note to give advice. Student A, turn to File U on page 152 to find out about your problems. Student B, look at File Z on page 154.

# 10.2 Responsibilities and regulations

| Grammar | Modals of obligation |
|---|---|
| | Asking and giving permission |
| Vocabulary | Company regulations |

**A** **Reading** `69`

1. Listen to two people describing their jobs. After each sentence try and decide what jobs are being described.

   Job 1 .......................................................

   Job 2 .......................................................

2. Roger Penn does both these jobs. Read this article about his company, Lloyds TSB, and answer these questions.

   1. Why do banks have to be open 24 hours a day?
   2. What does this mean for the staff?
   3. What are the advantages for Roger Penn?
   4. What are the advantages for Mr and Mrs Cox?

# Banks in Britain

and all over the world have a new problem – how to have enough staff present at the times customers want them. Banks now have to stay open all day and all night to deal with customers calling them by phone or conducting their business directly via the Internet. Many banks now offer flexible working hours to all their staff at all levels.

Roger Penn is a deputy manager. He works part-time for Lloyds TSB. He took a 50% cut in salary but now he can be free for his second job – he is a rugby referee. 'I can leave work at 1.00 and be on the rugby pitch by 2.00,' he says. He can also travel more without worrying about doing a full day's work the next day. All personnel at Lloyds can ask to reduce or change their contract.

Chris Cox is a Lloyds TSB manager in Reading (UK). He works four days a week from 8.00 a.m. to 7.00 p.m. This allows him to look after his children three days a week, while his wife Julie can continue her career as a manager in a leisure club.

**B Listening**

70 **1** Listen to this interview with Roger Penn. What expressions does he use which mean the following?

1 It is necessary for me to be at the bank for twenty hours.

*I have to* ...............................................................................

2 It is possible for me to train or referee in the afternoon.

*I can* ...................................................................................

3 It isn't necessary to be there in the afternoon.

*I don't have to* ......................................................................

4 It is necessary not to be too friendly.

*You can't* .............................................................................

**2** What is the difference between Roger Penn's customers and the players he referees?

**C Speaking**

**1** What are the advantages of working part-time? Make sentences using *can* and *don't have to* and the ideas below.

1 spend time with your family  *You can spend more time with your family.*

2 Monday to Friday  *You don't have to work Monday to Friday.*

3 continue your studies  ...............................................................

4 have more time to relax  ...............................................................

5 always work eight hours a day  ...............................................................

6 have two different jobs  ...............................................................

7 develop a hobby  ...............................................................

8 choose one employer for life  ...............................................................

9 work with the same people all the time  ...............................................................

**2** Can you add any disadvantages? Use *can't* and *have to*.

**LANGUAGE NOTE**

### Permission and obligation

1 To ask for and give permission we can use *can* or the more formal *be allowed to*.

*You can vote in the UK when you're eighteen.*   *We can't smoke here.*

*Can I go early?*   *No, you can't.*

*We're allowed to work at home.*   *I'm not allowed to smoke at work.*

*Am I allowed to have a holiday in July?*   *No, you're not.*

2 To talk about obligation we generally use *have to*.

*Do you have to go the meeting?*   *She doesn't have to work late.*

*Do I have to wear this uniform?*   *No, you don't.*

3 For very strong obligation, we use *must* or *mustn't*.

*You must stop at the red light.*

*You must switch off your mobile phone on a plane.*

*You mustn't argue with the referee.*

## D Speaking

**1** Think about your own job. Work with a partner and take it in turns to describe your job to each other, using the expressions below. Talk about, hours, dress, customers, smoking, company cars, and languages.

| I can | I'm allowed to | I have to |
| I can't | I'm not allowed to | I don't have to |

**2** Look at the photos a–f below. Match them with these jobs.

1 pilot      4 architect
2 waiter     5 receptionist
3 teacher    6 journalist

What are the advantages and disadvantages of each job?

e.g. Pilot – *He can travel a lot and visit interesting places.*
         – *He has to be away from his family a lot.*

**3** What are the advantages and disadvantages of your own job? Tell your partner.

## E Reading

**1** Match the words in 1–9 with their definitions, as in the example.

| 1 | pick up (the phone) | a | the way you look |
| 2 | punctuality | b | your desk and computer |
| 3 | break | c | matching jacket and trousers / skirt |
| 4 | absence | d | a beard or moustache |
| 5 | appearance | e | being on time |
| 6 | facial hair | f | time off for a coffee |
| 7 | suit | g | end a phone conversation |
| 8 | work station | h | answer |
| 9 | hang up | i | time away from work |

**2** Gregorio is a company which distributes office stationery. Read the company's regulations for its employees and see how many are similar to your company. Would you like to work in a company with these regulations?

| Customer Care | All phones are to be answered within three rings. |
| --- | --- |
| | Sound interested and happy to speak to the customer. |
| | Introduce yourself. |
| | Use the customer's name as often as possible. |
| | Promise something before you hang up. |
| **Appearance** | **No facial hair.** |
| | **Smart dress means a smart mind.** |
| Office | Tidy desks at the end of the day. |
| | No food or drink in the office. |
| | No smoking. |
| | A short break is a good break. |
| | No personal photos. |
| | No personal telephone calls. |
| | Absence is bad news for you and your customers. |

**71** **3** An employee at Gregorio is helping a colleague to understand all the regulations. Listen and complete her explanations.

1 *You have* ................................................................................................

2 *You must* ..............................................................................................

3 *I have* ....................................................................................................

4 *You have* ..............................................................................................

5 *I have* ....................................................................................................

6 *We aren't* ..............................................................................................

**F Speaking**

**1** Work in pairs. Explain the other regulations relating to personal appearance and to the office to each other. Make sure you use the verbs *have to, can, be allowed to,* and *must* correctly. When you have finished, exchange your ideas with other students. Then explain the rules of your own organization.

**2** You and your partner are taking over a company. What ten rules will you introduce immediately? Discuss your ideas and write them down.

**G Reading**

Look at these signs. What do they mean? Where would you see them?

1

2 **30**

3 SILENCE

4

5

6 *VISA*

7 **18**

8

# 10.3 Checking and correcting information

| Vocabulary | Ordering and supplying |
|---|---|
| Communication skills | Clarifying information |
| | Letter writing |
| Pronunciation | Contrastive stress |

## A Listening

Contact name:
*Stephanie Strahl*

Name of company:
..............................

Address:
..............................
..............................

Telephone:
..............................

Action:
..............................

1️⃣ Stephanie Strahl is a lawyer in Geneva. She wants some new furniture for her office. She phones Laporta, a furniture company in London. Note her details on the pad below.

2️⃣ The next day the brochure was sent with an accompanying letter. Read the letter and find three errors.

---

**LAPORTA**
24 Southwark Street London SE1 1TY

Ms Stephanie Strahl                      14 October 2001
STRAHL & FIRONI
30, Avenue de Frontenex
CA–1207 Geneva

Dear Ms Strahl

Following our conversation please find enclosed our latest brochure.

You will see we have a full range of office furniture to suit all budgets. You will find the Literatura range on pages 23–25.

Thank you for choosing our company. We look forward to being of service to you.

Yours sincerely

*Antonio Laporta*

Antonio Laporta

---

3️⃣ Answer the following questions.

1 Why does Antonio Laporta write *Ms Strahl* and not *Mrs Strahl*? Why *Yours sincerely* and not *Yours faithfully*?

2 Which expressions in the letter mean the following?
   a  I am sending ..............................
   b  a wide selection ..............................

## B Speaking

**1** Stephanie wants to compare products and prices before she places an order, so she asks her colleague to phone some other furniture companies. Complete the dialogue below with the following expressions. Then listen and check.

| Sorry, that's | Go ahead. | That's right. | Have you got that? |
|---|---|---|---|
| I've got that. | Go on. | I didn't catch ... | Can I read that back to you? |

A: Would it be possible to send me a brochure?

B: Yes of course. Let me take your details.

A: Ready?

B: Yes ................... ................... [1].

A: My name's Daniel Aubert.

B: Sorry, ................... ................... ................... [2] your last name.

A: Aubert.

B: Daniel Albert.

A: No, it's Aubert: A-U-B-E-R-T.

B: OK ................... ................... ................... [3]. ................... ................... [4].

A: And my phone number's 00 41 22 78 ...

B: ................... ................... [5] 00 41 22 ...

A: ... 78 24 60 54. ................... ................... ................... ................... [6] ?

B: Yes, I think so ................... ................... ................... ................... ...................
................... ................... [7] ? 00 41 22 78 24 60 94.

A: 54.

B: Sorry, 54.

A: ................... ................... [8].

**2** Now have similar conversations with a partner. Take it in turns to give:
- your name and telephone number
- a credit card or identity card number with expiry date or issue date
- the make of your car and the registration number.

## LANGUAGE NOTE

### Correcting and checking information

1 Here are some expressions we use on the telephone when we are noting information.

| Person giving information | Person noting information |
|---|---|
| *Ready?* | *Go ahead.* |
| *Have you got that?* | *I've got that. Go on.* |
| *That's right.* | *I'm sorry, I didn't catch that.* |
| *That's all.* | *Can I read that back to you?* |

2 When we want to correct someone, we stress the word or part of a word we are correcting.

| *You work for IBM, don't you?* | *No, I work for **Compaq**, actually.* |
| *You were born in 1958.* | *No, in fact I was born in fifty-**seven**.* |
| *She's German, isn't she?* | *No she isn't, she's **Dutch**.* |

3 To show you have understood, use these expressions.

| *OK. I've got that.* | *Right.* |

## C Reading

**Furniture**

1. Stephanie receives a quote from Laporta.

   1. What items of furniture does she want?
   2. What is the total price of these items?
   3. What does she have to decide about them?
   4. If she accepts the quote what does she have to do?

---

### LAPORTA
24 Southwark Street London SE1 1TY

**Customer: Strahl & Sironi**

By Fax
Quote

| *Items* | 1 x | Literatura desk 1800mm x 1500mm | £690 |
| | 1 x | Two drawer filing cabinet Available in beech or cherry | £310 |
| *Sub-total* | | | £1000 |
| | | VAT | £175 |
| | | Transport | £90 |
| *Grand total* | | | £1265 |

Delivery time 4–6 weeks.

We hope this offer suits you and we look forward to processing your order. Please confirm in writing.

---

2. Work in pairs. Take it in turns to read the following information aloud and correct each other, if necessary. When correcting, don't forget to stress the information you change.

   1. Stephanie is a doctor. *No, she's a lawyer actually.* ................
   2. She lives in Munich. ................................................................
   3. She wants to buy some stationery. .......................................
   4. Laporta is in Penny Lane. .....................................................
   5. The desk costs £790. ...........................................................
   6. It is one metre sixty. ............................................................
   7. The filing cabinet costs $310. ..............................................
   8. It has four drawers. ..............................................................

**D Listening** `74` Stephanie calls Laporta back. Listen and answer the following questions.

1 How much of a discount does Stephanie get?
2 Why does she decide to order a chair?
3 Why does Laporta say he can't give her a discount for the transport?
4 When does she have to pay?
5 How will Stephanie confirm the order?

**E Writing** Stephanie sends Laporta an e-mail. Read it and put the sentences in the right order.

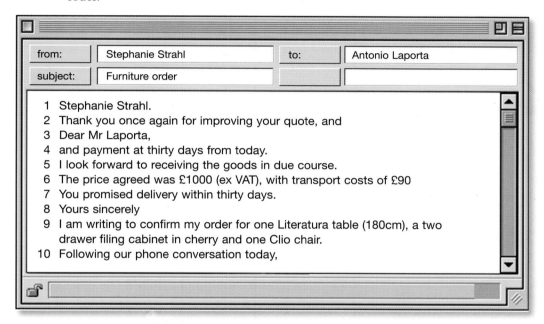

| from: | Stephanie Strahl | to: | Antonio Laporta |
| subject: | Furniture order | | |

1 Stephanie Strahl.
2 Thank you once again for improving your quote, and
3 Dear Mr Laporta,
4 and payment at thirty days from today.
5 I look forward to receiving the goods in due course.
6 The price agreed was £1000 (ex VAT), with transport costs of £90
7 You promised delivery within thirty days.
8 Yours sincerely
9 I am writing to confirm my order for one Literatura table (180cm), a two drawer filing cabinet in cherry and one Clio chair.
10 Following our phone conversation today,

**F Speaking** Work in pairs. Student A use the sentences below. Student B turn to File AA on page 154. Take it in turns to read your sentences to each other, and correct any information you hear which is wrong. Make sure you stress the information you are correcting. Use the expressions in the Language Note on page 123.

1 The legal age for voting in most countries is eighty.
2 New York is the capital of the USA.
3 There are 60,000 people in the UK.
4 Ferrari is a famous French company.
5 The President of the USA lives in a greenhouse.

# Unit 11 Getting a job

## 11.1 Recruitment processes

| | |
|---|---|
| **Grammar** | Verb + -*ing* |
| **Vocabulary** | Personal qualities |
| **Communication skills** | Talking about likes and dislikes |

**A** **Speaking**

**1** Write these verb phrases in the correct place in the diagram below.

| I don't really like | I don't mind | I really enjoy | I hate | I quite like |
|---|---|---|---|---|

|  |  |  |  |  |
|---|---|---|---|---|
| ..................... | ..................... | ..................... | ..................... | ..................... |

**2** Read what the five people below think about their jobs. Match the sentences 1–5 with the pictures a–e.

1 I *hate* telling clients they need to invest in new hardware. My job is to find software solutions, but it's not always possible.
2 I *really enjoy* working with figures, so this job is perfect for me.
3 I *don't mind* driving long distances. It's tiring, but if I don't visit customers regularly, our competitors will.
4 I *don't really like* working at nights. On some nights I have three or four calls.
5 I *quite like* receiving visitors. I usually only speak to them for a few seconds on the phone, so it's nice to meet them in person.

**3** Look at the expressions in italics above. Each one is followed by another verb. What form is it in?

**Verb + -ing**

Verbs used to talk about general preferences are usually followed by another verb ending -ing.
*I hate working late at night.*
*He enjoys meeting young people.*
*They don't mind travelling long distances.*

**4** Now think about your own job. Make similar sentences about aspects of your job that you like and don't like. Exchange information with a partner.

## B Vocabulary

**1** Here are three extracts from job advertisements. Which jobs in **A** are they describing?

**a** We are looking for outgoing and persuasive young people who are good with words. The post requires long hours of travel away from the office, so you must be energetic and independent.

**b** Do you like working with ideas? We are looking for creative people with a good knowledge of database management systems. You must be able to work well independently or as part of a team on large projects.

**c** *Are you good with figures, patient and attentive to detail?*

You will start as a junior clerk, but we offer you the opportunity to make quick progress in our firm.

**2** Now match the definitions (1–10) with the correct adjectives or phrases (a–j), as in the example.

| | | | |
|---|---|---|---|
| 1 | wants to get to the top | a | sensitive |
| 2 | thinks of other people's feelings | b | outgoing |
| 3 | doesn't get angry or irritated quickly | c | independent |
| 4 | can work alone | d | attentive to detail |
| 5 | open and friendly | e | energetic |
| 6 | doesn't mind changing his / her habits | f | ambitious |
| 7 | doesn't get tired easily | g | adaptable |
| 8 | can change people's opinions | h | patient |
| 9 | can produce new ideas | i | creative |
| 10 | regularly checks the quality of his / her work | j | persuasive |

**3** Write a short description of someone you like (or hate!) in your personal or professional life.

e.g. *My last boss was very energetic. He worked about 12 hours a day.*
*He was a patient man, who always had time to talk to us if we had a problem.*

## C Listening

**75a** ➊ Piet Smout works for a company which finds jobs for English-speaking people who want to work in other countries. Listen to the first part of an interview with him, and answer the questions.

1  In which parts of the world does the company find jobs?
2  What kind of jobs does it find? Give three examples.
3  What does Piet Smout's job consist of?
4  Why is it important to spend a long time in each company?

**75b** ➋ Now listen to the second part, and complete this table.

| What he likes about his job | What he dislikes about his job | Necessary qualities for working abroad |
| --- | --- | --- |
|  |  |  |

➌ Do you agree with the qualities that Piet Smout mentions? Can you think of any other qualities necessary for someone working abroad? Look again at the list in **B**.

## D Reading

➊ Look at this advertisement from a jobs website and answer the questions.

1  What job is it for?
2  Is it well-paid?
3  Where will the person work?
4  What qualifications, experience, and personal qualities will the person need?
5  If you're interested in the position, what do you have to do?

jobs@execnet.com

http://www.execnet.com

**jobs@execnet.com**     home     next     links     contact us

**European Sales Director**   Salary:          $90–110k + stock options
Ref: B112                     Location:        Lyon, France
                              Age range:       35–50
                              Qualifications:  Qualified doctor preferred
                                               Degree in Business Administration or similar
                                               Good level in three European languages, including English

Are you ambitious, energetic and adaptable? Based in Philadelphia, we are a leading American manufacturer of medical equipment. We are looking for someone with wide experience in the medical or pharmaceutical industry to manage our new European sales operation. You should have at least 10 years in the medical or pharmaceutical industry, of which five years in management. Please e-mail CV and covering letter to jobs@execnet.com.

➋ Now write a similar advertisement for your own job. If you don't work at the moment, choose a job you would like to do.

## E Vocabulary

**1** Here is a description of a typical procedure for recruiting a new manager. Complete the gaps in the flowchart with the phrases below.

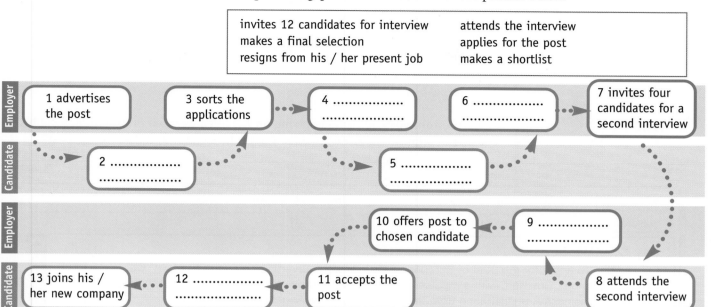

invites 12 candidates for interview  
makes a final selection  
resigns from his / her present job  
attends the interview  
applies for the post  
makes a shortlist

**Employer**

1 advertises the post

3 sorts the applications

4 ...................... ......................

6 ...................... ......................

7 invites four candidates for a second interview

**Candidate**

2 ...................... ......................

5 ...................... ......................

**Employer**

10 offers post to chosen candidate

9 ...................... ......................

**Candidate**

13 joins his / her new company

12 ...................... ......................

11 accepts the post

8 attends the second interview

**2** Complete the word-building table with words from the box below, as in the example. In the 'person' column, you will sometimes need two words, sometimes none.

employer  ~~interview~~  ~~interview~~  applicant  shortlist  employment  
application  advertise  employee  advertiser  shortlist  advertisement  
~~interviewer~~  apply for  resignation  resign  employ  ~~interviewee~~

| Verb | Noun | Person |
|------|------|--------|
| interview | interview | interviewer / interviewee |
| | | |
| | | |

**3** Which words in the list in **2** would you use to complete these sentences? Sometimes you will need to change the form.

1  We have received ........................ for this job from 3,000 people.

2  I saw the ........................ for this post in the *Sunday Times*.

3  OK, I think we've said enough about Mr Downing. Can you call the next ........................ ?

4  When she was offered the new job, she sent a letter of ........................ to her old ........................ .

5  Were you ........................ for the job?  
No, I didn't even get a first ........................ .

6  Nobody in the company ........................ for the job, so they had to ........................ the post in the newspaper.

7  His recent history of ........................ is very strange. He had six jobs between 1990 and 2000, and he ........................ from all of them.

# 11.2 Applying for a job

| Grammar | Present perfect and past simple |
|---|---|
| | Finished and unfinished actions |
| **Vocabulary** | CVs and covering letters |
| **Communication skills** | Talking about professional experience |

## A Reading

Luis António de Oliveira is applying for the job advertised on page 128. Read his letter of application below. In what ways is he a good candidate for the post?

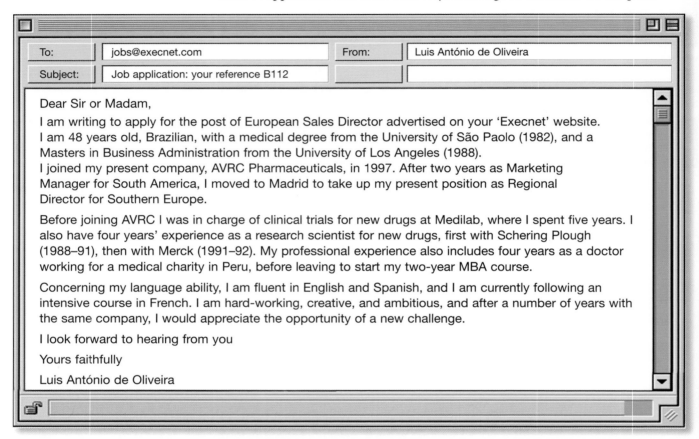

| To: | jobs@execnet.com | | From: | Luis António de Oliveira |
|---|---|---|---|---|
| Subject: | Job application: your reference B112 | | | |

Dear Sir or Madam,

I am writing to apply for the post of European Sales Director advertised on your 'Execnet' website. I am 48 years old, Brazilian, with a medical degree from the University of São Paolo (1982), and a Masters in Business Administration from the University of Los Angeles (1988).
I joined my present company, AVRC Pharmaceuticals, in 1997. After two years as Marketing Manager for South America, I moved to Madrid to take up my present position as Regional Director for Southern Europe.

Before joining AVRC I was in charge of clinical trials for new drugs at Medilab, where I spent five years. I also have four years' experience as a research scientist for new drugs, first with Schering Plough (1988–91), then with Merck (1991–92). My professional experience also includes four years as a doctor working for a medical charity in Peru, before leaving to start my two-year MBA course.

Concerning my language ability, I am fluent in English and Spanish, and I am currently following an intensive course in French. I am hard-working, creative, and ambitious, and after a number of years with the same company, I would appreciate the opportunity of a new challenge.

I look forward to hearing from you

Yours faithfully

Luis António de Oliveira

## B Speaking

1 Look again at Luis's letter and take turns with a partner to describe his career. Complete the time line below with details of his professional experience.

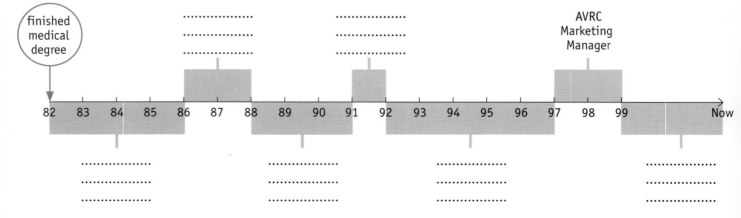

**2** Complete Luis's remarks about his career, then answer the questions using the same structures.

### Past simple + *in* or *ago*

4 When did he leave Peru?
5 How long ago did he resign from Schering Plough?
6 When did he move to Europe?

> I graduated from medical school ............[1] 1982.

> I ............[3] in 1997.

> I started my MBA ............[2] years ago.

### Past simple + *for* or *from ... to*

4 How long did he work for Schering Plough?
5 How long was he in charge of clinical trials?
6 How long did he live in Peru?

> I worked for Merck ............[1] year.

> I ............[2] at the University of Los Angeles from 1986 to 1988.

> I was a research scientist ............[3] years.

**3** Read the Language Note and then:
1 Complete sentences 1–3 below with the verb indicated, and *for* or *since*.
2 Answer questions 4–6 with complete sentences.

**LANGUAGE NOTE**

### The present perfect

1 The present perfect is formed with the present simple of the verb *have*, and the past participle of the main verb. For a list of irregular past participles, see page 157. For regular verbs, the past participle is the same as the past simple form.
   e.g. *to work – he worked – he has worked*.

2 We use the present perfect to talk about an action or a situation which started in the past, and is not finished now.
   *He's (he has) lived in Europe since 1999.* (And he lives there now.)
   *I've worked for this company for five years.* (And I still work there now.)
   *They've been married since 1985.* (And they're still married now.)

3 We use *since* with a moment in time, and *for* with a period of time.
   *since 1992, since June, since two o' clock*
   *for seven years, for a month, for half an hour*

> **1** He ............ a qualified doctor ............ many years. (be)

> **2** He ............ his MBA qualification ............ . (have)

> **3** He ............ for AVRC ............ 1997. (work)

### Present perfect + *for* or *since*

4 How long has he lived in Europe?
5 How long has he been Regional Director for Southern Europe?
6 How long has he worked in the pharmaceutical industry?

## C Listening

[ 76 ]

**1** Luis António de Oliveira meets an old friend at Madrid airport. Listen to their conversation. How do they know each other?

**2** What do we learn about Bill Pitt? Complete these notes. Listen again if necessary.

Present employer ......................... since .............

Married to ........................ since .............

First met his wife .........................

Lives in ......................... Moved there in .........................

## D Speaking

The present perfect tense is used to make a connection between the past and the present. We sometimes use different verbs to talk about when an action began (past simple tense) and its duration (present perfect tense).

**1** Complete the missing sentences using the verb indicated, as in the example.

| Past simple | Present perfect |
|---|---|
| I got married in 1987. | I've been married since 1987. (be) |
| She joined AVRC in 1999. | ................................................ (work) |
| ................................................ (move) | They've lived here for 10 years. |
| He met his wife three years ago. | ................................................ (know) |
| ................................................ (start) | I've had this job since January. |
| We arrived here about an hour ago. | ................................................ (be) |

**2** Now answer these questions.
1 How long have you lived in your present home, and when did you move there?
2 How long have you known your English teacher, and when did you first meet him / her?
3 How long have you been in this classroom, and what time did you arrive?

**3** Work in pairs. You're going exchange information to complete the CV (curriculum vitae) of another candidate for the post of European Sales Director.
1 Make a list of questions you have to ask to complete the missing information, e.g. *When was she born?*
2 Ask your partner your questions and answer his or her questions. When you've finished, discuss the following:
   a What similarities are there between Luis António's and Andrea's professional experience?
   b Who do you think is the better candidate for the job? Look again at the job advertisement on page 128.

Student A, look at the CV opposite. Student B, look at File CC on page 155.

# CURRICULUM VITAE

Name:           Andrea Paganini
Date of birth:      ...............................
Nationality:        British / Italian
Marital status:     Married

## QUALIFICATIONS

| | |
|---|---|
| 1987 | Obtained Degree in Pharmacology, University of London |
| 1994 | Obtained Diploma in Marketing Studies – London Institute of Marketing<br>( ........ – year correspondence course) |

## PROFESSIONAL EXPERIENCE

| | |
|---|---|
| 19 .... – 1989 | **University of London Hospital**<br>Research scientist in Pharmacology unit |
| 1989 – 1991 | **European Commission, Brussels**<br>Participated in European Community Drug Development Programme, co-ordinating and financing projects between hospitals and European pharmaceutical companies. |
| 1991 – 1998 | **AVRC Pharmaceuticals, Milan, Italy**<br>As Head of Research ( ........ years), I was responsible for the development of a new range of anti-depressant drugs. I then worked as Marketing Manager for Italy (4 years). |
| 1998 – present | **Pharmaline, Paris**<br>Pharmaline sells pharmaceutical products over the Internet. I joined the company as a product consultant. Since ................ I have been Marketing Manager for Europe. |

## LANGUAGES

English / Italian (native speaker)
................. (fluent)

## INTERESTS

Skiing, tennis, Modern European literature, architecture

---

 **Writing**      Write a short CV for yourself. Use Andrea Paganini's CV as a model.

# 11.3 Staff profiles

| Grammar | Present perfect and past simple |
| --- | --- |
| | Finished and unfinished time |
| Vocabulary | Staff movements |
| Communication skills | Expressing preferences |

## A Vocabulary

Match 1–7 with a–g to make seven sentences.

1  You can sometimes take early retirement …
2  You resign from your job …
3  You are transferred …
4  You are dismissed …
5  You usually retire …

6  You are made redundant …
7  You are taken on …

a  … to another part of the same company.
b  … by a new company.
c  … if your job no longer exists.
d  … between 60 and 65.
e  … to take up a position in another company.
f  … between 50 and 60.
g  … if your job performance hasn't been satisfactory.

## B Listening

**1** The administrative department of a company is trying to reduce its staff by 10% this year. The Personnel Manager is discussing the new staffing figures with the Head of Administration. Listen and complete the table. Have they achieved their objective of a 10% reduction?

| | Last year | This year |
| --- | --- | --- |
| **Total at start of year** | 564 | 600 |
| New employees | 60 | ............. |
| Transfers to other divisions | ............. | ............. |
| Resignations | 5 | ............. |
| Redundancies | 0 | ............. |
| Dismissals | 2 | 0 |
| Early retirement | ............. | ............. |
| Retirement | 7 | 12 |
| **Total at end of year** | 600 | ............. |

**2** Listen to the first part again and complete this extract.

> Well, the number of new employees ............. .............[1] dramatically this year.
> Last year we ............. .............[2] sixty people, but this year we've only
> .............[3] on sixteen. We .............[4] all new recruitment six months ago.

1  Which tense do we use when the time mentioned (last year / six months ago) is finished?
2  Which tense do we use when the time mentioned is not finished (this year)?

**3** Now describe the other changes between last year and this year. Continue as in the example.

*Last year the company transferred ...    This year they have ...*

LANGUAGE NOTE

### Present perfect and past simple

1 We also use the present perfect when the time of reference is not finished, even if the action itself is finished.
  *We've taken on sixteen people this year.* (But we're only in August.)
  *He's written three letters today.* (It's only 4 p.m. now.)
  *In my professional career, I've worked in three foreign countries.*
  (I'm only forty now, so my career is not finished.)

2 Compare the time expressions used with the present perfect and past simple.

| Present perfect | Past simple |
| --- | --- |
| *I've worked ...* | *I worked ...* |
| *this year / month / week* | *last year / month / week* |
| *today* | *yesterday* |
| *since 1997* | *in 1997* |
| *in the last ten years* | *ten years ago* |
| *recently* | *a long time ago* |

## C Speaking

**1** A candidate is attending a job interview. Match questions 1–4 below with his / her answers.

1 Have you ever had a difficult boss?
2 Have you worked abroad in the last five years?
3 Have you ever managed a team?
4 Have you studied any other languages apart from English?

a 'Yes, I have. I was in charge of ten technicians when I worked for Olivetti.'

b 'No, I haven't. But I lived in Spain for a year, so I can speak Spanish quite well.'

c 'Yes. I spent six months on a construction project in Delhi.'

d 'Yes. In fact that's why I resigned from my first job after only six months.'

**2** Which tense is used for the questions? Which tense is used for the candidate's answers?

**3** Ask and answer similar questions with your partner. Student A, use the prompts below to ask a question with *Have your ever . . . . ?* If Student B answers *Yes, I have,* ask a follow-up question using *When, What, Where,* or *Why.* Student B, turn to File X on page 154.

**When?**     **Where?**

- visit England or the USA
- play a musical instrument
- be made redundant
- run in a long-distance race
- do a computer course
- learn any other languages
- read any good books recently

**What?**     **Why?**

## D Reading

**1** Do you prefer working for a male boss or a female boss? Or do you have no preference?

The table below shows the preferences of American women for male or female bosses. Does anything surprise you?

| 'Do you prefer a male or a female boss?' | | | |
|---|---|---|---|
| **Table A** | **Women's answers (%)** | | |
| | *Male* | *Female* | *No preference* |
| Today | 42 | 22 | 35 |
| 1993 | 44 | 29 | 24 |
| 1982 | 52 | 15 | 30 |

Source: Gallup

**2** Complete this summary of table A, using the verbs below. Use each verb once, and put it in its correct form – present perfect or past simple, as in the example.

| increase | rise | go down | be | go up |
|---|---|---|---|---|
| decrease | start | prefer | fall | have |

1 The number of women who prefer to have a male boss *.has..gone..down..*[1] by 10% since 1982. Between 1982 and 1993 the number ........................[2] by 8%, and in the last few years it ........................[3] by another 2%.

2 Since 1982, the number of women who prefer a female boss ........................[4] . In 1982, only 15% ........................[5] a woman. In 1993, the number ........................[6] to 29%, but recently it ........................[7] to fall again.

3 30% of women ........................[8] no preference in 1982, but there ........................[9] a fall in numbers to 24% in 1993. Since then, the number ........................[10] to 35%.

78

Listen to this presentation of table B, and complete the missing figures. What similiarities are there with table A?

### 'Do you prefer a male or a female boss?'

| Table B | Men's answers (%) | | |
|---|---|---|---|
| | *Male* | *Female* | *No preference* |
| Today | — | — | 52 |
| 1993 | — | 16 | 49 |
| 1982 | 40 | — | — |

Source: Gallup

**F** Reading

Companies often use aptitude tests to evaluate candidates' intellectual, logical, mathematical or word skills. How quickly can you do this test? The answers are in File R on page 153.

**1** Which of these words is different from the others?
a level
b train
c madam
d refer
e stats

**2** If you rearrange the letters 'Sinodanie', you have the name of a:
a continent
b ocean
c country
d city
e animal

**3** Using all four mathematical symbols (+ - / x) make this sum correct:

11 ..... 4 ..... 3 ..... 9 ..... 5 = 6

**4** Which word can be added before all the following words to make common two-word expressions?

...................... qualities
...................... computer
...................... interests
...................... questions

**5** There are 30 monkeys in a banana tree. Some have orange and purple stripes, a third are all purple, and some are all green. Is it true that 10 monkeys are definitely green?

**6** Which letter comes next in this series of letters?

G  F  H  G  I  H  J  I  K

**7** Which consonant is midway between I and O?

**8** Use all the letters in this letter chain to make one word of eight letters.

E
R        A
C                S
N        E
I

..............................

**9** 'Brothers and sisters have I none. But that man's father is my father's son.'

Who is 'that man' in relation to the speaker?

# Unit 12 | The world of work

## 12.1 Changing careers

| Grammar | Revision of tenses |
| --- | --- |
| Vocabulary | Work |
| Pronunciation | Word stress |

**A** **Reading**

**1** Find words in the text below which have these meanings.

1 stop working at the end of your career
2 work for yourself
3 have no job
4 lose your job usually for economic reasons
5 a move to a better-paid or more important job in the same company
6 opportunities to make progress and improve your position
7 a meeting between a candidate and a potential employer
8 monthly pay
9 a company which finds jobs for people and people for jobs
10 an arrangement for two companies to join together

### *Twenty years ago ...*

most people *have started* / *started*[1] work around the age of twenty and *retired* / *have retired*[2] at the age of sixty-five. Normally they worked for the same company all their life. In the last twenty years things *are changing* / *have changed*[3]. Today people often *work* / *are working*[4] for different employers, many are self-employed and many, unfortunately, are unemployed. Companies employ fewer people and many processes *computerize* / *are computerized*[5].

**P**EOPLE change jobs for different reasons. 'I was forty,' says Jürgen Klimmer, an IT engineer. 'I liked my job, but the prospects weren't good, and there was very little chance of promotion. I read the papers and wrote one or two letters. One day I got a telephone call and an offer from Lufthansa. I said immediately, *'I'll / I*[6] take it'. The job offered a better salary and excellent prospects, but I had to move which was a problem for my family.' Jürgen took the job and *is* / *has been*[7] with the company for the last three years.

**Sergio Laguardia**, an accountant in Milan, was less fortunate. 'I *am* / *was*[8] made redundant six months ago. I am over fifty and it is hard to get another job. People think I am too old. I read the papers every day. I *have written* / *write*[9] a lot of letters of application in the last few weeks. Next week I *will go* / *I'm going*[10] to Turin for an interview but I am not confident. If they offer me the job I *will* / *would*[11] take it but the salary is not really high enough.'

**Patrizia Rojas** lives in Madrid. She is a secretary with a pharmaceutical company, but she *is looking* / *looks*[12] for another job. She has registered at a recruitment agency. 'I like my job but there was a merger between my company and another one last year. I am employed by a large multi-national now, instead of a small Spanish firm. There are too many people in my department now, and *I'll* / *I would*[13] probably leave quite soon.'

**Karel Sudek** lives in Prague where he works for himself. 'I *worked* / *have worked*[14] for a car manufacturing company for six years. I liked my job, but I had a bad relationship with my boss and I wanted to be more independent. In 1995 I left to start my own business. It is very stressful, but I like it. At least I know that I am responsible for my own future.'

**2** Read the article opposite and choose the correct form of the verbs in *italics*.

**3** Look at the text again and answer these questions.

1 Which of the people in the text is:
  a  unemployed
  b  employed
  c  self-employed?
2 Why did Jürgen change companies?
3 Why is Sergio looking for a new job?
4 What is Patricia's problem?
5 Why did Karel start his own business?

## B Speaking

**1** Complete the table below with an example sentence from the text.

| Active form | Use | Example from text |
|---|---|---|
| Present simple | Regular repeated actions or situations | *Patricia lives in Madrid.* |
| Present continuous | Present actions<br>Future arrangements | ....................................<br>.................................... |
| Future with *will* | Predicting<br>Stating a condition<br>Decision | ....................................<br>....................................<br>.................................... |
| Past simple | Finished actions | .................................... |
| Present perfect | Unfinished action or time period begun in the past | ....................................<br>.................................... |
| **Passive form** | | |
| Present simple passive<br>Past simple passive | Situations where who is / was responsible is unknown or unimportant | ....................................<br>....................................<br>....................................<br>.................................... |

**2** Work in pairs. Use the information in the text to ask and answer the following questions about Jürgen, Patricia, Sergio, and Karel.

1 What / do / Patricia? *What is Patricia doing?* ...............................................
*She is looking for* ........................................................... another job.

2 What / do / Jürgen? ..............................................................................
............................................................................................ Lufthansa.

3 Where / go / Sergio next week? ..............................................................
........................................................................................................ Turin.

4 How long? ...............................................................................................
........................................................................................... for six years.

5 How long? ...............................................................................................
.......................................................................................... for three years.

6 When? .....................................................................................................
............................................................................................... in 1995.

7 What? .......................................................................................................
.................................................................................... a lot of letters.

8 Where? .....................................................................................................
.......................................................................... at a recruitment agency.

9 Who / Patricia / employ / by? ..................................................................
...................................................................... a large multi-national.

10 When / make redundant / Sergio? .........................................................
......................................................................... six months ago.

## C Listening

**1** Sergio Laguardia is looking for another job. He is interviewed by a business magazine about the problems of being unemployed. Look at the interviewer's notes and predict her questions.

SERGIO LAGUARDIA

age?
Profession?
Married?
Wife / work?

Last job?

Where?
How long?
How / lose job?
How long unemployed?

79a   **2** Now listen. How does Sergio answer the questions? Make some notes.

## D Speaking

**1** Here is some advice for someone who is unemployed and looking for a new job. Look at these ideas and say if you agree or disagree. Can you think of any other advice?

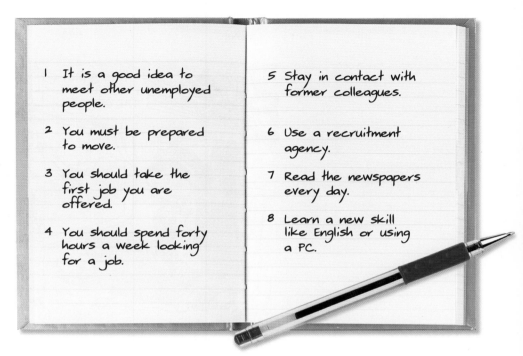

1 It is a good idea to meet other unemployed people.

2 You must be prepared to move.

3 You should take the first job you are offered.

4 You should spend forty hours a week looking for a job.

5 Stay in contact with former colleagues.

6 Use a recruitment agency.

7 Read the newspapers every day.

8 Learn a new skill like English or using a PC.

`79b` **2** In the second part of the interview Sergio talks about his experience of unemployment. Listen and tick (✓) the things in the list above that Sergio himself is doing to find a job.

## E Pronunciation

**1** Look at some of the vocabulary from this unit section. Put the words in the correct column according to the stress pattern, as in the example.

| | | | |
|---|---|---|---|
| unemployed | accountant | manufactured | company |
| recruitment | optimistic | pharmaceutical | psychology |
| ~~interview~~ | redundant | psychological | responsible |
| information | secretary | fortunate | confident |

○○● .................................................................

●○○ *interview* ...........................................................

○●○ .................................................................

○○●○ .................................................................

○●○○ .................................................................

○○●○○ .................................................................

`80a` **2** Listen and check your answers.

`80b` **3** Mini-dictation. Write down these sentences. Then read them aloud with the correct stress.

# 12.2 Work environments

| Grammar | *Too* and *not enough* |
|---|---|
| Vocabulary | Computers |

## A Listening

**1** Rebecca Long is a market analyst. Johann Koops does the same job. They are both being interviewed by a business magazine. Listen to the interviews and complete the table below.

|  | **Rebecca** | **Johann** |
|---|---|---|
| Place of work | ................................... | ................................... |
| Type of office | ................................... | ................................... |
| Hours | ................................... | ................................... |
| Lunch | ................................... | ................................... |
| Equipment | ................................... | ................................... |
| After-work activities | ................................... | ................................... |

**2** In pairs look at these remarks. Who makes them? Mark them (J) Johann or (R) Rebecca.

1 In fact sometimes there is too much information. .......
2 My wife thinks it's too late! .......
3 This gives me enough time to go and pick up the children. .......
4 If you don't arrive early enough you don't get the best places. .......
5 It's not really big enough for me and all my equipment. .......
6 Sometimes it's too quiet in my office. .......
7 When I have enough data I write my reports. .......
8 Because in an office there are too many distractions. .......
9 My doctor says I spend too much time in front of a screen. .......

**3** Look at the sentences again.

1 Where do we put *enough*? Before or after a noun? What about adjectives?
2 What kind of words can we put after *too*?

## Too / not enough

### Too

1 *Too* means 'more than necessary'. It is used in front of adjectives and adverbs.
*He didn't take the job because the salary was too low.*
*She couldn't do the job well because she worked too slowly.*

2 *Too* is also used in front of *much / many* when the quantity is larger than is wanted.
*There were too many people on the first day so I went back the next day.*
*I didn't get the job because I asked for too much money.*

### Enough

1 *Enough* means the 'right amount'. *Not enough* means 'less than necessary'. It is used after adjectives and adverbs.
*She wasn't old enough to vote.*
*He didn't work hard enough so he failed his exams.*

2 *Not ... enough* is also used with nouns. *Enough* goes before the noun.
*I don't have enough money to buy a new car.*
*There's not enough space in this office for more people.*

**B Speaking**

① We can say the same thing in different ways. Say these sentences in different ways using the prompts provided, as in the example.

1 I don't earn enough.              My salary ..*is too low*..................................

2 My office isn't large enough.      I don't have ........................................

3 She is too busy to see you.        She has ..............................................

4 He was too tense at the
  interview.                        He wasn't ..........................................

5 He wasn't young enough.            He .................................................

6 My computer is too slow.           It doesn't have ....................................

7 He made too many mistakes.         His English ........................................

8 He laughs too much.                He .................................................

② In pairs talk about your own working or study conditions. What aspects are you not happy about? Use the ideas below to help you.

| A | B |
| --- | --- |
| Travel | Homework |
| Hours worked | Exams |
| Length of day | Class size |
| Office – size, number of people | Social life |
| Responsibility | Teachers |
| Salary | Money |
| Boss | |

③ Write down some sentences about your partner and tell the rest of the class.

## C Vocabulary

In *Business Basics* we have shown you a number of ways to learn, record, and revise vocabulary.

**1** You can draw a picture. Look at the picture below and label it correctly using the words in the box.

| | | | |
|---|---|---|---|
| keyboard | printer | central unit | screen |
| scanner | socket | mouse mat | mouse |

**2** You can make a word chain or flowchart.

Rebecca has to write a weekly article, and then send it to her editor with an e-mail message. Complete this flow chart using the expressions below.

| | | |
|---|---|---|
| send to editor | connect modem | ~~save any changes~~ |
| ~~shut down~~ | ~~attach article~~ | save document |
| check spelling | write article | open application |
| write e-mail message | disconnect modem | ~~switch on computer~~ |

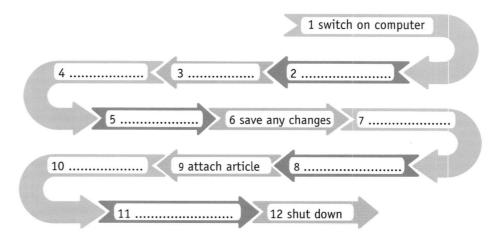

**3** You can record collocations and compounds as well as individual words. Add to the lists using the words in the box, as in the example. Some words can be used more than once.

| open | paste | copy | enter | word-processing |
| database | rename | attach | print | spreadsheet |

1 a _word-processing_ application    3 to ................................ text

................................

................................

2 to ................................ a document    4 to ................................ a folder

................................      ................................

................................      ................................

................................      ................................

................................      ................................

................................

**4** You can record words in the same family. Complete the table below.

| Verb | copy | print | ............ | attach | ............ | ............ |
|------|------|-------|---------|--------|------------|----------|
| Noun | copy, copier | ............ | scanner | ............ | connection | computer |

**5** You can write example sentences.

The table below shows some words from exercises 1–4. Complete the missing words for 2 and 3. Then write your own example sentences for 4, 5, and 6.

1 computerize    _Our language tests are computerized so they are easier to mark._

2 ...................    _We have the records of all our customers on a_ ................................................................

3 ...................    _I_ ........................ _the document to my e-mail and then sent it._

4 printer    ................................................................

5 scan    ................................................................

6 spreadsheet    ................................................................

**6** You can do a mind map. Look back at page 29 for an example. Close your books and try and do one for COMPUTER.

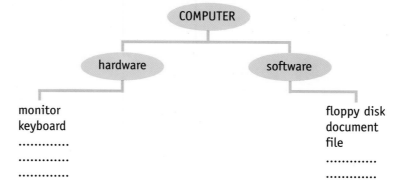

COMPUTER

hardware        software

monitor                 floppy disk
keyboard              document
............                  file
............                  ............
............                  ............

# 12.3 Saying goodbye

| Grammar | Functions review |
|---------|------------------|
| **Communication skills** | Saying goodbye |

## A Listening
82

Listen to these dialogues and match them to the situation described below, as in the example.

a   the end of a presentation .......
b   ending negotiations .......
c   the end of a meal with a client at a restaurant .......
d   saying goodbye at the end of a sales visit .......
e   saying goodbye to colleagues at the end of the day .......
f   saying goodbye to colleagues on an intensive language course .......

## B Speaking

1   Complete the dialogues below using these words.

| thank   thanks   speak   see   soon   calling   been   coming |
|---|

1   'OK. Thank you very much for ..............[1] Mr Jones.'
'Well thank you for asking me. When will you decide?'
'We'll send you a letter within a week.'
'Well, ..............[2] you for your time. See you again, maybe?'
'Yes of course. Goodbye.'

2   'I think that brings us to the end of the agenda. Thank you all for coming.'
'It's been a good day. ..............[3] you all next month.'

3   '..............[4] very much for your help.'
'Not at all. Thanks for ..............[5]'
'OK ..............[6] to you soon. Bye.'
'Bye.'

4   'Thanks very much. It's ..............[7] a lovely day.'
'Thanks for coming. Drive safely. See you ..............[8]'
'Yes. Definitely. Good bye.'
'Good bye.'

2   Match each dialogue with one of the pictures above.

3   Practise the dialogues in pairs.

## Polite goodbyes

1 **Saying goodbye**
*Goodbye (Bye).*
*Good night.*

2 **Thanking and responding to thanks**
*Thanks.*                                                  *You're welcome.*
*Thank you.*                                            *Don't mention it.*
*Thank you for everything / coming /*      *It was a pleasure.*
  *the invitation.*

3 **Commenting on the event**
*It's been very interesting / a pleasure.*
*It was nice to meet you / see you again.* (face-to-face)
*It was nice to speak to you / hear from you.* (telephone)

4 **Referring to a future journey**
*Have a good / safe trip / journey.*
*Drive carefully.*

5 **Referring to future contact**
*See you.*                                     *See you soon / next year / tomorrow.*
*Speak to you soon.*                   *I'll be in touch.*
*You must come again.* (host)      *You must come to us next time.* (guest)

## C Speaking

Work in pairs. Practise saying goodbye and thank you in the following situations.

| | | Student A | Student B |
|---|---|---|---|
| 1 | It is the end of a party. Student B is the host, Student A is leaving. | thank your host<br>offer an invitation<br>say goodbye | reply<br>thank<br>reply |
| 2 | In a restaurant. Student B is Student A's boss. | comment on the meal<br>offer to pay<br>thank | agree<br>refuse the offer<br>reply |
| 3 | It is the end of an annual conference. | say goodbye<br>reply<br>thank | ask about next year<br>wish a good journey<br>say goodbye |
| 4 | It is the end of the day. You are leaving work. | say goodbye to your colleague<br>reply – invite for a drink later<br>agree – say goodbye | say you are on holiday tomorrow<br>agree – fix time for 7 o'clock<br>say goodbye |

## D Listening

 83a

**1** Listen to these prompts and reply in a natural way.
e.g. *Thanks for coming.*     *Thanks for the invitation.*

83b

**2** Now listen to the completed dialogues and compare the replies with your own answers.

Your English is now good enough to go around the world! Play in teams or pairs. Use dice or toss a coin to move forward. Each square asks you to make a sentence in English; (T) means 'on the telephone'. If the expression is in *italics* you have to reply

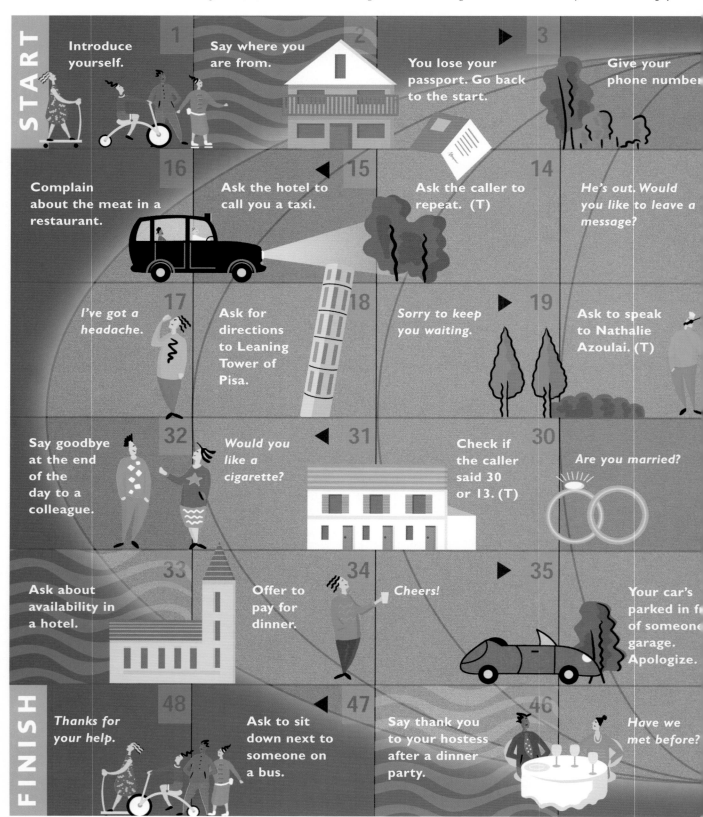

**START**

1. Introduce yourself.
2. Say where you are from.
3. You lose your passport. Go back to the start. ▶ Give your phone number

16. Complain about the meat in a restaurant.
15. Ask the hotel to call you a taxi. ◀
14. Ask the caller to repeat. (T) / *He's out. Would you like to leave a message?*

17. *I've got a headache.*
18. Ask for directions to Leaning Tower of Pisa.
19. *Sorry to keep you waiting.* ▶ Ask to speak to Nathalie Azoulai. (T)

32. Say goodbye at the end of the day to a colleague.
31. *Would you like a cigarette?* ◀
30. Check if the caller said 30 or 13. (T) / *Are you married?*

33. Ask about availability in a hotel.
34. Offer to pay for dinner. / *Cheers!* ▶
35. Your car's parked in front of someone's garage. Apologize.

**FINISH**

48. *Thanks for your help.*
47. Ask to sit down next to someone on a bus. ◀
46. Say thank you to your hostess after a dinner party. / *Have we met before?*

to what is written. If your answer is perfect you can throw again. If it is average you can stay on the square, but if it is inappropriate you must go back to where you came from! Your opponents will judge your answers, so speak and listen carefully.

**5** hat do you do?

**6** Count from 77 to 98.

Ask politely for a coffee.

Compare the USA to the UK. **8**

**7**

**12** friend loses wallet. Give vice.

**11** Count backwards from 101 to 94.

**10** Invite a friend to dinner.

How do you do? **9**

**21** Thanks for coming.

**22** The caller is speaking too quickly. (T)

**23** How are you?

Use since yesterday in a sentence.

**24**

**28** se if in a entence.

**27** Ask a caller to wait. (T)

**26** Offer to answer the telephone.

Ask a friend about their plans for tomorrow.

**25**

Tuesday 23

**37** k the distance m Tokyo Osaka.

A
B

**38** Ask about the price of a one-way ticket from Wellington to Sydney.

WELLINGTON | SYDNEY
TKT 1

Ask to receive a brochure. (T)

**39**
HOLIDAYS ABROAD

Use for three years in a sentence. **40**

**44** k for the nslation of erkraut in glish.

Ask someone's place of birth.

**43** Your bed is not long enough. Tell reception.

**42** Say alphabet from F to S.

**41**

# Information files

## File A page 95

1. In 1999 A had 600 shares = 60%.
   B had 75 shares = 7.5%.    C had 50 shares = 5%.
   D had 200 shares = 20%.    E had 75 shares = 7.5%.

2. 1  A £12,000    B £1,500    C £1,000    D £4,000
      E £1,500
   2  Yes. D received £4,000 in dividends and his stake
      is now worth £40,000. He has to repay the bank.
   3  A, with 60% of the shares.
   4  £15,000

## File B page 150

1  Over 6,400 km
2  432.3 metres
3  1.4 kg
4  3,926 m
5  About 29 km
6  10.3 cm
7  7–10 cm

## File C page 19

IN THE CENTRE OF OLD BANGKOK

*Royal Princess Hotel*

## File D page 27

The answers are not in the same order as the questions.
Can you match them?

a  You can't take any alcohol if you are a Moslem. Non-
   Moslems can take six bottles.
b  You can't take any plants or vegetables – they carry
   viruses.
c  1 kg. This country wants to protect agriculture, its
   main industry.
d  As many as you want, but they must be disinfected.
e  Two litres, if you live outside the European
   Community. If you travel from a country inside the
   EU, you can take up to 90 litres.
f  If your personal jewellery weighs more than 100g
   you must leave it at customs until you leave the
   country or complete a temporary importation form.
g  As many as you want, but the total value must not be
   more than US $300.
h  One bottle of 57 ml.

*170 rooms all with:*
- safe
- minibar and refrigerator
- air conditioning
- TV (cable and satellite channels)
- IDD (International Direct Dial) telephone.

*Other facilities:*
- Meeting and conference rooms
- Business centre with computers, mobile
  phones, fax machines
- Outdoor swimming pool
- Fitness centre
- Garden
- Specialty shops

*Restaurants and cafés:*

**Mikado** – Japanese restaurant
**Piccolo** – Italian cuisine
**The Empress** – Cantonese cuisine
**Princess Cafe** – Thai and continental cuisine

| Name | Arrive | Stay | From | Time | Hotel |
|------|--------|------|------|------|-------|
| Jack Scott | 26.07 | ............. | Seattle | 21.30 | Sheraton |
| Thérèse Blanc | 27.07 | 4 nights | Paris | 20.30 | Ramada |
| Giovanni Costa | 27.07 | 3 nights | Rome | 18.30 | Sheraton |
| Michel Lenoir | 27.07 | 3 nights | Geneva | 20.30 | ................... |
| Yoshi Omura | 26.07 | 4 nights | .............. | ............. | Holiday Inn |
| Patricia Lingwood | ......... | 2 nights | Boston | 22.30 | Ramada |

**THURSDAY 16TH JULY**

| | |
|---|---|
| 8.00–10.00 a.m. | Breakfast meeting |
| 10.30–12.00 p.m. | Presentation |
| 1.00–2.00 p.m. | Lunch with Mr Felipe Delaserra |
| 2.30 p.m. | Playing golf with new Saudi client(s) |
| 5.30–7.00 p.m. | Meeting with the Chairman |
| 7.15 p.m. | Taxi to the airport (15 minutes) |
| 9.00 p.m. | Plane to Rome |

| Company A | Estée Lauder |
|-----------|--------------|
| Founded | 1946 |
| Founder | An American woman |
| Location | New York |
| Activity | Cosmetics |
| Famous products | Clinique, Aramis |
| Key date | 1948 First counter at Saks department store on 5th Avenue New York |

Use the information below to help you answer Student A's questions.

– On Monday you were late, so you travelled to Manchester by taxi.
– You stayed in a luxury suite at the Royal Hotel.
– You telephoned your girlfriend / boyfriend.
– On Wednesday you were tired so you stayed at home. (You worked at home.)
– On Thursday you visited a customer near your girlfriend / boyfriend. (S/he lives in Scotland.).
– You played golf at St Andrews with a good friend (an important future customer).

| | |
|---|---|
| Activity: | food and drink |
| Employees: | 230,929 |
| Location: | headquarters in Switzerland, branches all over the world |
| Products: | Nescafé coffee, Perrier mineral water, Kit Kats |
| Company name: | Nestlé |

Here are the 'down' words for the crossword. Make clues for these words to give your partner.

| | | | |
|---|---|---|---|
| 1 | envelope | 4 | window |
| 2 | coin | 5 | plate |
| 3 | snow | 6 | car |

This is what you did last week. Answer Student B's questions, and ask questions to complete his / her diary on page 49.

| February | Week 6 2001 | 2001 | February |
|----------|-------------|------|----------|
| **5 Monday** Train from London to Paris Hotel Concorde Dinner at Pizza Pino | | Buy presents for the family | **Friday 9** |
| **6 Tuesday** Visit Versailles Train to London Home | | | **Saturday 10** |
| **7 Wednesday** Tennis – Wimbledon | | | **Sunday 11** |
| **8 Thursday** Interview 11.00 a.m. at Trafalgar House Mr Jones | | | |

| Concorde | 1969 | It was the first supersonic passenger plane. |
| Eiffel Tower | 1889 | It was built to celebrate the 100th anniversary of the French Revolution. |
| Walkman | 1979 | It was originally called the Soundabout. |
| Guggenheim | 1959 | There is now one in New York, Bilbao, Venice and Berlin. |
| London Eye | 1999 | It offers the best view of London. |
| Empire State Building | 1931 | It was featured in King Kong. |
| Escalator | 1891 | It was originally designed as a fairground attraction. |
| American Express Card | 1958 | It was the original plastic money. |
| Levis | 1890 | They were originally made for cowboys and gold prospectors. |

1. Your partner works for a small company in the UK. Listen to a description of sales for last year, and mark them on this graph. What do your think your partner sells. Is it:
   - skis
   - sun cream
   - Christmas decorations?

2. You work for a company in the USA which sells children's toys. Your partner doesn't know this. Describe your sales figures for last year, then ask your partner to guess your product. Start like this:

   *In January we had sales of $1 million. Sales remained stable in February*

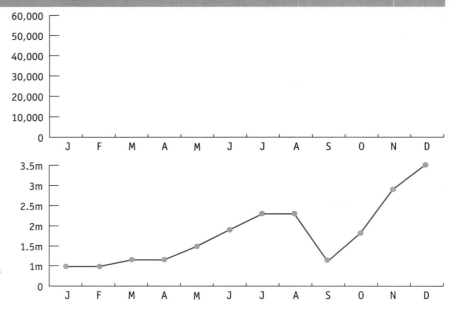

**THURSDAY 16TH JULY**

| 9.00–11.00 a.m. | Sales meeting |
| 11.30 a.m.–12.30 p.m. | Tennis |
| 12.30–1.30 p.m. | Lunch with Anita Chung |
| 2.30–3.30 p.m. | Video conference |
| 3.45–5.30 p.m. | Marketing meeting |
| 6.00 p.m. | Taxi to the airport |
| 9.30 p.m. | Departure for London |

| Activity: | cars, planes, engines |
| Employees: | 428,000 |
| Location: | headquarters in Stuttgart (Germany) and Auburn Hills (USA) |
| Products: | Mercedes Benz, Eurofighter Typhoon, Dodge Pickup |
| Company name: | Daimler Chrysler |

You are a travel agent. Look at the information below about flights to Warsaw. Ask your customer when he / she wants to travel, and give the plane times. When the customer makes a decision, note the reservation details (flight time and day, customer name and telephone number).

| LONDON HEATHROW TO WARSAW Daily flight schedule | | | |
|---|---|---|---|
| Departure | Arrival | Flight No. | Airline |
| 07:05 | 10:30 | BA4454 | LOT – Polish Airlines |
| 10:35 | 14:00 | BA4450 | LOT – Polish Airlines |
| 11:40 | 15:00 | BA850 | British Airways |
| 17:30 | 20:55 | BA4452 | LOT – Polish Airlines |
| 18:35 | 21:55 | BA852 | British Airways |

| Name | Arrive | Stay | From | Time | Hotel |
|------|--------|------|------|------|-------|
| Jack Scott | 26.07 | 4 nights | Seattle | 21.30 | Sheraton |
| Thérèse Blanc | 27.07 | 4 nights | Paris | 20.30 | Ramada |
| Giovanni Costa | 27.07 | 3 nights | Rome | 18.30 | Sheraton |
| Michel Lenoir | .......... | 3 nights | Geneva | 20.30 | Ramada |
| Yoshi Omura | 26.07 | .......... | Tokyo | 17.30 | .............. |
| Patricia Lingwood | 27.07 | 2 nights | .............. | .......... | Ramada |

## File R page 137

1 train (the others read the same backwards as forwards)
2 c (Indonesia)
3 $11 - 4 \times 3 + 9 \div 5 = 6$
4 personal
5 no
6 J
7 L
8 increase
9 his son (the speaker is male)

## File S page 81

Use the table to calculate your score.

| | | | | |
|----|-------|-------|-------|-------|
| Q1 | a = 3 | b = 4 | c = 0 | d = 1 |
| Q2 | a = 4 | b = 2 | c = 2 | d = 1 |
| Q3 | a = 4 | b = 3 | c = 2 | d = 1 |
| Q4 | a = 1 | b = 2 | c = 3 | d = 4 |
| Q5 | a = 0 | b = 3 | c = 2 | d = 4 |
| Q6 | a = 3 | b = 0 | c = 0 | d = 4 |
| Q7 | a = 0 | b = 4 | c = 0 | d = 0 |
| Q8 | a = 4 | b = 3 | c = 0 | d = 4 |

**What was your score?**

| | |
|----|----|
| *Less than 10* | You have a nice relaxed life – at home and at work. |
| *10 – 18* | You work hard, but you know when to stop. |
| *19 – 27* | Be careful. If you take on more work, you'll be very stressed. |
| *28 – 32* | Oh dear! Time to take a long holiday – now! |

## File T page 100

| Company B | Sony |
|-----------|------|
| Founded | 1946 |
| Founder | Two Japanese men |
| Location | Tokyo |
| Activity | Electronics |
| Famous products | Walkman |
| Key date | 1970 first Japanese firm on New York Stock Exchange |

## File U page 117

You run your own small business. These are your problems.
1 Your staff want a salary rise of 10%.
2 Your turnover is down 20%.
3 Your company car is five years old!
4 Your best customer wants a 5% discount.
5 You work seven days a week.
6 You cannot relax.

## File V page 88

Here are the 'across' words for the crossword. Make clues for these words to give your partner.

2 can
5 pencil
7 wine
8 door
9 computer
10 watch

## File W page 49

This is what you did last week. Answer Student A's questions, and ask questions to complete his / her diary on page 49.

February Week 6 2001

**5** Monday
Plane from Berlin to Paris
Hotel Bristol
Dinner at Marty's restaurant

**6** Tuesday
Visit Fontainebleau
Plane to London
Dinner at Hard Rock Café

**7** Wednesday
Visit British Museum

**8** Thursday
Interview 12.00 p.m. at Trafalgar House.
Mr. Jones

2001 February

Friday **9**
Return home

Saturday **10**

Sunday **11**

Use these ideas to ask Student A questions, e.g. *Have you ever done a part-time or holiday job?*

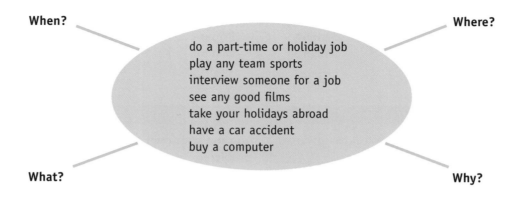

**When?**  **Where?**

do a part-time or holiday job
play any team sports
interview someone for a job
see any good films
take your holidays abroad
have a car accident
buy a computer

**What?**  **Why?**

**1** You are Pierre Crenn, Chief Accountant at EMN. You received an invoice from SIMCO for $900. You are sure this is too high.

1 Phone Simco and ask to speak to Mrs Powell, the Accounts Manager. Explain the problem. The invoice number is 6748, and it is dated the 23rd of February.
2 Mrs Powell phones you back. When she has finished, offer to send back the original invoice.

**2** You are Ms Geraldo, Sales Manager of Funglass Inc.

1 You receive a call from John Miller-Jones. He has a problem with an order of champagne glasses. Promise to look into the problem and call back.
2 Call back. Apologize – the order was sent to the wrong address, and returned to the factory this morning. Ask for the correct address. If he asks about delivery, tell him it will take 3 days.

You are the Sales Director of a small business founded by your father. These are your problems.

1 Your father is 72, and still CEO of the company.
2 The staff never want to have a drink with you after work.
3 You don't like the colour of your new BMW.
4 You cannot choose between Florida and Hawaii for your next holiday.
5 You work five days a week, but would like longer weekends.
6 An American firm wants to buy the businesss for $1,000,000 but your father wants more.

1 In most countries you stop working around the age of seventeen.
2 The best football team in the world is Iceland.
3 BMX is a famous German car company.
4 In the UK people eat a lot of fish and ships.
5 The River Danube flows through Paris.

You went on a sales trip to London. Your experience wasn't very positive.

- Your journey was long and tiring, and your flight was late.
- The weather was cold and windy, your hotel was clean and modern but cold and a long way from the centre.
- You visited three new clients. They were difficult meetings.
- You went to a presentation of the Millennium Dome given for foreign businessmen at the Chamber of Commerce. The cocktail party after was very nice.
- At the weekend you took a boat trip on the River Thames to see the sights of London and went on the London Eye. The view was spectacular.
- You ate out in a restaurant. It wasn't very good. The food was dull and you didn't like it much.

# CURRICULUM VITAE

Name:               Andrea Paganini
Date of birth:      1st June 1963
Nationality:        ......................................
Marital status:     Married

## QUALIFICATIONS

1987            Obtained Degree in Pharmacology, University of London
19.......       Obtained Diploma in Marketing Studies – London Institute
                of Marketing
                (2–year correspondence course)

## PROFESSIONAL EXPERIENCE

1987 – 1989     **University of London Hospital**
                Research scientist in Pharmacology unit

1989 – 1991     ........................................................................
                Participated in European Community Drug Development
                Programme, co-ordinating and financing projects between
                hospitals and European pharmaceutical companies.

1991 – 1998     **AVRC Pharmaceuticals, Milan, Italy**
                As Head of Research (3 years), I was responsible for the
                development of a new range of anti-depressant drugs.
                I then worked as Marketing Manager for Italy ( ........ years).

............ – now    **Pharmaline, Paris**
                Pharmaline sells pharmaceutical products over the Internet. I
                joined the company as a product consultant. Since 2000 I
                have been .................................................. for Europe.

## LANGUAGES

                English / Italian (native speaker)
                French (fluent)

## INTERESTS

                Skiing, tennis, Modern European literature, architecture

# Language file

## Comparison of adjectives  *See 7.1*

| Category of Adjective | Adjective | Comparative | Superlative |
|---|---|---|---|
| One syllable | old | older | the oldest |
| Ending in -*y* | easy | easier | the easiest |
| Two syllables or more | expensive | more expensive | the most expensive |
| | | less expensive | the least expensive |
| Irregular forms | good | better | the best |
| | bad | worse | the worst |
| | far | further | the furthest |

**Comparing two things**

*The ferry **is cheaper than** the plane.* = *The ferry **isn't as expensive as** the plane.*
*English **is easier than** Chinese.* = *English **isn't as difficult as** Chinese.*
*Your handwriting **is better than** mine.* = *Your handwriting **isn't as bad as** mine.*

## Countable and uncountable nouns  *See 2.3, 3.3*

| Countable nouns [C] | Uncountable nouns [U] |
|---|---|
| **❶** Countable nouns have a singular and a plural form.<br><br>singular:  *a book, a cigarette.*<br>    *There is a book on the table.*<br>plural:  *some books, some cigarettes*<br>    *There are some books on the table.* | **❶** Uncountable nouns have only one form. They take a singular verb, but they cannot be used with the indefinite article *a / an*. The article we use with uncountable nouns is *some*.<br><br>*some money, some information, some water*<br>*There is some money on the table.* |
| **❷** In the plural form, we usually use *any* in negative sentences and in questions.<br><br>*There aren't any faxes from Tokyo.*<br>*Have you got any cigarettes?*<br>*Are there any faxes from Tokyo?* | **❷** We usually use *any* in negative sentences and in questions.<br><br>*There isn't any news from Tokyo.*<br>*I don't have any flight information.*<br>*Has he got any money?*<br>*Is there any news from Tokyo?* |
| **❸** We use *many* to express quantity.<br><br>*How many weeks do we have? Not many.*<br>*I don't have many suitcases.* | **❸** We use *much* to express quantity.<br><br>*How much time do we have? Not much*<br>*I don't have much luggage.* |

**Countable nouns [C] and uncountable [U] nouns**

**❹** We use *some* (and not *any*) to ask 'questions' that are really offers or requests.

Offer:     *Would you like some coffee [U] / some biscuits [C] ?*
Request:  *Could I have some information [U] / some advice [U] / some magazines [C] to read?*

**❺** In spoken English *a lot* often replaces *much* and *many* in simple positive and negative statements.

*I have a lot of books. I don't have a lot of suitcases.* (instead of *many*)
*He has a lot of experience. I don't have a lot of luggage.* (instead of *much*)

## Future with *will*   See 9.1, 9.2, 9.3

The future with *will* is used for: making predictions about the future / making decisions at the time of speaking. For talking about our fixed plans, we don't use *will*, we use the present continuous (see page 160).

| Affirmative* | | Negative* | | | Question | | |
|---|---|---|---|---|---|---|---|
| I'll | work. | I | won't | work. | Will | I | work? |
| You'll | | You | | | | you | |
| He'll | | He | | | | he | |
| She'll | | She | | | | she | |
| We'll | | We | | | | we | |
| They'll | | They | | | | they | |

*In the affirmative and negative form, we generally use the contraction (*I'll = I will; we'll = we will; he won't = he will not*, etc.) in both spoken and informal written English.

## Irregular verbs   See 4.2

| stem | past tense | past participle | stem | past tense | past participle |
|---|---|---|---|---|---|
| be | was/were | been | lend | lent | lent |
| become | became | become | let | let | let |
| begin | began | begun | lose | lost | lost |
| break | broke | broken | make | made | made |
| bring | brought | brought | mean | meant | meant |
| build | built | built | meet | met | met |
| buy | bought | bought | pay | paid | paid |
| catch | caught | caught | quit | quit | quit |
| choose | chose | chosen | read | read | read |
| come | came | come | ride | rode | ridden |
| cost | cost | cost | ring | rang | rung |
| cut | cut | cut | rise | rose | risen |
| deal | dealt | dealt | run | ran | run |
| do | did | done | say | said | said |
| draw | drew | drawn | see | saw | seen |
| drink | drank | drunk | sell | sold | sold |
| drive | drove | driven | send | sent | sent |
| eat | ate | eaten | set | set | set |
| fall | fell | fallen | show | showed | shown |
| feel | felt | felt | shut | shut | shut |
| find | found | found | sing | sang | sung |
| fly | flew | flown | sit | sat | sat |
| forbid | forbade | forbidden | sleep | slept | slept |
| forget | forgot | forgotten | speak | spoke | spoken |
| get | got | got (US *gotten*) | spend | spent | spent |
| give | gave | given | spread | spread | spread |
| go | went | gone | stand | stood | stood |
| grow | grew | grown | steal | stole | stolen |
| have | had | had | swim | swam | swum |
| hear | heard | heard | take | took | taken |
| hit | hit | hit | teach | taught | taught |
| hold | held | held | tell | told | told |
| keep | kept | kept | think | thought | thought |
| know | knew | known | throw | threw | thrown |
| lay | laid | laid | understand | understood | understood |
| lead | led | led | wear | wore | worn |
| lend | lent | lent | win | won | won |
| learn | learnt | learnt | write | wrote | written |
| leave | left | left | | | |

## Letter-writing expressions *See 2.1, 3.1, 4.2, 6.3, 9.3, 11.2*

We use different expressions for formal letters (e.g. to companies or to people we haven't met) and informal letters, faxes or e-mails to friends or business acquaintances.

| | **Formal** | **Informal** |
|---|---|---|
| **Opening** | *Dear Sir / Madam*<br>*Dear Mr / Ms Jones* | *Dear Maria* |
| **Saying thank you** | *Thank you for …* | *Thanks for …* |
| **Reason for writing** | *I am writing to inform you that …*<br>*I am writing to ask you about /*<br>*apologize for …* | *I'm writing to tell you …*<br>*I'm writing to say sorry for …* |
| **Asking for help** | *Please could you …?*<br>*I would be grateful if*<br>*you could …* | *Could you …?*<br>*Can you …?* |
| **Offering help** | *We will be pleased /*<br>*happy to (send you) …* | *I'll (send you) …* |
| **Enclosed documents** | *I enclose …*<br>*Please find enclosed (my CV) …* | *I'm sending you …* |
| **Closing remark** | *I look forward to hearing from you /*<br>*meeting you / seeing you.* | *(I'm) looking forward to hearing from you /*<br>*seeing you again.* |
| **Finishing** | *Yours faithfully** (UK)<br>*Yours sincerely**<br>*Sincerely yours* (US) | *Best wishes*<br>*Best regards*<br>*Yours* |

*In British English, *Yours faithfully* is used for letters which begin *Dear Sir / Dear Madam*. *Yours sincerely* is used when the letter begins *Dear Mr / Ms (Jones)*.

## Modal verbs *See 2.1   3.2   9.1   9.3   10.1   10.2*

| **Verb** | **Use / Meaning** | **Example** |
|---|---|---|
| have to / must | obligation / necessity | *I have to work 5 days a week.*<br>*I must leave at 4 o'clock to catch my train.* |
| mustn't | not permitted | *You mustn't smoke here – it's a non-smoking office.* |
| don't have to | not necessary | *I don't have to work on Sundays.* |
| can (can't) | possibility | *I can meet you next week.* |
| | ability | *I can't swim.* |
| | permission | *Can I leave early?* |
| | request | *Can you help me, please?* |
| may | permission | *May I smoke?* |
| could (couldn't) | request | *Could you tell me the address?* |
| should (shouldn't) | recommending / advising | *I think we should accept the proposal.*<br>*You shouldn't do that, it's not a good idea.* |
| shall | suggesting | *Shall we finish now and go for coffee?* |
| | offering | *Shall I do that?* |
| would | offering | *Would you like some coffee?*<br>*Would you like me to help you?* |

## Numbers *See 1.3, 5.2, 6.1, 8.2*

| Cardinal numbers | | Ordinal numbers (e.g. for dates) | | Cardinal numbers | | Ordinal numbers | |
|---|---|---|---|---|---|---|---|
| 1 | one | 1st | first | 21 | twenty-one | 21st | twenty-first |
| 2 | two | 2nd | second | 22 | twenty-two | 22nd | twenty-second |
| 3 | three | 3rd | third | 30 | thirty | 30th | thirtieth |
| 4 | four | 4th | fourth | 31 | thirty-one | 31st | thirty-first |
| 5 | five | 5th | fifth | 40 | forty | 40th | fortieth |
| 6 | six | 6th | sixth | 50 | fifty | 50th | fiftieth |
| 7 | seven | 7th | seventh | 60 | sixty | 60th | sixtieth |
| 8 | eight | 8th | eighth | 70 | seventy | 70th | seventieth |
| 9 | nine | 9th | ninth | 80 | eighty | 80th | eightieth |
| 10 | ten | 10th | tenth | 90 | ninety | 90th | ninetieth |
| 11 | eleven | 11th | eleventh | 100 | a hundred | 100th | hundredth |
| 12 | twelve | 12th | twelfth | | | | |
| 13 | thirteen | 13th | thirteenth | 110 | a hundred and ten | | |
| 14 | fourteen | 14th | fourteenth | 1,000 | a thousand | | |
| 15 | fifteen | 15th | fifteenth | 5,342 | five thousand three hundred and forty-two | | |
| 16 | sixteen | 16th | sixteenth | | | | |
| 17 | seventeen | 17th | seventeenth | 100,000 | a hundred thousand | | |
| 18 | eighteen | 18th | eighteenth | 1,000,000 | (1m) a million | | |
| 19 | nineteen | 19th | nineteenth | 1,000,000,000 | a billion | | |
| 20 | twenty | 20th | twentieth | | | | |

## Past simple *See 4.1, 4.2, 5.2, 8.1, 8.3*

**1** The past simple is used for talking about past actions which have no relation to now.

| Affirmative* | | Negative | | Question | | |
|---|---|---|---|---|---|---|
| I | worked. | I | didn't work. | Did | I | work? |
| You | | You | | | you | |
| He | | He | | | he | |
| She | | She | | | she | |
| We | | We | | | we | |
| They | | They | | | they | |

*Regular verbs all finish in -*ed* in the affirmative past simple form (for past simple irregular forms see **Irregular verbs**).

**2** The passive form of the past simple is often used to describe the history of people, companies or products. It is formed with the verb *to be* and the past participle.

| Affirmative | | Negative | | Question | |
|---|---|---|---|---|---|
| It was | introduced in 1970. | It wasn't | introduced. | Was it | introduced? |
| They were | | They weren't | | Were they | |

## Prepositions  *See 3.1*

**① Prepositions of place**

Prepositions of place are often used with the verb *be*.
*The report is on my desk, under the red file.*
*It's on the left, opposite the bank.*

**② Prepositions of movement**

Prepositions of movement are normally used with verbs of movement.
*Come out of the office, and walk along the street.*
*Go out of the front door and down the steps.*

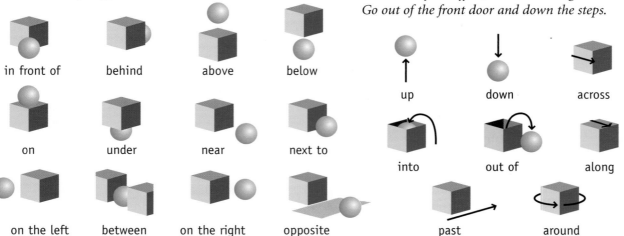

in front of  behind  above  below

on  under  near  next to

on the left  between  on the right  opposite

up  down  across

into  out of  along

past  around

## Present continuous  *See 5.1, 5.2, 6.1, 6.2*

The present continuous is used for talking about: actions happening now, at this moment; present projects; fixed plans and appointments in the future.

| Affirmative* | | Negative | | | Question | | |
|---|---|---|---|---|---|---|---|
| I'm | working | I'm | not | working. | Am | I | working? |
| You're | | You | aren't | | Are | you | |
| He's | | He | isn't | | Is | he | |
| She's | | She | | | | she | |
| It's | | It | | | | it | |
| We're | | We | aren't | | Are | we | |
| They're | | They | | | Are | they | |

*In the affirmative form, we generally use the contraction (*I'm = I am; we're = we are,* etc.) in both spoken and informal written English.

## Present perfect  *See 11.2, 11.3*

The present perfect is used for talking about actions which started in the past and are continuing now:  *I've lived here for ten years;* past actions which may have finished, but where the time of reference is not finished: *I've worked on three different projects this year.*
The present perfect is formed with the verb *have* plus a past participle (for irregular past participles see **Irregular verbs**).

| Affirmative* | | Negative | | | Question | | |
|---|---|---|---|---|---|---|---|
| I've | gone | I | haven't | gone. | Have | I | gone? |
| You've | | You | | | | you | |
| He's | | He | hasn't | | Has | he | |
| She's | | She | | | | she | |
| It's | | It | | | | it | |
| We've | | We | haven't | | Have | we | |
| They've | | They | | | | they | |

*In the affirmative form, we generally use the contraction (*I've = I have; he's = he has; she's  = she has etc.*) in both spoken and informal written English.

## Present simple *See 1.1, 1.2, 1.3, 4.3, 7.2*

**1** The present simple is used for talking about permanent states or regular actions.

| Affirmative | | Negative* | | | Question | | |
|---|---|---|---|---|---|---|---|
| I | work. | I | don't | work. | Do | I | work? |
| You | | You | | | | you | |
| He | works. | He | doesn't | | Does | he | |
| She | | She | | | | she | |
| It | | It | | | | it | |
| We | work. | We | don't | | Do | we | |
| They | | They | | | | they | |

*In the negative form, we generally use the contraction (*I don't = I do not; he doesn't = he does not*) in both spoken and informal written English.

**2** The passive form of the present simple is often used to describe systems and processes.

| Affirmative | | Negative | | Question | |
|---|---|---|---|---|---|
| It's | made in England. | It isn't | made … | Is it | made …? |
| They're | | They aren't | | Are they | |

## Pronouns and determiners

**A** Subject pronouns *I live in Paris. **She** works here.*
**B** Object pronouns *I see **him** every week. Give it to **her**.*
**C** Possessive pronouns *Whose car is that? It's **mine**.*
**D** Possessive determiners *It's **my** book. It's **their** idea.*

| A | B | C | D |
|---|---|---|---|
| I | me | mine | my |
| you | you | yours | your |
| he | him | his | his |
| she | her | hers | her |
| it | it | its | its |
| we | us | ours | our |
| they | them | theirs | their |

## Social expressions *See 1.1, 2.1, 3.2, 3.3, 4.1, 5.3, 9.3, 12.3*

**Introducing**
*I'm Mr / Ms … How do you do?*  ·  *How do you do? / Pleased to meet you. My name's …*

**Greeting**
*How are you?*  ·  *Fine, thank you. (And you?)*
*How's business?*  ·  *Not so bad, thank you. / Pretty good.*

**Offering**
*Would you like some coffee?*  ·  *Yes, please. / No, thank you.*
*Please take a seat. / Have a biscuit.*  ·  *Thank you. / No, thank you.*
*Would you like me to send it today?*  ·  *Yes, please. / That's very kind of you.*
*Shall I phone the hotel?*  ·  *No, that's OK. / No, thank you, it's not necessary.*

**Making a request**
*Can I leave early?*  ·  *Yes, of course.*
*May I smoke?*  ·  *No, I'm afraid … (this is a no-smoking area).*
*Could you help me for a minute?*  ·  *Yes of course. / I'm afraid I can't because …*

**Apologizing**
*I'm sorry I'm late.*  ·  *That's OK. / Never mind. / It doesn't matter.*
*I'm afraid I can't come.*

**Thanking**
*Thank you very much (for …)*  ·  *You're welcome. / It's a pleasure. / Don't mention it. / Not at all.*
*Thanks for inviting me / looking after me / etc.*

## Telephone Expressions *See 3.2, 6.2, 6.3, 9.3, 10.3*

| | |
|---|---|
| **Asking to speak to someone** | *Could I / I'd like to speak to Lisa, please.* |
| | *Can you put me through to Diana Carter?* |
| | *Hello, is that Mr. Mancini?* |
| **Identifying yourself** | *This is Mario Kantel (speaking).* |
| | *Mario Kantel here.* |
| **Identifying the caller** | *Who's calling / speaking please?* |
| | *Could you give me your name, please?* |
| **Asking the caller to wait** | *Hold on, please / Hold the line, please* |
| | *I'm trying to connect you / I'll transfer you.* |
| | *Could you call back later?* |
| | *Can Ms Lee call you back?* |
| **Explaining absence** | *I'm sorry but / I'm afraid he's in a meeting / with a client / off sick / on holiday.* |
| **Leaving a message** | *Could you take a message?* |
| | *Could / Can I leave a message?* |
| **Taking a message** | *Can I take a message?* |
| | *Would you like to leave a message?* |
| | *I'll give him/her the message.* |
| | *I'll pass on the message.* |
| **Dealing with problems** | *I think you've got the wrong number / extension.* |
| | *Could you speak up please, it's a bad line.* |
| | *Could you speak more slowly, please?* |
| | *I'm sorry, I didn't catch that.* |

## Time and date expressions *See 4.1, 6.1, 6.2, 8.1, 11.2*

**1** Describing a point in time

| | |
|---|---|
| on | *Sunday, Monday* |
| | *Sunday morning, Tuesday afternoon, Monday evening* |
| in | *the morning / the afternoon / the evening* |
| | *January, February* |
| | *1970, 1985* |
| at | *3 o'clock, half past five* |
| | *Easter / Christmas* |
| | *night* |
| — | *this morning, next Tuesday, next year* |
| | *last month, last week* |
| | *every day, every year* |

**2** Describing duration

| | | | |
|---|---|---|---|
| 7 a.m. | **ago** | 10 a.m. | *The train left three hours **ago**.* |
| (the train left) | | (the time now) | |
| **from** | **for** | **to / until** | *We spoke **from** 3 **to** / **until** 5 p.m.* |
| 3 p.m. | | 5 p.m. | *We spoke **for** two hours.* |
| **since** | **for** | Tuesday | *I've been here **since** Sunday / **for** two days.* |
| Sunday | | (today) | |

# Tapescript

**1**

A: Her name is Lorella Braglia.
B: OK. Where does she live?
A: She lives in Italy. In Reggio Emilia.
B: Who does she work for?
A: She has her own company.
B: Really? What's the name?
A: Dielle. D-I-E-double L-E.
B: And what does this company do?
A: They produce knitwear, you know pullovers, etc. She's the main designer.
B: Oh, and does she speak English?
A: Yes. She and her husband speak excellent English.
B: Her husband?
A: Yes. He's the Marketing Director.
B: So they work together?
A: That's right.
B: How old are they?
A: I think they're both about thirty.

**2**

Lorella Braglia is the founder of Dielle, and also the main designer. Her husband, Danilo, works for the company as Marketing Director. Lorella designs two collections every year, and presents them at fashion shows in London, Paris, and New York. Dielle makes everything in Italy, and uses very modern equipment in its workshops. The company employs the services of 70 workshops in and around Reggio Emilia. It produces 100,000 units per year.

**3**

A B C D E F G H I J K L M
N O P Q R S T U V W X Y Z

**4**

1 A: Who do you work for?
   B: BA. That's British Airways.
2 B: What about you?
   A: GM – General Motors, the American car company.
3 C: What does HP stand for?
   D: It stands for Hewlett Packard.
4 E: What is BASF?
   F: It's a German chemical company.
5 G: What is your name?
   H: Sanz. That's S-A-N-Z.
   G: And your initial?
   H: E for Enrique.
6 I: What does AOL mean?
   J: America Online.
7 K: What kind of a qualification is a BA?
   L: It stands for Bachelor of Arts. It's a university degree.
8 M: So you work for the FBI. What does that mean?
   N: Well, the FBI is the Federal Bureau of Investigation.

**5a**

A: What's your name?
B: Gonzague Lepoutre.
A: Could you spell that, please?
B: Sure. G-O-N-Z-A-G-U-E, new word, L-E-P-O-U-T-R-E.
A: Mmhm. Where do you work?
B: I work in London.
A: Who do you work for?
B: I work for UBS.
A: Mm. What is your job?
B: I'm a Human Resources Manager.
A: And where are you from?
B: I'm from France but I live in England, near Oxford.

**5b**

1 What is your job?
2 Where do you work?
3 Are you married?
4 Where do you live?
5 Do you live in a house or a flat?
6 What do you do in your free time?

**6**

A: Alessandra, let me introduce you to my colleague, Simon Hastings.
B: How do you do? Pleased to meet you.
C: How do you do?
B: Do you work here, Alessandra?
C: No, I work for SAP. I'm a consultant. This is my colleague Akiko Takajima.
D: Nice to meet you.
B: Nice to meet you, too, Akiko. Where are you from?
D: I'm from Osaka. In Japan.
B: Where do you work?
D: I work for SAP in Frankfurt. I'm a software engineer. And you?
B: I'm a journalist. I work here at Business Monthly. Sally's my boss.

**7**

A: Can you begin by telling us a bit about Nokia? What does the company do?
B: Nokia mainly produces and sells mobile telephones. We also build base stations – they transmit the signals.
A: And where are you based?
B: The Head Office is in Helsinki. We also have a research centre in Tampere. That's about 150 kilometres north of Helsinki. We have research centres in other countries as well.
A: I see. How many people do you employ?
B: About 53,000 worldwide. We have factories in about ten countries and offices in many more.
A: What languages do you speak in the company?
B: Finnish. And English, of course.
A: What are your biggest markets?
B: China. We sell a lot of telephones in China. I go there a lot. The US is also a big market and Europe too. There's a lot of competition.
A: Who are the competitors?
B: Motorola and Ericsson.
A: Where do you advertise?
B: On TV, in magazines, and on buses. We also sponsor sports events.

**8**

1  France, French
2  Brazil, Brazilian
3  Italy, Italian
4  China, Chinese
5  Portugal, Portuguese
6  Australia, Australian
7  Germany, German
8  Japan, Japanese
9  Spain, Spanish
10 Mexico, Mexican

**9**

A: What do you do at the weekends?
B: I often go to my cabin near Lake Pukkala.
A: What do you do there?
B: I swim or play tennis.
A: Who do you play with?
B: My sons.
A: And where do you swim?
B: In the lake. It's very cold but very refreshing.
A: What do you do in the evenings?
B: I listen to music or take a sauna.
A: Thank you.

**10a**

Good morning, ladies and gentlemen, thank you for coming. My name is Sarah James, and I'm here to give a brief presentation on the company. My talk is very short so please keep your questions for the end.

The first part of my presentation is about the company structure of Pizza Hut (UK). The second part looks at the present activity of the company in the UK, and in the last part I want to talk about our future plans. First, the structure. Let's start with the parent company. As you know, Pizza Hut (UK) is a subsidiary of Tricon Global Restaurants. There are other brands in the group, such as KFC and Taco Bell. The President of Pizza Hut (UK) is Jon Prinsell.

Now, let's look at our present activity. Business is very good. People in Britain like pizza! We have sales of over £300 million from 400 outlets. We employ about 16,000 people. In Britain our brand is very well-known. 80% of the population eat at Pizza Hut at least once a year. On top of that, we deliver 75,000,000 pizzas to people's homes. Pizzas are our main product, but we also sell a lot of pasta, salads, desserts, and drinks.

Finally, the future. In the next ten years we plan to open at least another hundred restaurants. At the moment, our market share of all meals in restaurants in Britain is 6%. We would like to increase that number to 10% in the next ten years. With our customers and our staff, that aim is possible. Thank you for listening. Do you have any questions?

**10b**

1 My name is Sarah James, and I'm here to give a brief presentation on the company.
2 The first part of my presentation is about the company structure of Pizza Hut (UK). The second part looks at the present activity of the company in the UK, and in the last part I want to talk about our future plans.
3 First, the structure. Let's start with the parent company.
4 Now, let's look at our present activity.
5 Do you have any questions?

**11**

1 Where do you work?
2 How much does he earn?
3 What does she do?
4 He doesn't speak English.
5 A: Does she work here now?
   B: Yes, she does.
6 A: Do you use a PC?
   B: Yes, I do.

**12**

1 What's the company called?
2 Could you spell that?
3 Is it a private company?
4 What's the turnover?
5 Where is it based?
6 Who are the competitors?
7 How many people does it employ?
8 Who's the Managing Director?
9 What does the company produce?

**13**

A: Royal Princess hotel. Good morning.
B: Good morning. Could I reserve a room for next week, for three nights, from Monday the first of November?
A: Certainly, sir. Three nights from Monday the first, you say?
B: Yes, that's right.
A: Single or double room, sir?
B: Single, please.
A: OK. Let me check. Yes, we have a room free. May I have your name, please?

B: It's Gervais. That's G-E-R-V-A-I-S.
A: Sorry, that's G-E-R …
B: … V-A-I-S. But the reservation is in the name of my company, Cambridge Management Consulting. That's CMC.
A: OK. I've got that. Can you confirm your reservation in writing please, sir?
B: I'm afraid I'm not in my office today. Can I fax you tomorrow?
A: Yes, of course. That's fine.
B: Could you tell me your fax number?
A: Yes, it's 662–238–1999.
B: OK. Thanks. Goodbye.
A: Goodbye.

**14**

1 S: Excuse me. Is this Mr Maleta's office?
R: Yes it is. Can I help you?
S: Yes, I'm Chris Sutton. I have an appointment to see Mr Maleta.
R: I'm afraid he's in another meeting at the moment, Mr Sutton. Could you wait a few minutes?
S: Yes, of course.

2 S: Hello, could I speak to Mario Maleta, please? It's Chris Sutton here.
R: Hello, Mr Sutton. I'm sorry, but Mr Maleta isn't here today.
S: OK, it doesn't matter. Could you ask him to call me back?
R: Yes, certainly. Can I have your number?

**15a**

| | |
|---|---|
| think | thank |
| that | three |
| the | this |
| other | there |
| bath | theatre |
| month | thirty |

**15b**

1 Is that the theatre?
2 It's not this month, it's the other month.
3 I think there are three rooms with a bath.

**16**

1 A: Do you have the time, please?
B: Yes, it's quarter past three.
A: What time does the meeting start this afternoon?
B: At half past five. And it finishes at seven o'clock.

2 C: Oh no! It's time to go. It's already twenty past nine.
D: What time's your train?
C: At ten to ten.

3 E: This is the last call for flight Number LO 532 to Warsaw, leaving at fourteen forty-five. All passengers for the fourteen forty-five flight to Warsaw, flight number LO 532, please go to Gate 25.

**17**

A: How far is it from the city centre to the airport?
B: Not far. About ten kilometres, I think.
A: And what's the best way to get to the centre?
B: Well, airport taxis are quite expensive, so I always take the airport shuttle bus. It's cheap and quick.
A: How long does it take to get there?
B: About twenty-five minutes.
A: And how often does the bus go? My flight's on a Sunday.
B: I think there are buses every half an hour at weekends. And they run all day, from about half past five in the morning to eleven at night.
A: OK, I'll take the bus, then. I also want to go shopping in Warsaw, if I've got time. When are the shops and banks open?
B: The banks open at eight or nine in the morning. Shops are usually open from eight to six.
A: From eight o'clock. That's good – I can shop early in the morning, before my meetings.
B: Yes, but be careful. Some specialist boutiques open late, at about eleven in the morning. And if you're there on Saturday, most shops close at two.
A: Right, I'll remember that. Thanks for all your help. I'll send you a postcard.

**18**

1 There are seventy rooms in the hotel.
2 It's eighteen kilometres from the airport.
3 My plane is at three fifteen.
4 We have thirty companies in the group.
5 It takes fourteen hours by road.
6 There are ninety people at the conference.
7 The bus comes every sixteen minutes.

**19**

1 A: Good afternoon. Could I see your passport, please?
B: Yes, of course.
A: Thank you. Are you here on business?
B: Yes, I am.
A: How many days are you here for?
B: Just three.
A: And how much money do you have with you?
B: Uhm … about $500.
A: OK, thank you. Enjoy your stay.
B: Thank you.

2 A: Could you come here, sir?
B: Yes, sure.
A: How much luggage do you have?
B: Just this one bag.
A: Do you have any perfume, cigarettes, tobacco?
B: No, I have some duty-free wine. That's all.
A: How many bottles do you have?
B: Two.
A: Thank you, sir. Could you just open your suitcase for me?

**20**

A: Good afternoon, sir.
B: Good afternoon. I'd like a single room for tonight, please, if you have one.
A: Have you got a reservation, sir?
B: No, I haven't.
A: Just one moment. Let me check. Yes, we have a single room.
B: Does it have a shower?
A: Yes, it does, sir. It's got a shower and a bath.
B: That's fine. I'll take it.
A: Very good, sir. Could I have your credit card, please?

Unit 3

**21**

L: Leanne Sands. How can I help you?
V: Hi, Leanne. This is Vernon.
L: Vernon. Where are you?
V: I'm in your building. I have a great view of the Empire State Building. But I can't find your offices.
L: Are you on the fourteenth floor?
V: No, I'm on the fourth. In reception they told me to go the fourth.
L: No, we're on the fourteenth, Vernon. Are you near an elevator?
V: Yes, there's one just next to me. It's Elevator … D.
L: Elevator D, OK. So take the elevator to the fourteenth floor. When you come out of the elevator, turn left. You'll see the Conference Center in front of you. Then take the first right.
V: One second. So that's left at the elevator, then first right.
L: Yeah. Go along the corridor, past the Conference Center. At the end of the corridor you come to a small escalator. Go up the escalator, and Glick and Warburg is immediately on the right, just opposite the Business Center.
V: So that's along the corridor, up the escalator, and you're on the right.
L: Yeah – just opposite the Business Center. It's easy to find. There are signs everywhere.
V: OK, thanks Leanne. I'll be with you in a moment. Bye.
L: Good luck, Vernon!

**22**

| | |
|---|---|
| thirty | thirteen |
| it | eat |
| live | leave |
| sit | seat |
| this | these |

**23**

B: Hello.
A: Hello. Could I speak to David Payton, please?
B: Certainly. Who's calling, please?
A: This is Monique Dumont, from Execo.
B: Hold on one moment, please … Hello, I'm afraid David's in a meeting at the moment. Can I take a message?
A: Yes, could you ask him to call me back? It's about his trip to France.
B: Yes, of course. Could you tell me your number?
A: Yes, it's 33 – that's the code for France – then 2–51–25–89–74.
B: 89–74. OK. I'll give him the message.
A: Thank you for your help. Goodbye.

**24**

1 Could I have your name?
2 Can I leave a message?
3 Hold on a moment.
4 Could you ask Ellen to call me back?
5 I'm afraid she's not in the office at the moment.

**25**

A: Hello. Is that David?
B: Yes, speaking. Is that Monique?
A: Yes. Hello David. How are you?
B: I'm fine.
A: It's about your trip to France next week.
B: Yes?
A: Would you like to stay on for the weekend – as a guest of Execo, of course?
B: Well, that's very kind of you, but I'm afraid I have a flight to England on Friday evening.
A: Can you change it?
B: Uhm, yes, I'm sure that's possible. I don't have any meetings at the weekend.
A: Because we'd like to take you to the Loire valley. What do you think?
B: Well, that would be very nice.
A: We can have dinner in a château, we can go wine-tasting, and … would you like to go ballooning?
B: I'm sorry?
A: The best way to go sightseeing in the Loire is in a hot-air balloon, David.
B: Well, yes, I'd love to.
A: OK. I'll make all the reservations and I'll call you back.
B: Yes, but …

**26**

A: What would you like, Katrin?
B: I can't decide. What do you recommend?
A: Well, it's difficult to say. There's a different menu every day, but it's always good. I'll have the green curry myself. I really like Thai food. Do you like spicy dishes?
B: No, not really.
A: Then I suggest you try the lasagne as a main course. Italian dishes are always very good here.
B: OK, I'll have that. Ah, just a second … there's paella on the menu. That's my favourite. Yes, I'll have the paella.
A: OK, good. And what will you have to start?
B: Well, um, the Japanese and Mexican dishes look very spicy. So I think I'd like the onion soup. What about you?

A: Well, sushi's very nice, but that's rice again. So I'll have the guacamole.
B: Great, so are we ready to order?
A: Yes, I think so. Excuse me, could we order please?

### 27

C: More coffee, madam?
B: No, thank you.
C: Would you like some more coffee, sir?
A: No, thanks. Could you bring me the bill, please?
C: Certainly, sir.
B: Please, let me get this.
A: No, you're my guest! This is on me.
B: That's very kind of you. Um, thank you for inviting me.
A: You're very welcome.
B: It's an excellent restaurant. Good food and friendly service.
A: I'm pleased you like it.
C: Here's your bill, sir.
A: Thank you. Do you accept credit cards?
C: Yes, we do.
A: And could I have a receipt?
C: Yes, of course.

## Unit 4

### 28

A: Thomas Hart.
B: Hi, Thomas. This is Martin.
A: Martin! Welcome back. How was your course?
B: Really good. I called yesterday evening, but there was no answer. Were you all out?
A: Actually, yes. I was in a restaurant with a client. I wasn't home until midnight.
B: Was Angela with you?
A: No she was at a friend's house, I think. The children were at the cinema with friends.
B: Right. Well, are you free now? Can I come and see you?
A: Yes, of course.

### 29

1 A: Where were you? I called but there was no answer on this number.
B: I was in Paris from Thursday to Saturday.
A: Were you?

2 C: There were three of us at the conference.
D: Was Christian there?
C: Yes, he was.

3 E: How was the conference?
F: It was interesting, but by eight we were all very tired.
E: I'm sure you were.

### 30

*Example*
A: Did you enjoy the course?
B: Yes, I did. It was really interesting.
1 A: Did you improve your English?
B: Yes I did – and I improved my Spanish too!

2 A: Did you attend any Spanish classes?
B: Yes, I did to start with. I attended classes for two weeks. After that I learned Spanish from my friends.

3 A: Did you do any sport?
B: No, I didn't do any sport, but I started to learn the tango.

4 A: Really! Did you live on the university campus?
B; No, I didn't. I lived in a flat in the city.

5 A: And did you like the city?
B: Yes, I did. I really liked the people.
A: And did you pass all your exams?
B: Mm, no. I failed my statistics exam the first time. But I passed it the second time.

### 31

A: Excuse me. Are you Yuji Ishiguro?
B: Yes, that's right. You must be Paco Reverte. Thanks for coming.
A: No problem. Is this your first visit here?
B: Yes it is.
A: What time did you arrive?
B: About midnight. My plane was late.
A: Oh I'm sorry to hear that. Did you sleep well?
B: Yes, thanks, I did. What time is our meeting?
A: At ten. Shall we go? We can have a coffee in the city centre.
B: That would be nice. Do we get to the centre by car or on foot?
A: By car. I parked just outside the hotel. This way.

### 32

1 Do you smoke?
2 Did you have a good journey?
3 How's the hotel?
4 Would you like a coffee?
5 Here you are.
6 Thank you for coming.
7 I'm afraid that a lot of people are away today.
8 Would you like a quick tour?
9 Is this your first visit?
10 We are very happy with your company's work.

### 33

A: Hi Piera, this is Charles. How are you?
B: Fine, thanks.
A: When did you get back from Washington?
B: I got home on Sunday morning.
A: How was the meeting at Citibank?
B: Oh, it was very long. We didn't finish until six, but it was a good meeting.
A: Did you go out in the evening?
B: Yes, I went out on Thursday evening – to the theatre.
A: Where did you stay?
B: I stayed at the Madison.
A: Did you go shopping?
B: Yes, I bought some perfume and some shoes.

A: What did you do yesterday?
B: Oh, I was at the office. In the afternoon I wrote my report and in the evening I answered my e-mail.

### 34

1 PM: Hello, William. Could I introduce you to Isaac Cady from Washington? This is William Bernstein. He's an accountant.
WB: Nice to meet you, Isaac. Do you know Marianna Tardelli? She's our Marketing Director.
MT: How do you do.
IC: How do you do.

2 PM: Hello, Carla. Meet Isaac Cady. This is Carla Dendena. Carla's in charge of Human Resources.
IC: Nice to meet you, Carla. Are you busy at the moment?
CD: Very.

3 PM: Isaac. I'd like you to meet Gianni Baresi, our company lawyer, and Daniel Jones, our Sales Director, who I think you met last year.
GB: Nice to meet you.
IC: Nice to see you again.
PM: Oh and this is Erika Chang. She's Daniel's Personal Assistant.
EC: How do you do.

4 PM: Can I introduce you to Frank Jensch? Frank here is our Head of Research.
IC: A very important job. Pleased to meet you.
FJ: Pleased to meet you. Come and see my laboratory if you have time.
IC: Thank you. I'd like to.

### 35a

1 Thank you very much. I would like to talk about the Research Department. As you know there are four scientists in the department plus ten technicians. Our main activity is software research. We have a well-equipped laboratory and four offices. We are not in the main building. We work a lot with computer companies in the USA, so we spend a lot of our budget on travel.

2 I am in charge of the Purchasing Department. There are five managers in the team and seven administrative staff. We are responsible for all purchases, raw material, components, and other supplies. We travel a lot to China, the Philippines, and Korea. We have a large open-plan office on the second floor and two more offices on the top floor. We use fax and e-mail a lot.

3 My department is the Human Resources Department. We are on the first floor of the main building. We are responsible for recruitment and training. As you know, we spend a lot of our budget on computer and language training. There are six of us in the department, plus the Director.

4 Hello. I am the Head of the Communications Department. It's very small. There are three of us in one large open-plan office on the ground floor. We are in charge of internal and external communications and public relations. Our main projects are the company newsletter, which we produce four times a year, and we are also responsible for the publication of the annual report.

### 35b

1 We work a lot with computer companies in the USA, so we spend a lot of our budget on travel.
2 We are responsible for all purchases, raw material, components, and other supplies.
3 There are six of us in the department, plus the Director.
4 We are in charge of internal and external communications and public relations.

## Unit 5

### 36

A: Which company are you with, Alicia?
B: I work for Repsol YPF.
A: So you're in the oil business?
B: Yes, that's right. Oil and petrol are our main products. But the company also manufactures and distributes gas, petrochemicals, and electricity.
A: And what job do you do at Repsol?
B: I work in the training department. I train new employees. We're investing a lot of money in training at the moment.
A: Is the company expanding very quickly, then?
B: Yes, it is. Repsol YPF is developing its activity in Latin America. And in Spain, we're building a big technology centre for all our research and development work.
A: Really? Where in Latin America does Repsol operate, then?
B: Well, mostly in Argentina. Recently, Repsol bought the Argentinian company YPF, and the company has a new South American headquarters in Buenos Aires.
A: Sounds exciting. And what are you working on at the moment?
B: Well, we're organizing specialized training programmes because the company's introducing a lot of new technology and computer tools.
A: I see.

### 37

A: So, What company are you with?
B: I work for a company called ATC.

A: And what does ATC do?
B: We sell perfumes and beauty products.
A: And where do you work?
B: In our head office, in the centre of Stockholm.
A: So where are you travelling today?
B: I'm flying to Brussels.
A: Oh really. My mother comes from Belgium, so I know the country well.
B: Really? Uhm, please excuse me. I have to go. My flight's at two o'clock.

38

Good morning, ladies and gentlemen. I am here to tell you how the Internet can help you to do business in the Asia-Pacific region. Let's have a look at this first slide. Can everybody see? Good.

This table shows the number of Internet users in different parts of the world. On the third line, you have the figures for Asia-Pacific. Notice that the number of Internet users is rising rapidly, an increase of 878% – yes, 878 – in the five-year period. What does that mean for e-commerce in Asia Pacific? The column on the right shows the estimated revenue for e-commerce in 2002. For Asia-Pacific, the figure is 34.5 billion dollars. Not bad, when you compare with Western Europe at 55.5 billion, and Japan at 26 billion.

Let's look at my next slide. This pie chart compares the number of Internet users in 1997 and 2001. These figures are only for Asia-Pacific. I'd like to draw your attention to the white and green segments. Can everybody see? These show the percentage of Internet users in the region. In 1997, only 19% of the population had an Internet connection. For 2001 the figure is 35%. That's 28% in the highly-developed countries – Australia, Hong Kong and so on – and 7% in the developing countries like Malaysia and Thailand.

So, as you can see, consumption is increasing dramatically in all Asia-Pacific countries. There is a big market in Asia-Pacific, ladies and gentlemen, and it's waiting for you.

39

| | |
|---|---|
| recruitment | figures |
| diagram | compare |
| percentage | remain |
| India | consumer |
| Japan | period |
| column | segment |

40

1 A: Good morning.
   B: Good morning, Mrs Turner. Which floor?
   A: The third, please.
   B: And how are you?
   A: Very well, thank you, Mr Trenton. And you?
   B: Very well too. It's a beautiful day, isn't it?
   A: Yes, it is. It's nice to see the sun.
   B: Yes, it is – particularly in January. And how's your new job?
   A: Fine, thank you. I'm enjoying it a lot.
   B: I'm pleased to hear that ... Ah, I think this is my floor.
   A: Goodbye, Mr Trenton. Have a nice day.
   B: Yes, you too.

2 C: Hello, Brigitte.
   D: Igor, what a surprise! Great to see you again. How are you?
   C: Not so bad.
   D: And are you still working for MVC?
   C: Yes, for the moment.
   D: And how are things?
   C: Well, not very good, I'm afraid. Business is very slow. There's a lot of competition these days.
   D: Sorry to hear that, Igor. These seem to be difficult times for everyone. But how's the family?
   C: Fine, thanks. Oleg is starting university this year.
   D: Really? Is he eighteen already?
   C: Yes, he is.
   D: That's incredible. So, what are you doing here at Sema?
   C: Well, I'm looking for a new job. And I think Sema wants to offer me one. I'm going to see the head of IT this morning.
   D: Are you ? Well, that's great news, Igor. I'm really happy to hear that. I ...
   C: Ah, I think this is my floor.
   D: Well very good luck for today, Igor!
   C: Thanks Brigitte!

41

A: Danuta, hi. Welcome back. Did you have a good trip?
B: Yes, thanks, I did. It was great.
A: So what was New York like?
B: Very noisy, but it's an exciting city to visit.
A: Yes, everybody says that. What was your hotel like?
B: Well, my room was quite small, but the hotel itself was very clean. And really convenient – only two minutes' walk from the conference centre.
A: How was the conference?
B: I loved it. People were really friendly, and I made two or three very useful contacts. I'll tell you about them later.
A: And what were the presentations like?
B: Well, actually, the talks that I went to were a little boring. I fell asleep in one of them.
A: You didn't!
B: Yes, I did. But that was the only negative thing. Generally, it was a fantastic visit. I'd love to go again.
A: No! Next time, I want to go! You can stay here!

Unit 6

42

A: So, we are nearly ready.
B: Right. Let's just check the programme.
A: Who's the Guest Speaker for the Welcome Dinner?
B: Elizabeth Cortes.
A: How do you spell that?
B: C-O-R-T-E-S.
A: When is she arriving?
B: She's flying in from Boston on Wednesday morning. Miguel is meeting her at the airport at midday.
A: Where is she staying?
B: At the Ramada. She's leaving on Thursday. She and her husband are only staying one night.
A: What about Professor Lingwood? What time is she speaking on Thursday?
B: She's starting at two thirty.
A: What is she talking about?
B: T-E-R-N. Trans European Road Networks. It'll be very interesting.
A: What about Professor Denier?
B: He's not coming this year. He's too busy.

43a

A: Is that Jaime?
A: Hello Jaime. This is Tim Railton. Are you going to the conference?
A: When are you going?
A: How long are you staying?
A: Where are you staying?
A: I'm staying at the Ramada. Are you speaking at the conference?
A: What are you speaking about?
A: That's interesting. Are you going to the cocktail party?
A: What are you doing on Thursday evening?

43b

A: Is that Jaime?
B: Speaking.
A: Hello, Jaime. This is Tim Railton. Are you going to the conference?
B: Yes, I am.
A: When are you going?
B: I'm going on the twenty-sixth of July.
A: How long are you staying?
B: Four nights. I'm leaving on Saturday.
A: Where are you staying?
B: At the Sheraton.
A: I'm staying at the Ramada. Are you speaking at the conference?
B: Yes. On Friday morning.
A: What are you speaking about?
B: Underground train systems.
A: That's interesting. Are you going to the cocktail party?
B: No, I'm not free.
A: What are you doing on Thursday evening?
B: I'm meeting Thérèse Blanc.

44a

| | |
|---|---|
| sixtieth | twentieth |
| twelfth | twenty-first |
| eighteenth | thirteenth |
| third | fifteenth |

44b

1 May is the fifth month of the year.
2 Twelve point five per cent is one eighth.
3 The last day of April is the thirtieth.
4 The person who finishes first gets a gold medal.
5 October to December is the fourth quarter of the year.

45

1 The film Titanic starring Leonardo di Caprio last night won ten Oscars. The film is based on the true story of the ship which sank on April the fifteenth 1912.
2 A: So, how did you see in the Millennium? Can you remember?
   B: Of course I can! We were up in the mountains in Switzerland drinking champagne. We had a great time! What did you do?
3 Here is the news. It is eight o'clock on June the second 1953. The first two men to climb Mount Everest arrived at the summit yesterday. Edmund Hilary and Sherpa Tensing sent a radio message today to confirm their achievement.
4 Many countries have one minute's silence at eleven o'clock on the eleventh day of the eleventh month to celebrate the end of the First World War.
5 This is the news on WKLG. Amelia Earhart today became the first woman to fly the Atlantic solo. This day, the twenty-first of May 1932 will become famous in the history of flight.
6 There is a full moon over Paris. It is July the twelfth 1998 and President Chirac hands the World Cup to Didier Deschamps. France are World Champions of Football.

46

1 A: HK Oil & Gas. How can I help you?
   B: Could I speak to Diana Wong, please?
   A: I'm sorry, sir, but the line is busy. Would you like to hold?
   B: Yes, please.
   *HK Oil & Gas. Hold the line please. We're trying to connect you.*
   A: HK Oil & Gas. How can I help?
   B: I wanted to speak to Diana Wong.
   A: Her line is busy. Would you like to hold?
   B: No thanks. I'll call later.

2 A: HK Oil & Gas. How can I help you?
   B: Could I speak to Diana Wong, please?
   A: Certainly. I'll put you through. (*pause*)
   I'm sorry, sir, but there is no reply from her office.

B: Oh, do you have her mobile number, by any chance?
A: Yes. I think we do. Let me see, it's 04345 then 4631.
B: Thanks very much.

3 C: Hello. Sales Department. Diana Wong's phone.
B: Is that you Diana?
C: Sorry but Diana's out of the office today.
B: When are you expecting her back?
C: Tomorrow. Can I take a message?
B: Yes, please. Could you tell her Jordi Marrero rang? I'd like to see her on Friday. My direct line is 663–4562.
C: OK. I'll give her the message. Thanks for calling.
B Thanks for your help. Bye.
C: Bye.

4 B: Hello. Is that Diana Wong?
D: I'm sorry. You've got the wrong extension. She's in the Sales Department.
B: Could you transfer me to her?
D: Yes, of course. Hold the line. I'll transfer you.
E: Hello.
B: Is that Diana?
E: Speaking.
B: Hi it's Jordi Marrero ...

47

1 I'm arriving in Hong Kong on Friday.
2 Where's he staying?
3 When's she due back?
4 You're welcome.
5 No thanks. I'll call back later.
6 I'm afraid she's out this afternoon.
7 He's in a meeting this morning.
8 He's got a meeting this morning.

48

1 This is a message for Ms Diana Wong. It is May the twenty-sixth at seven thirty. This is Suntours Travel. Your ticket for Manila is ready. We'll put it in the mail for you tomorrow.
2 Mrs Wong. This is Patricia Lopez. I am calling to cancel our dinner on the ninth of June. I have to go to Australia that week. My apologies.
3 Hello Diana, this is James Lee. Could you call me back this afternoon. It's now three p.m. on the twenty-seventh of May. My number is 452–98577. Bye.
4 Hi Diana. This is Jordi Marrero. I am at the Royal Garden hotel. Please call me today, Friday May the twenty-seventh, before nine p.m. My number is 453–49823.

49

1 A: Hello, Erika, this is Natasha.
B: Natasha, what a surprise! I didn't think what you were coming this year. How are you?
A: I'm fine. What about you? When did you get here?

B: Oh, about an hour ago. It would be great to see you – can we meet up?
A: Well, let me see, are you free tomorrow evening?
B: Er, well, I'm going to the dinner.
A: OK, well are you doing anything afterwards? We could meet up then.
B: Yes, that would be nice.
A: What time do you think you'll be free?
B: Um, is ten thirty OK?
A: Sounds good. Let's meet at the restaurant at ten thirty.
B: OK, ten thirty tomorrow, then. I'll look forward to it. Bye.

2 C: Hello. Mikael Stefansson speaking.
A: Hello, Mr Stefansson. My name is Natasha Hall. I work for Roche.
C: Oh yes, Ms Hall. I know your work. What can I do for you?
A: I'm working on a project which might interest you. Would it be possible to meet ?
C: Certainly. When would be convenient?
A: Wednesday would suit me.
C: I'm afraid I'm giving a paper on Wednesday morning.
A: What about the evening?
C: I'm going to the jazz concert at ten. Could we make it before dinner?
A: Yes. Is seven all right?
C: That sounds fine. So that's seven o'clock on Wednesday. Shall we meet in the lobby?
A: That's fine with me. I look forward to meeting you.
C: I look forward to meeting you too. Thank you for calling.

3 D: Hello?
A: Hello. Could I speak to Dr Jung, please?
D: Speaking.
A: This is Natasha Hall. I don't know if you remember me – we met last year.
D: Oh, yes. Of course I remember. It was in Berlin, wasn't it? I can't believe that was a year ago! So, how are things with you?
A: Everything is fine. I was wondering if you would like to meet up?
D: That would be nice. Are you doing anything tomorrow evening?
A: I'm sorry, I've got something else on tomorrow. Are you free this evening?
D: Yes I am. Is nine o'clock OK?
A: That's fine. Downstairs in the bar at nine. It'll be nice to see you again.
D: Lovely. See you then. Thanks for calling.

4 A: Hello. Is that Ms Aoki?
E: Speaking.
A: This is Natasha Hall. I'm calling to confirm our

appointment on Wednesday.
E: Oh, I'm glad you called. I have a problem on Wednesday. I have another engagement. Could we cancel our meeting? Could we meet at another time?
A: Of course. When would be convenient for you?
E: I'm free on Thursday at lunchtime.
A: Could we have lunch together?
E: That would be nice. Shall we meet in the restaurant at twelve thirty?
A: That's fine. So that's Thursday the sixth at twelve thirty. I look forward to meeting you.
E: Thank you for calling. Bye.
A: Bye.

50

A: Hello Mr Stefansson. This is Natasha Hall again.
C: Hello, Ms Hall. What can I do for you?
A: We have an appointment tomorrow at seven. Would it be possible to change it?
C: Yes, I think so. What time would suit you?
A: Could we bring it forward a couple of hours?
C: Five o'clock? I'm afraid I'm busy.
A: Could we postpone it to Friday?
C: I'm going on the tour of New Orleans in the morning. Are you doing anything in the afternoon?
A: I'm afraid I'm leaving for Washington at three. How about another day? Are you free on Thursday?
C: On Thursday morning, yes.
A: I am free before nine. How about breakfast?
C: That would be fine. Eight o'clock in the coffee shop.
A: Fine. So that's eight o'clock on the sixth, then.

## Unit 7

51

1 The car's quicker than the bus.
2 The train's more tiring than the car.
3 The bus is slower than the train.
4 The train's more dangerous than the car.
5 The country isn't as stressful as the town.

52

1 Here in Japan, we live in very small apartments. The average living area is just thirty-one square metres per person. And it's particularly expensive to live in Tokyo. The average rent here is higher than in New York and Paris.
2 As you know, the USA is a very big country. Space is very important for us. The average American has a living area of fifty-nine square metres. And prices are not always high, even

in big cities. Renting an apartment in New York, for example, is cheaper than in Tokyo or Paris.
3 I've lived in Tokyo and New York, but now I live in Paris. Flats in Paris are more expensive than in New York, but cheaper than in Tokyo. And we have more space than in Japan. In France our average living area is thirty-seven square metres per person.

53

1 Travelling by train is less tiring than driving.
2 Renting a flat is cheaper than buying.
3 I think the most important thing in life is money.
4 Learning English is difficult, but it's easier than learning Japanese.
5 The biggest problem in the world today is pollution.
6 Life is more stressful than fifty years ago.
7 The best holiday is one where you do nothing for two weeks.

54a

A: So what is 'Veggie Vision'?
B: It's a computerized scanner system for supermarkets. It's used to identify fruit and vegetables and to give the price.
A: Ah! Is it used by customers or by cashiers?
B: By cashiers at the checkout. So when a customer is buying some apples or some tomatoes, the cashier uses the Veggie Vision scanner to identify the items.
A: So, the main advantage here is speed, I suppose.
B: Yes, absolutely. Veggie Vision can identify fruit and vegetables faster than the cashier.
A: And how is it different from the supermarket scanners we see today?
B: It's an intelligent system. It learns all the time, just like you or me.

54b

A: So how does Veggie Vision work exactly?
B: Well, let's take this melon. First of all the product is scanned by the cashier. A photo of the product is taken, and then information about the melon's size, shape, and colour is recorded.
A: What happens then?
B: Next, the product details are compared with the database. That's the database of all the fruit and vegetables in the supermarket.
A: OK. I'm with you.
B: After this, Veggie Vision selects the correct item on the database. Then the cashier is shown a picture of the melon with the price.
A: And finally, the cashier confirms the choice.

B: Yes, she pushes this button.
A: Mm. Does Veggie Vision make mistakes sometimes?
B: No, but sometimes it finds it difficult to identify the item. This can happen when two types of fruit or vegetable are very similar in shape and size. Like a grapefruit and an orange, for example.
A: What happens in that case?
B: Veggie Vision shows the cashier the two different fruits, and she chooses the right one. This is how it 'learns'. Next time it identifies the correct fruit immediately.

55

1 It's rectangular.
  It's made of plastic.
  It's eight centimetres long and five centimetres in width.
  It's about one millimetre thick.
  It weighs about five grams.
  It's multicoloured.
  It's used for calling people.
  (beep)
  It's a phone card.
2 It's round.
  It's made of metal.
  It's about seventy centimetres in diameter.
  It's about eight kilograms in weight.
  It's often white.
  Maybe you have one on the roof of your house.
  It's used for receiving TV programmes.
  (beep)
  It's a satellite dish.
3 It's more or less rectangular.
  It's made of plastic.
  It's about ten centimetres in length and seven centimetres wide.
  It weighs about one hundred grams.
  It's usually grey.
  It has a little round ball inside.
  It's used for working on a computer.
  (beep)
  It's a mouse.

56

A: Let's discuss the promotional gift. As you know, the marketing department have suggested three different products: the pedometer, the calorie counter, and the Relax Max CD. Anna, would you like to start?
B: Yes, I think the calorie counter is the best. It's cheap, and there's lots of interesting information in it. It also doesn't weigh much, so it's a good product to put in the cereal packet.
A: What do you think, Ned?
C: I don't agree with Anna. I don't like the calorie counter. I think it's a product that only interests women. Men want to be healthy, but they don't want to count calories.
A: Mm, yes, I think you're right, Ned. So which product do you prefer?

C: Well, in my view, the pedometer is the best. It's very original as a promotional gift, and it's very useful for men – and women – who go running.
B: Sorry, Ned, but I disagree. I think cost is a problem here. It's original, that's true. But if a lot of people want it, it will be very expensive for us. Don't you agree, Carmen?
A: Yes, I do. And I don't think it gives the right image. This cereal isn't only for people who do sport, it's for people who want a healthy diet.
B: Yes, I agree.
C: OK. I see you both disagree with me. So, how about the Relax Max CD? It's not very expensive.
B: And it interests both men and women.
A: Yes, I think so too. And it's not just a sports product.
C: Yes, You can imagine people eating our breakfast cereal, then sitting down to listen to the CD.
B: And doing their relaxation exercises!
A: Good. So do we all agree?
B: C: Yes.

## Unit 8

57

In March 1997 Robert Ayling, the Chairman of British Airways, decided to create a low-cost airline. He asked Barbara Cassani to run it. Six months later she presented her business plan to the board of BA, who agreed to invest $25,000,000 in the project. In November 1997, she announced the start of a new airline, but it still had no name. In December, she chose Stansted Airport in South East England as the base for the new airline, and the following month she chose the name 'Go'. The first passengers took off in May 1998, and by 1999, Go had thirteen aircraft in the air.

58a

A: Well, first of all, where was she born?
B: In the US – in 1960, I think.
A: What about her studies?
B: She got her first degree at a college in Massachusetts, and her Masters at Princeton.
A: What about her husband? He's British, isn't he?
B: Yes he is. She met him at Princeton.
A: OK. Now, what was her first job?
B: I believe she worked for a US senator when she was still a student. So that was in 1981. But her first real job was in 1984 when she was a consultant with Coopers and Lybrand – you know, the Management Consultants.
A: So when did she move to England?
B: She was transferred here by Coopers and Lybrand in 1986, and then joined British Airways the following year.

A: In 87.
B: Mm, that's right. She worked in Sales and Marketing for five years and then had her first baby in 1992.
A: And then?
B: The following year she was offered the job of General Manager in New York.
A: And from there she moved to Go, right?
B: That's right. In a way she was Go's first employee. She was appointed CEO in 1997.

58b

1 She was transferred here by Coopers and Lybrand in 1986.
2 She was offered the job of General Manager in New York.
3 She was appointed CEO in 1997.

59

1 In 1977 Michael Jordan earned $78,300,000.
2 In 1899 a bottle of Coca Cola cost 5 cents.
3 In 1867 Russia sold Alaska to the USA for $7,000,000.
4 The first American millionaire was Cornelius Vanderbilt who left $100,000,000 when he died in 1877.
5 In 1995 the company secretary of Glaxo wrote a cheque for £2,474,655,000.
6 In 1986 Dr Ronald Dante earned $3,080,000 for a 2-day lecture course.

60

1 The Starbird Group received good news this morning. The company, which owns over a hundred hotels in Great Britain, has agreed to sell 30% of its shares to Italian entrepreneur Luigi Vieri. The shares were valued at £70 million. Shares in the group rose on the London Stock Exchange. They closed at £3.50.
2 The Swedish furniture company IKEA has a new way of paying its employees their annual bonus. The money from all of today's sales will be shared between the staff.
3 The Bank of England today announced an increase of a quarter of one per cent in its base rate. Banks immediately announced increases in interest rates. Shares fell as a result of this news.
4 It was announced today that AGF, France's second largest insurance company, will be taken over by Allianz to create a large pan-European insurance company. The headquarters of the new group will be in Germany.

61

Good morning everybody. I'd like to look at brands this morning and as an example I have chosen McDonald's. McDonald's is famous

all over the world. It serves forty million customers every day. A new McDonald's opens somewhere in the world every five hours. The restaurants look the same, the menus are the same and the clients get the same service. A McDonald's customer is always served in no more than ninety seconds.

It all started in 1955 when a man called Ray Kroc opened his first restaurant in Illinois. He bought the name from two brothers called McDonald. To increase sales he started advertising on TV in 1963 and a clown called Ronald McDonald appeared in the first ads. The clown was friendly and helpful and gave good advice to children. To raise more money for expansion, the company was floated on Wall Street in 1965. Incidentally 100 shares cost $2,250. They are now worth $2.5 million.

In 1967 Kroc opened his first restaurants outside the US in Canada and Puerto Rico and in 1968 his most famous product, the Big Mac™ was launched. By the end of the seventies they were ready for a new idea. The 'Happy Meal', a special menu for children, was introduced in 1979.

Five years later, the founder Ray Kroc died at the age of 82. At the start of the nineties McDonald's opened in Beijing and Moscow. In 1995, Burghy, the Italian fast food chain, was acquired and within one month turnover increased by 50%. In 1996, Belarus became the hundredth country to have a McDonald's, and three years later, the twenty five thousandth McDonald's was opened in Chicago.

## Unit 9

62a

A: Hello Rosalind. Any mail this morning?
B: Good morning, Tony. Yes, there is – a letter from our head office in Germany. Astrid Köhnen is coming to England next month.
A: What? To see us?
B: Well, she's coming for a sales conference in London, but she also wants to visit us here in Manchester. She would like to meet the key staff in the Manchester office, and one or two of our British clients.
A: When's she arriving?
B: On the fourth of March. And she's staying all week until the eleventh.
A: But that's in two or three weeks. That doesn't give us much time. Um, how long is she staying with us?
B: Just a day. The afternoon of the Wednesday, then Thursday morning.
A: Is she spending the night here in Manchester?

B: I don't know. All I know is that she's arriving here at about one in the afternoon.

62b

A: Rosalind, can I ask you to organize Frau Köhnen's visit?
B: Yes, of course. I'll phone Katya Muster in Germany first of all. I'll see if we need to reserve a hotel room. And I'll ask her about Frau Köhnen's travel arrangements.
A: Yes, and can you offer to meet her at the station or airport?
B: Yes, sure.
A: Great. And we also need to know what time she's leaving on Thursday.
B: OK, I'll check that. Then I'll reserve a room for her at the Palace Hotel, if necessary.
A: Good. And what about the visit schedule? Can you ask Joseph to do that?
B: Yes, he's good at organizing these things. I'll ask him to prepare a provisional schedule for the end of this week.
A: Thanks Rosalind. We'll talk about this again on Friday.

63

1 I'll give her a call.
2 She's arriving on the five fifty train.
3 They aren't coming to see us next week.
4 We'll see you at two p.m. on Thursday.
5 You're staying at the Palace Hotel.
6 He's not meeting her on the first day.
7 When's he giving an answer?

64

A: So what about the hotel rooms? Can you book them or shall I?
B: Can you do that? You're good at negotiating prices.
A: Sure. How about the guest speakers? Shall I invite them?
B: No, I'll do that. I have all their addresses.
A: Great. And can you ask them to send a summary of their talk?
B: Yes, of course.

65

A: How about this watch, the DBCV501?
B: I like it. But I'm not sure about the market. Who'll buy it? Business people, I suppose.
A: Yes, particularly business people who travel a lot. It has some great features, like the world time indicator, and the memo function.
B: Any particular type of business person?
A: Well, I think you'll have more success with men in the twenty to thirty-five age group. The product has a younger high-tech image. Older men won't be interested.

B: OK, so that's business men under forty. How about sales outlets? Will supermarkets buy it?
A: No, they won't. It's too specialized.
B: But I'm sure we'll have customers in airport shopping centres.
A: Yes, absolutely.
B: And by mail order?
A: Yes, I think you'll probably have your best sales by mail order.
B: What about advertising, then?
A: I would say the specialist press. You'll get a lot of sales if you advertise in business magazines, for example.
B: And if we want to sell by mail order, it'll be necessary to do some direct mailing.
A: Yes, of course. We have some very useful customer lists on computer. We can send them to you.
B: That would be great. So when do I have to make a decision?
A: Very quickly, I'm afraid. My client wants a distributor as soon as possible. If you don't decide now, you won't have another chance later.
B: Give me a week.
A: Fine.

66

1 I haven't got any children.
2 She's not thirty, but forty.
3 I won't sell many in Europe.
4 Who'll work in the head office?
5 We buy all our products from one supplier.
6 I'd like this model.
7 Would you like coffee or tea?
8 They're not very expensive.

67a

A: Customer Service. Stephanie Rowe speaking.
B: Hello. This is Steve Meehan of TPS.
A: Sorry, I didn't catch your name.
B: Steve Meehan. That's M-double E-H-A-N. From TPS.
A: Mr Meehan. Sorry, I didn't recognize your voice. What can I do for you?
B: I'm calling about my order for the calculators, the model RK 529.
A: Yes, we sent them two days ago, I think. Did you receive them?
B: Yes, they arrived yesterday evening. But there were no instruction manuals in the boxes.
A: No instruction manuals. That's very strange. I'm very sorry about that.
B: Can you look into the problem?
A: Yes, of course. Can you give me the order number?
B: Yes, it's 4189 / JG.
A: 4189 / JG. And it was twenty calculators, model RK 529.
B: That's right.
A: OK, Mr Meehan. I'll look into it, and I'll call you back in ten to fifteen minutes.
B: Thanks. Speak to you soon.

67b

A: Hello, is that Mr Meehan?
B: Yes, speaking.
A: This is Stephanie Rowe again. I'm calling about your instruction manuals. I'm sorry, but we found them here in our factory.
B: So you have them. Can you send them today?
A: Yes, of course. Shall I send them by express mail?
B: Yes, please, if you could.
A: OK, I'll do that. And I do apologize once again for the mistake.
B: That's OK. Goodbye.

## Unit 10

68

A: Our next caller is Astrid Heiner, who has a translation agency in Essen in Germany. Her letter is on page thirty-five of this week's magazine. Hello, Frau Heiner.
B: Hello, Dr Biz.
A: Now, just to remind everybody, your problem is that you don't have enough work all year round, but you don't have much money for advertising.
B: Yes, that's right.
A: Well, first, I think you should use your present customers more. Ask them to tell other companies about the good work you do.
B: Well, we ask our clients to do that now, but I don't think they have the time, or they forget. So I don't think that's the answer.
A: Then how about advertising your agency on the Internet? It's not so expensive, and maybe it's a good way to find new business in other parts of Germany.
B: Well, I'm not sure about that. Some translator friends of ours have an Internet website, and they say the response isn't so good. I think we really need to offer other services to our present customers.
A: OK. Why don't you offer language training in their companies? Lessons, I mean.
B: No, that's out of the question. As you know we work from home, and we live about eighty kilometres from Essen. Most of our customers are in Essen, and it's just too far.
A: Yes, I can understand that. You only offer translation in three languages, is that right?
B: Yes.
A: That's not very many. I'd advise you to offer more unusual languages, like Chinese or Japanese, for example.
B: Ah, yes, that's a possibility. But we can't afford to employ any more people.
A: No, but many translators work for themselves. It's not always necessary to employ them. What about looking for specialist translators on the Internet? I'm

sure many of them advertise their services on the Net, like your friends.
B: Yes, that's a good idea. Mm. A very good idea. I think I'll try that.
A: Well let us know what happens, Frau Heiner. Good luck, and goodbye.
B: Goodbye, and thank you.
A: OK. Can we have our next caller?

69

1 I wear a suit and tie.
   I work for a large company with branches in nearly every town in Britain.
   The public visit us every day.
   Customers come inside, or use the machines outside our premises.
   If they want to borrow money they make an appointment to see us.
   I am in charge of about seventy people.
   I use a computer for my work.

2 I wear shorts for my job.
   I travel to different places.
   Each job lasts about two hours.
   The public watch me doing my job.
   People often shout at me.
   I am in charge of thirty men.
   I use a whistle for my work.

70

A: So, Roger, you are a bank manager and a rugby referee.
B: That's right. In fact I am deputy manager of two branches of Lloyds TSB.
A: How do you organize your time?
B: I have to twenty hours per week for the bank and then the rest of the time is free, so I can referee or train most afternoons.
A: Do you work long days?
B: Well, I have to be in the office by eight most days, but I don't have to work after lunch or at weekends.
A: And which is more difficult, managing a bank, or refereeing?
B: They're both great jobs. In both you have to be polite, friendly, and firm.
A: But you can't be too friendly, I suppose.
B: No, that's true, but you must be fair. I suppose players have to do what I say but customers can decide for themselves.

71

A: These regulations are not all that clear to me. Could you explain them to me?
B: Sure, Dino. The first one means that you have to answer the phone immediately. Three rings maximum. This gives the caller a good impression.
A: OK. That's clear. What about the next one?
B: 'Sound interested?' Well, this means you must never sound

bored or angry, even if the caller is difficult.
A: I see. And I have to introduce myself to every caller.
B: Yes. At the start of every call you have to give your name. So you say 'Good Morning. Gregorio. Sophie speaking.' Or 'Dino speaking' in your case.
A: And I have to call the customer by name too?
B: Yes, that's right. It's more personal, and more polite.
A: Mm, and this last one. What do we have to promise, exactly?
B: At Gregorio we aren't allowed to end a call without promising to do something. So you say 'I'll send you the catalogue today,' for example. Or 'I'll see what I can do, and I'll call you back.'
A: I see.

### 72

A: Good Morning, Laporta. How can I help you?
B: Hello. My name is Stephanie Strahl. I'm calling from Geneva. I understand you distribute furniture made by a Swedish company called Literatura.
A: In fact it's a Spanish company. But we are the distributors.
B: Oh, OK. Could you send me a brochure, please?
A: Yes, of course. Could I have your name again, please?
B: Strahl. Stephanie. Strahl is S-T-R-A-H-L.
A: OK. I've got that. And the name of the company?
B: STRAHL and SIRONI. That's S-I-R-O-N-I.
A: One moment, please. R-O-N-I. OK, I've got that. Could I have a phone number?
B: 022–787 …
A: … 022–787. Go on.
B: 0540.
A: 0540. Right. And, can I have your address, please?
B: Mm. 13, Avenue de Frontenex, CH 1207, Geneva.
A: Sorry, I didn't catch that.
B: 13, Avenue de – D-E – Frontenex – F-R-O-N-T-E-N-E-X.
A: Geneva.
B: That's right. And the postcode is CH 1207.
A: Fine. I'll put the brochure in the post today.
B: Thank you very much. Goodbye.

### 73

C: Would it be possible to send me a brochure?
D: Yes, of course. Let me take your details.
C: Ready?
D: Yes. Go ahead.
C: My name's Daniel Aubert.
D: Sorry. I didn't catch your last name.
C: Aubert.
D: Daniel Albert.
C: No, it's Aubert – A-U-B-E-R-T.
D: OK. I've got that. Go on.
C: And my phone number's 00 41 22 78 …

D: Sorry, that's 00 41 22 …
C: … 78 24 60 54. Have you got that?
D: Yes, I think so. Can I read that back to you? 00 41 22 78 24 60 94.
C: 54.
D: Sorry, 54.
C: That's right.

### 74

A: Good morning. Laporta.
B: Mr Laporta? This is Stephanie Strahl. Thank you very much for your quote for the Literatura furniture. I'd like to place an order, but I find it a bit expensive. Is that your best price?
A: For two items, yes, I'm afraid it is.
B: Aha. What about three items? Could you perhaps offer me a discount on a desk, a filing cabinet and a chair to go with the desk?
A: I think I could give you 15%.
B: So. 15% off £1000 makes £800.
A: No, that's not quite right. Actually, I said 15% not 20% – So I make that £850.
B: Oh, yes, sorry. You're right. 15% off each item. And the chair?
A: I have a very nice one in stock at £150. Leather and chrome.
B: OK, that sounds good. What about the transport? Is there any chance of a discount on that?
A: I'm afraid I can't reduce that because it's another company which does the delivery.
B: Ah, and the delivery time of eight weeks?
A: Well, we have everything in stock, so if you order today I can get everything to you within thirty days.
B: Oh, excellent. Payment thirty days after delivery?
A: Oh, I think thirty days after the order would be better.
B: Mm. Fine. I'll send an e-mail to confirm.
A: Thank you, Ms. Strahl. I look forward to receiving your confirmation.

## Unit 11

### 75a

A: Where do you send people? All over the world?
B: No, not exactly. Most of our contacts are in Europe, particularly southern Europe. But we're also now developing an activity in South-east Asia, particularly in Japan, Thailand, and China.
A: And do you specialize in particular types of jobs?
B: No, we don't. You see, we always work with big companies, who need new staff in many different areas. So we recruit computer technicians, teachers, construction workers, project managers, engineers. We've even recruited a personal bodyguard for the President of a European company.

A: That's quite a range. Now, tell me about the work you do.
B: Well, like all the consultants in my firm, I specialize in one particular country. I'm working in Thailand at the moment, one of our new markets. I go there regularly, visit companies, and listen to their needs. I spend at least three days in each company – that's an important point.
A: Why's that?
B: Because we provide a very personalized service. We have to know the company well, and the person who's going to work there. We don't want to recruit someone for Thailand who then leaves after two weeks because he's not happy.

### 75b

A: I can see you enjoy your job.
B: Yes, very much. I really enjoy learning about new cultures, when I visit companies abroad. I also really like interviewing people for jobs, particularly younger people.
A: Why's that?
B: Because younger people are generally very interested in the country, not only the job, and that's very important.
A: Mm. What about the travelling?
B: Well, I love visiting new countries, but I don't really like taking the plane.
A: You don't like flying. Isn't that rather difficult for someone who works in Thailand?
B: Yes, a little.
A: Is there anything else you don't like?
B: Yes, I hate telling people we can't help them. Sometimes we say no because we feel a person doesn't have the right personal qualities to work in a certain country.
A: What qualities do you think are necessary for someone working abroad?
B: I think there are three. First, they have to be adaptable, ready to change their working habits and their living habits. Secondly, they have to be sensitive people. That means they have to respect the culture of the country they are in. Finally, it's better if they are outgoing. Outgoing people will make friends easily, and learn the local language more quickly.

### 76

A: Hey, Luis Antonio!
B: Bill Pitt. I don't believe it! Bill, how are you?
A: Just fine. You're looking good, Luis.
B: You too, Bill. It's been a long time.
A: Yes, it has. When did we finish in LA?
B: In 1988. You went to Washington and I went back to Rio.
A: That's right.
B: So what are you doing now, Bill?
A: Well, I'm a Project Director with

Sun Microsystems in Silicon Valley.
B: Sun Microsystems. That's great! How long have you worked there?
A: Since 97.
B: And where do you live?
A: In San Francisco. We moved there in 1994.
B: And I guess you are married now.
A: Yes, with three beautiful children. Two sons and a daughter.
B: So where did you meet your wife?
A: Well, Luis, do you remember a girl on our MBA course in Los Angeles? Her name was Melissa Norton. She always had the best grades.
B: Melissa Norton. Of course I remember.
A: Well, we got married in 1991.
B: Well, congratulations, Bill.
A: Thanks. What about you? Do you have a family now?
B: Well, it's a long story. Do you have time for a drink before your flight?

### 77

A: Can we talk about staffing levels now? Our objective was to reduce our staff by ten per cent. How are we doing for the moment?
B: Well, the number of new employees has fallen dramatically this year. Last year we took on sixty people, but this year we've only taken on sixteen. We stopped all new recruitment six months ago.
A: Mm, what about the number of transfers?
B: Transfers have gone up too. This year we've transferred thirteen people to other divisions of the company. Last year it was only four. But the number of resignations is down. Last year five people left the company, but this year only two have resigned.
B: Have we managed to persuade more people to take early retirement?
A: Yes, that's been a success. Twenty employees have taken early retirement this year; that's fourteen more than last year.
B: But we've had some redundancies.
A: Yes, unfortunately. But it could be worse. We've made six people redundant this year. I hope there won't be any more.
B: Well, let's add up the figures and see.

### 78

Let's start with men's view of male bosses. You will notice that the number of men who prefer to have a male boss has gone down since 1982. But let's look at the figures in detail. Between 1982 and 1993, the number fell by 7% to reach 33%. What is interesting is that since

1993, the number has risen again by 2%. How does this compare with men's opinions of female bosses? In 1982, only 9% of men preferred a woman boss. In 1993, the number rose by 7% to 16%, but in the last few years it has decreased by 4%, back to 12%. As you can see, in recent years, there has been some kind of reaction against the idea of female bosses. The best news is perhaps that we now have a small majority of men – that's 52% – who have no preference. The numbers have increased by 6% since 1982.

## Unit 12

### 79a

A: Sergio. Thank you for agreeing to this interview. How old are you?
B: Um, I'm fifty-one.
A: And what is your profession?
B: I'm an accountant.
A: Are you married?
B: Yes, I am.
A: Does your wife work?
B: Yes, luckily. She's a teacher.
A: Could you tell me about your last job? Who did you work for?
B: Um, I worked for a chemical company near Milan.
A: How long did you work there?
B: Um, for fourteen years.
A: How did you lose your job?
B: The company was taken over by a Swedish firm and I was made redundant.
A: So, how long have you been unemployed?
B: Um, for about six months.

### 79b

A: So, Sergio. It must be difficult being unemployed at your age.
B: Of course. Many people don't want to employ someone over fifty.
A: So how do you spend your days?
B: I get the newspaper every day and look at the job advertisements. When I see something interesting I apply.
A: Any luck so far?
B: Yes, I was offered something last month, but the job was not very interesting.
A: Do you meet other unemployed people?
B: Not really. Um, I prefer to stay at home and work on my PC. I'm also studying psychology.
A: That's an interesting idea. What else do you do?
B: I have lunch with my former colleagues about once a month. They often hear about jobs and so on. They often have useful information.
A: Have you registered with a recruitment agency?

B: No, I haven't. I think they already have too many people on their books.
A: So how much time do you spend looking for a job?
B: Oh, about ten, fifteen hours per week. The rest of the time I do the housework and other things.
A: Are you optimistic?
B: Yes. But I really don't want to leave Milan.
A: I see. Thank you.

### 80a

| | |
|---|---|
| unemployed | interview |
| accountant | redundant |
| manufactured | psychological |
| company | responsible |
| recruitment | information |
| optimistic | secretary |
| pharmaceutical | fortunate |
| psychology | confident |

### 80b

1 She was made redundant by a pharmaceutical company.
2 I'm confident about the interview.
3 Who's responsible for recruitment?
4 I'm the company accountant's secretary.
5 This information makes me more optimistic.

### 81

1 A: So, what is your job exactly?
B: I write market reports about the chemical industry.
A: How do you do that?
B: I talk to people in the industry. I read articles and obviously I follow the markets.
A: What sort of equipment do you use?
B: Well, there are some good Internet sites which give a lot of information. In fact sometimes there is too much information. And I also use teletext on my TV. My doctor says I spend too much time in front of a screen, but I don't really have a choice.
A: Where do you work?
B: I work at home near Oxford. When I lived in France I had an office in Paris, but I moved to England two years ago, and found I could do the job from home. I have a very small office with my fax, my phone, and my PC. In fact, it's not really big enough for me and all my equipment, but I manage somehow.
A: And do you work normal office hours?
B: Yes. I start at about nine and work until three thirty. This gives me enough time to go and pick up the children.

A: So no business lunches?
B: No, unfortunately. It's usually a quick sandwich in the kitchen, then back upstairs. It was nice before to have lunch with contacts or colleagues, but now I waste less time. Now, I only speak to colleagues on the phone. Sometimes it's too quiet in my office.
A: So do you prefer the traditional way of working?
B: It depends. I feel I work more efficiently at home because in an office there are too many distractions, but I do miss the contact with colleagues.
B: Thank you.

2 A: You are a market analyst I believe.
C: That's right. I work in Brussels and I analyse the petroleum market.
A: What sort of office do you have?
C: It's a very modern open-plan office. It has work-stations for about twenty people in one large area.
A: Surely that's too many people?
C: Not really. In the morning there are usually about fifteen people, but after lunch there are fewer. When you arrive you take a space that is free. If you don't arrive early enough, you don't get the best places – next to the window!
A: Isn't it very noisy?
C: Not really. And anyway it is good to hear other conversations. It helps you to know what's happening on different markets and with different customers.
A: What about lunch?
C: We usually take customers and contacts to lunch. It's a good way of getting information. When I have enough data I write my reports.
A: What sort of equipment do you have?
C: Computer screens with direct online data from the markets. Everyone has a lap-top and a phone. That way they can work anywhere.
A: So what are your normal hours?
C: I start really early at about seven, and I finish at about seven p.m. And then I go for a drink with my colleagues. I get home at about nine, which my wife thinks is too late!

### 82

1 A: That was very nice. I'll get the bill.
B: No, this is on me. You can pay next time.

A: Oh, that's very kind of you. It's been a very pleasant evening.
B: I enjoyed it too.

2 C: See you tomorrow!
D: Yes. Have a nice evening.

3 E: OK. I've really enjoyed studying with you.
F: Me too. See you next year, maybe.
E: I hope so. Anyway, have a safe journey back.
F: You too. Bye.
E: Bye.

4 G: Thank you very much for coming. It was very interesting.
H: Thank you for giving me the time. Shall I call you next week?
G: No, that's OK. Just send the price list. I'll get back to you.

5 I: So, is that your best offer?
J: I'm sorry, I can't go any lower.
I: In that case, we accept your terms.
J: Thank you. I'll write to confirm everything.

6 K: So that brings me to the end of what I have to say. Now, does anybody have any questions?

### 83a

1 Thanks for coming.
2 Goodnight. See you tomorrow.
3 I hope to see you next week.
4 Thanks for everything.
5 Have a safe journey.
6 See you on Monday.
7 It's been a lovely evening.
8 This is on me.

### 83b

1 A: Thanks for coming.
B: Thanks for the invitation.
2 C: Goodnight. See you tomorrow.
D: Yes. Sleep well.
3 E: I hope to see you next week.
F: I hope so too.
4 G: Thanks for everything.
H: It was a pleasure.
5 I: Have a safe journey!
J: Thanks.
6 K: See you on Monday.
L: Yes. Have a nice weekend.
7 M: It's been a lovely evening.
N: Thank you. It was nice to see you again.
8 O: This is on me.
P: That's very kind of you.

# Glossary

| (abbrev) | abbreviation | (adv) | adverb | (Brit) | British English | (n pl) | plural noun | (n) [U] | uncountable noun |
|----------|--------------|-------|--------|--------|-----------------|---------|--------------|----------|------------------|
| (adj) | adjective | (Am) | American English | (n) | noun | (n) pers | noun to describe a person | (vb) | verb |

an **accountant** (n) pers 4.3 /ə'kaʊntənt/ a person who keeps or checks the financial records of a business. Also an **accounts** department (n)

to **acquire** (vb) 8.3 /ə'kwaɪə(r)/ to buy another company, e.g. *Vodafone acquired Mannesmann in 2000.* Also an **acquisition**

**advertising** (n) 1.2 /'ædvə,taɪzɪŋ/ information used to sell a product or service. Also to **advertise** (vb) an **advertisement / advert / ad** (n)

to **afford** (vb) 8.2 /ə'fɔːd/ to be able to do something because you have enough money, e.g. *I can't afford to go on holiday this year.*

**age group** (n) 9.2 /'eɪdʒ gruːp/ people of the same age, e.g. *the 18-25 age group*

an **agenda** (n) 7.3 /ə'dʒendə/ a list of points to be discussed at a meeting

to **agree** (vb) 7.3 /ə'griː/to have the same opinion, e.g. *I agree with you. Do you agree? I don't agree.*

an **analyst** (n) 11.1 /'ænəlɪst/ a person who examines something in detail to learn something about it, e.g. *a systems / market analyst*

to **apologize** (n) 6.3 /ə'pɒlədʒaɪz/ to say sorry. Also an **apology** (n) e.g. *to make an apology*

an **application** (n) 12.2 /,æplɪ'keɪʃn/ a computer program, e.g. *a word-processing application*

to **apply for** (vb) 11.1 /ə'plaɪ ,fɔː(r)/ to ask formally in writing, e.g. *to apply for a job.* Also an **application** (n) an **applicant** (n) pers

to **appoint** (vb) 8.1 /ə'pɔɪnt/ to choose a person for a job. Also an **appointment** (n), e.g. *Congratulations on your new appointment.*

an **appointment** (n) 2.1 /ə'pɔɪntmənt/ a meeting at an agreed time and place, e.g. *I have an appointment with my bank manager.*

an **arrangement** (n) 6.1 /ə'reɪndʒmənt/ an agreed plan. Also to **arrange** (vb), e.g. *We arranged to meet at 6 p.m.*

to **attend** (vb) 4.1 /ə'tend/ to be present at, e.g. *to attend a meeting / conference, etc.*

**attractions** (n pl) 2.2 /ə'trækʃnz/ the places of interest in a city, region or country, e.g. *tourist attractions*

**baggage** (n) [U] 2.3 /'bægɪdʒ/ suitcases, travel bags, etc., e.g. *At*

*the end of the flight, you collect your suitcase from the baggage claim.*

to be **based** (vb) 1.3 /'beɪst/ where an organization (or person) has its main office, e.g. *The company is based in Geneva.*

a **bill** (n) 3.3 /bɪl/ (in a restaurant, hotel, etc.) the piece of paper which shows the price to pay

to **board** (vb) 2.3 /bɔːd/ to get on a plane. Also a **boarding** card (n)

to **book** (vb) 4.1 /bʊk/ to reserve a flight, hotel, etc. Also **booked** (adj), e.g. *This hotel is fully booked.*

to **borrow** (vb) 8.2 /'bɒrəʊ/ to take something for a short time and give it back later, e.g. *Can I borrow your pen for a minute?*

a **branch** (n) 9.2 /brɑːntʃ/ an office, shop etc. which is part of a larger organization, e.g. *We have branches in 30 cities.*

a **brand** (n) 8.3 /brænd/ a commercial name used by a company for itself or its products, e.g. *Nescafé is a famous brand of coffee.*

a **break** (n) 10.2 /breɪk/ a pause or interruption in an activity, e.g. *We have a 15-minute coffee break every morning.*

to **bring forward** (vb) 6.3 /,brɪŋ 'fɔːwəd/ to change a meeting, etc. to an earlier time or date

a **brochure** (n) 10.3 /'brəʊʃə(r)/ a document of several pages with illustrations, used to advertise a company's products or services

to **build** (vb) 5.1 /bɪld/ to construct a house, factory, etc. Also a **building** (n)

a **business centre** (n) 2.1 /'bɪznɪs ,sentə(r)/ a special room, often in a hotel, equipped with fax machines, computers, telephones, etc.

**busy** (adj) 4.2 /'bɪzi/ not free (for a person or telephone line)

to **cancel** (vb) 6.3 /'kænsl/ to decide that something you have arranged will not happen, e.g. *We have to cancel the meeting.* Also a **cancellation** (n)

a **candidate** (n) pers 11.1 /'kændɪdət/ a person who applies for a job

a **career** (n) 10.2 /kə'rɪə(r)/ the development and progress of your professional life

to **carry out** (vb) 7.2 /,kæri'aʊt/ to do (a job or task), e.g. *We carried out a market study.*

**cash** (n) [U] 9.2 /kæʃ/ money in notes and coins, e.g. *Payment in cash only. No cheques or credit cards.*

a **cashier** (n) pers 7.2 /kæ'ʃɪə(r)/ the person who receives your payment in a shop or supermarket

a **cashpoint** (n) 2.2 /'kæʃpɔɪnt/ an automatic machine, usually outside a bank, for giving or receiving money

**catering** (n) [U] 9.1 /'keɪtərɪŋ/ the business of serving food, e.g. *McDonald's is a catering business.*

a **central unit** (n) 12.2 /,sentrəl 'juːnɪt/ the main part of a computer which processes information

**charge** (n) 4.3 /tʃɑːdʒ/ responsibility for, e.g. *He's in charge of the Personnel Department.*

to **check** (vb) 3.1 /tʃek/ to look at something to see if it is correct, e.g. *I'll check the reservation details on the computer.*

to **check in** (vb) 2.1 /tʃek 'ɪn/ to arrive and register at a hotel, airport, etc. Also to **check out** (vb), e.g. *You pay your hotel bill when you check out.*

a **checkout** (n) 7.2 /'tʃekaʊt/ the place in a shop or supermarket where you pay

a **competitor** (n) 1.2 /kəm'petɪtə(r)/ another company which sells the same products or services as you. Also to **compete** (vb) **competitive** (adj) a **competition** (n)

to **complain** (vb) 9.3 /kəm'pleɪn/ to say you are not happy with something. Also a **complaint** (n), e.g. *to make a complaint*

a **component** (n) 1.3 /kəm'pəʊnənt/ a basic part or element of a machine

to **computerize** (vb) 12.1 /kəm'pjuːtəraɪz/ to make a process automatic with the help of computers

a **conference** (n) 2.1 /'kɒnfərəns/ a special meeting where a lot of people discuss their work or interests, e.g. *an annual sales conference*

to **confirm** (vb) 2.1 /kən'fɜːm/ to say again that you agree with a date, meeting, reservation, etc. Also **confirmation** (n), e.g. *a letter of confirmation*

**consumption** (n) [U] 5.2 /kən'sʌmpʃn/ the quantity of products used, e.g. *Consumption of wine is decreasing in France.* Also a **consumer** (n) pers to **consume** (vb)

a **contract** (n) 5.3 /'kɒntrækt/ a written legal agreement between two people or companies, e.g. *a work / sales contract*

**convenient** (adj) 6.3 /kən'viːnɪənt/ easy or suitable, e.g. *Is Thursday convenient for a meeting?*

to **co-ordinate** (vb) 11.2 /kəʊ'ɔːdɪneɪt/ to manage all the different parts of a task and the people doing them

a **cost** (n) 5.2 /kɒst/ the amount of money you pay for something, e.g. *the cost of living.* Also to **cost** (vb), e.g. *The ticket costs £35.*

a **course** (n) 4.3 /kɔːs/ a series of lessons, e.g. *a management training course*

a **covering letter** (n) 11.1 /,kʌvərɪŋ 'letə(r)/ a letter, usually handwritten, that you send with your CV when you apply for a job

to **create** (vb) 8.3 /kri'eɪt/ to make something new, e.g. *He created the company in 1988.* Also **creative** (adj), e.g. *A writer has to be creative.*

a **credit note** (n) 9.3 /'kredɪt ,nəʊt/ a document you send to a customer when they have paid too much, as an alternative to paying the money back

a **currency** (n) 9.2 /'kʌrənsi/ the money of a country, e.g. *The dollar is the currency of the USA.*

a **customer** (n) pers 1.2 /'kʌstəmə(r)/ a person or company who buys your products or services, e.g. *a customer service department*

**customs** (n) [U] 2.3 /'kʌstəmz/ the place in an airport, port, etc. where your luggage is sometimes checked, e.g. *He's a customs officer at JFK Airport.*

**CV** (abbrev) 11.2 /ˌsiː 'viː/ a curriculum vitae - a document with information about your education and work experience, used when applying for a job

a **database** (n) 7.2 /'deɪtə,beɪs/ an organized list of information (names, addresses, etc.) on a computer

to **deal with** (vb) 10.2 /'diːl wɪð/ to do what is necessary to resolve a problem, complaint, etc.

to **decrease** (vb) 5.2 /dɪ'kriːs/ to go down, e.g. *Our turnover decreased from 3m to 2m last year.* Also a **decrease** (n) /'diːkriːs/

a **degree** (n) 11.1 /dɪ'griː/ an official diploma from a university or similar institute, e.g. *an MBA / a Law degree*

to **deliver** (vb) 1.3 /dɪ'lɪvə(r)/ to take or send goods to a particular place, e.g. *We will deliver the new machine on 13th August.* Also a **delivery** (n)

a **department** (n) 4.3 /dɪ'pɑːtmənt/ a part of a company which has a particular function, e.g. *the sales / personnel department*

a **department store** (*n*) 2.3 /dɪˈpɑːtmənt ˌstɔː(r)/ a big shop which sells many different kinds of goods

**departure** (*n*) [U] 2.3 /dɪˈpɑːtʃə(r)/ the action or time of leaving, e.g. *Our departure time will be 2.30 p.m.* Also a **departure** gate / lounge (in an airport) (*n*)

to **design** (*vb*) 1.1 /dɪˈzaɪn/ to draw plans for something, e.g. *An architect designs new houses.* Also a **designer** (*n*) *pers*

a **dessert** (*n*) 3.3 /dɪˈzɜːt/ a sweet dish or course in a meal, usually served last

to **develop** (*vb*) 5.1 /dɪˈveləp/ to change something to make it better or larger, e.g. *We are developing faster and more efficient machines.* Also **development** (*n*)

**direct mailing** (*n*) [U] 9.2 /ˌdaɪrekt ˈmeɪlɪŋ/ a form of advertising where you send information by post to specific people or companies

to **disagree** (*vb*) 7.3 /ˌdɪsəˈɡriː/ to have a different opinion, e.g. *I disagree with you.*

a **discount** (*n*) 10.1 /ˈdɪskaʊnt/ an amount of money taken off the normal price, e.g. *We can give you a discount of 20%.*

to **discover** (*vb*) 8.1 /dɪˈskʌvə(r)/ to find something new, often by accident, e.g. *Columbus discovered America.*

a **dish** (*n*) 3.3 /dɪʃ/ a particular kind of food, prepared in a certain way, e.g. *Paella is a Spanish dish.*

to **dismiss** (*vb*) 11.3 /dɪsˈmɪs/ to tell someone they can no longer keep their job, e.g. *The company dismissed him for bad results.*

to **dispatch** (*vb*) 9.3 /dɪˈspætʃ/ to send something to a destination

a **distributor** (*n*) *pers* 9.2 /dɪˈstrɪbjətə(r)/ a person or company who transports or sells the goods (usually of another company) Also to **distribute** (*vb*) **distribution** (*n*)

a **dividend** (*n*) 8.2 /ˈdɪvɪdend/ a part of a company's profits paid to shareholders, usually once or twice a year

a **division** (*n*) 4.3 /dɪˈvɪʒn/ a part of a company that is responsible for a certain product, service or area, e.g. *the telecommunications / Asia Pacific division*

**due** (*adj*) 6.2 /djuː/ expected (at a particular time), e.g. *He's due back in the office at 2 pm. The train is due at 11.37.*

**early** (*adj*) 7.1 /ˈɜːli/ before the agreed time, e.g. *There was no traffic on the road, so he arrived 15 minutes early.*

to **earn** (*vb*) 8.2 /ɜːn/ to receive money for work or in payment for a loan, e.g. *to earn a salary / interest*

an **elevator** (*n*) 3.1 /ˈelɪveɪtə(r)/ (*Am*) an apparatus in a building that carries you from one floor to another (*Brit* = lift)

an **employee** (*n*) *pers* 1.2 /ɪmˈplɔɪiː/ a person who works for a company. Also to **employ** (*vb*) an **employer** (*n*) *pers*

**engaged** (*adj*) 9.1 /ɪnˈɡeɪdʒd/ busy, not free (on the telephone), e.g. *I'm afraid the line's engaged.*

to **enjoy** (*vb*) 3.2 /ɪnˈdʒɔɪ/ to take pleasure in something, e.g. *I enjoy playing tennis at weekends.*

to **enter** (1) (*vb*) 5.1 /ˈentə(r)/ to start selling products (in a market), e.g. *We want to enter the South American market.* (2) (*vb*) to put information on a computer, e.g. *to enter text / data*

an **estimate** (*n*) 9.2 /ˈestɪmət/ a calculation of cost, measurement, etc. Also to **estimate** (*vb*) /ˈestɪmeɪt/

an **executive** (*n*) 4.3 /ɪɡˈzekjətɪv/ a person in a management position in a company, e.g. *a senior executive*

to **expand** (*vb*) 1.3 /ɪkˈspænd/ to get bigger, e.g. *Our market in Eastern Europe is expanding.* Also **expansion** (*n*)

to **expect** (*vb*) 6.2 /ɪkˈspekt/ to believe / think that something will happen, e.g. *We expect him to be back by 3.00.*

**experience** (*n*) [U] 11.1 /ɪkˈspɪəriəns/ knowledge and skills obtained by practice of an activity, e.g. *He has a lot of experience of sales.*

**express** (*adj*) 9.3 /ɪkˈspres/ delivered quickly, e.g. *We sent the letter by express mail.*

an **extension** (*n*) 6.2 /ɪkˈstenʃn/ a telephone number in a person's office, e.g. *Can I have extension 243, please?*

**facilities** (*n pl*) 2.1 /fəˈsɪlɪtiz/ buildings, equipment, etc. for a particular function, e.g. *hotel / conference / sports facilities*

a **factory** (*n*) 1.2 /ˈfæktəri/ a building with machines where goods are made

to **fail** (*vb*) 4.1 /feɪl/ to be unsuccessful, not to obtain what was wanted, e.g. *to fail an exam / test*

to **fall** (*vb*) 5.2 /fɔːl/ to go down, e.g. *Sales fell from 3m to 2 m last year.* Also a **fall** (*n*)

a **figure** (*n*) 5.2 /ˈfɪɡə(r)/ a number in a table, graph, etc., e.g. *sales / production figures*

a **filing cabinet** (*n*) 10.3 /ˈfaɪlɪŋ ˌkæbɪnət/ a piece of furniture with drawers used for keeping documents organized

a **fitness room** (*n*) 2.1 /ˈfɪtnəs ˌruːm/ a small gymnasium, usually in a hotel, with equipment for taking exercise

**flexible** (*adj*) 10.2 /ˈfleksɪbl/ (of schedules, etc.) can be changed easily, e.g. *flexible working hours*

a **flight** (*n*) 2.2 /flaɪt/ a journey by plane. Also to **fly** (*vb*)

a **floor** (*n*) 3.1 /flɔː(r)/ a level in a building, e.g. *My office is on the ground / first floor.*

**fluent** (*adj*) 11.2 /ˈfluːənt/ able to speak easily and without hesitation, e.g. *a fluent English speaker*

to **forecast** (*vb*) 9.2 /ˈfɔːkɑːst/ to predict, usually based on experience or scientific study. Also a **forecast** (*n*)

a **founder** (*n*) *pers* 1.1 /ˈfaʊndə(r)/ the person who creates a company or organization. Also to **found** (*vb*)

**friendly** (*adj*) 5.3 /ˈfrendli/ pleasant, ready to help, e.g. *The staff in the hotel are very friendly.*

the **general public** (*n*) [U] 9.2 /ˌdʒenrəl ˈpʌblɪk/ ordinary people who are not members of a special group, e.g. *We sell to the general public.*

to **get back** (*vb*) 4.2 /ɡetˈbæk/to return (to your starting point) , e.g. *I got back to my house at 11 p.m.*

to **graduate** (*vb*) 8.1 /ˈɡrædʒuˌeɪt/ to finish your studies at university, e.g. *He graduated from Harvard in 1988.* Also a **graduate** (*n*) *pers* /ˈɡrædʒuət/

a **graph** (*n*) 5.2 /ɡrɑːf/ a diagram showing the relationship between two changing quantities, e.g. *This graph shows our sales month by month last year.*

a **guest** (1) (*n*) *pers* 3.3 /ɡest/ someone you have invited to your house for a meal, etc. (2) (*n*) *pers* a person staying in a hotel

to **hang up** (*vb*) 10.2 /hæŋ ˈʌp/ to put the phone down at the end of a call

the **head office** (*n*) 1.2 /ˌhed ˈɒfɪs/ the main office of a company. Also **headquarters** (*n*)

**hire** (*vb*) 9.1 /ˈhaɪə/ to pay money for something or someone for a short time, e.g. *to hire a car / temporary staff*

a **hoarding** (*n*) 9.2 /ˈhɔːdɪŋ/ (*Brit*) a large board, usually in the street, used for displaying advertisements (*Am* = billboard)

**illegible** (*adj*) 9.3 /ɪˈledʒəbl/ (of a letter or document) impossible to read

to **improve** (*vb*) 4.1 /ɪmˈpruːv/ to get better or make something better, e.g. *He wants to improve his English.* Also an **improvement** (*n*)

an **income** (*n*) 8.2 /ˈɪnkʌm/ the money you earn from all sources (not just salary), e.g. *annual income / income tax*

to **increase** (*vb*) 5.2 /ɪnˈkriːs/ to go up, e.g. *Inflation increased from 1% to 1.5% last year.* Also an **increase** (*n*) /ˈɪŋkriːs/

an **interview** (*n*) 1.1 /ˈɪntəvjuː/ a meeting where someone has to answer questions, e.g. *a job / radio interview.* Also to **interview** (*vb*) an **interviewer** (*n*) *pers*

to **introduce** (1) (*vb*) 1.1 /ˌɪntrəˈdjuːs/ (when people meet, etc.) to tell each person the name of the others, e.g. *Can I introduce you to my boss?* (2) (*vb*) to bring something into use for the first time, e.g. *We introduced this product on the market last year.* Also an **introduction** (*n*)

to **invent** (*vb*) 8.3 /ɪnˈvent/ to plan or make something new, e.g. *Akio Morita invented the Sony Walkman.*

to **invest** (*vb*) 8.2 /ɪnˈvest/ to spend money in order to make a profit, e.g. *to invest in the stock market / new machines for the factory.* Also an **investment** (*n*) an **investor** (*n*) *pers*

to **invite** (*vb*) 3.2 /ɪnˈvaɪt/ to ask someone to come somewhere or to do something, e.g. *She invited me for dinner.* Also an **invitation** (*n*)

an **invoice** (*n*) 9.2 /ˈɪnvɔɪs/ a bill, usually between two companies, showing the goods sold and the price to be paid

**IT** (*abbrev*) 9.3 /aɪ ˈtiː/ information technology - relating to computers, e.g. *He's the IT Manager, he's responsible for the IT department.*

an **item** (*n*) 9.3 /ˈaɪtəm/ one in a list of things, e.g. *an item on an order form / invoice / agenda*

to **join** (*vb*) 8.1 /dʒɔɪn/ to start working (for a company), e.g. *She joined Compaq in 1995.*

a **journey** (*n*) 3.1 /ˈdʒɜːni/ the act of going from one place to another, e.g. *The journey took three hours by car.*

a **keyboard** (*n*) 12.2 /ˈkiːbɔːd/ the part of the computer you use to type words and numbers

to **land** (*vb*) 2.3 /lænd/ (of a plane) to arrive at your destination

**late** (*adj / adv*) 7.1 /leɪt/ after the expected or usual time, e.g. *They arrived late, so they missed the meeting.*

to **launch** (*vb*) 7.3 /lɔːntʃ/ to start selling (a new product or service). Also a **launch** (*n*), e.g. *the launch of a new product*

a **lawyer** (*n*) *pers* 4.3 /ˈlɔɪjə(r)/ someone whose job is to help people with legal problems

a **lease** (*n*) 10.1 /liːs/ a written agreement to rent land or property (factory, house, etc.)

to **lend** (vb) 8.2 /lend/ to give for a short time, e.g. *Can you lend me £5, and I'll give it back to you next week?*

a **lift** (1) (n) 2.1 /lɪft/ an apparatus in a building that carries you from one floor to another (*Am* = elevator) (2) (n) transport of a person in another person's car, e.g. *I'll give you a lift to the airport.*

to be **located** (vb) 1.3 /ləʊ'keɪtɪd/ where a building or company is, e.g. *Our factory is located near London.* Also a **location** (n)

to **look for** (vb) 5.1 /'lʊk fɔː(r)/ to try to find, e.g. *He's looking for a new job.*

to **look into** (vb) 9.3 /ˌlʊk'ɪntə/ to investigate or make a study of something, e.g. *I'll look into the problem.*

**luggage** (n) [U] 2.3 /'lʌgɪdʒ/ suitcases, travel bags, etc.

**mail order** (n) [U] 9.2 /ˌmeɪl 'ɔːdə(r)/ the buying of goods (often from a catalogue) which are delivered by post

a **main course** (n) 3.3 /meɪn 'kɔːs/ the principal part of a meal, usually with meat or fish

to **manage** (1) (vb) 6.3 /'mænɪdʒ/ to be free (for a meeting or appointment), e.g. *I can't manage Monday.* (2) (vb) to be in charge of a company, department, etc.

the **Managing Director** (n) *pers* 4.3 /ˌmænɪdʒɪŋ daɪ'rektə(r)/ a top manager in a company, just under the Chairman or President (*Am* = CEO [Chief Executive Officer])

a **manual** (n) 9.3 /'mænjʊəl/ a book that tells you how something works, e.g. *an instruction manual*

to **manufacture** (vb) 1.3 /ˌmænjʊ'fæktʃə(r)/ to make something in large quantities using machines, e.g. *We manufacture cars.* Also a **manufacturer** (n) *pers*

a **market** (n) 1.2 /'mɑːkɪt/ a geographical area, or section of the population, where you can sell products, e.g. *We operate in the Asian / export / under-25s market.*

a **market share** (n) 1.3 /ˌmɑːkɪt 'ʃeə(r)/ a percentage of the total sales of a product obtained by one company, e.g. *We have a 20% share of the PC market in Europe.*

**marketing** (n) [U] 1.1 /'mɑːkɪtɪŋ/ the theory and practice of selling (in large quantities)

a **meal** (n) 3.2 /miːl/ food that you eat at a certain time of day, e.g. *Breakfast, lunch and dinner are meals.*

a **meeting** (n) 2.1 /'miːtɪŋ/ an occasion when two or more people come together to discuss something. Also to **meet** (vb)

a **menu** (n) 3.3 /'menjuː/ a list of things to eat in a restaurant, hotel, etc.

a **mouse** (n) 12.2 /maʊs/ part of the computer you use to select an operation without using the keyboard

to **move** (vb) 10.1 /muːv/ to change your house, business address, etc., e.g. *The company moved to Seattle in 1979.*

a **need** (n) 11.3 /niːd/ what a company / person wants, e.g. *You have to listen to meet the needs of your customers.* Also to **need** (vb), e.g. *We need some more photocopy paper.*

to **notice** (vb) 5.2 /'nəʊtɪs/ to see or observe, e.g. *I noticed that his car wasn't in the car park.*

**open-plan** (adj) 4.3 /ˌəʊpən 'plæn/ (of an office building) having no walls between individual offices

to **operate** (vb) 5.1 /'ɒpəreɪt/ to do business, e.g. *ICL operates in three different markets.*

to **order** (vb) 3.3 /'ɔːdə(r)/ to make a request for goods, e.g. *to order a meal in a restaurant / something from a company.* Also an **order** (n)

an **outlet** (n) 1.3 /'aʊtlət/ a place where goods can be sold, e.g. *a sales / distribution outlet*

to **overcharge** (vb) 9.3 /ˌəʊvə'tʃɑːdʒ/ to ask a price which is too high, e.g. *They overcharged me for the wine.*

an **overhead projector** (n) 9.1 /ˌəʊvəhed prə'dʒektə(r)/ an apparatus for projecting images, text, etc. on the wall at presentations (*abbrev* = OHP)

to **owe** (vb) 8.2 /əʊ/ to be in a situation where you have to pay (back) money to someone, e.g. *We owe our suppliers $3,000.*

to **own** (vb) 5.1 /əʊn/ to have something which is yours, e.g. *Do you own your house, or do you rent it?* Also an **owner** (n) *pers*

to **park** (vb) 2.3 /pɑːk/ to put or leave your car, lorry, etc. somewhere for a time.

a **parent company** (n) 1.3 /'peərənt ˌkʌmpəni/ the head company in a group

to **participate** (vb) 11.2 /pɑː'tɪsɪpeɪt/ to play a part or role in something, e.g. *He participated in the meeting.*

to **pass** (vb) 4.1 /pɑːs/ to be successful, e.g. *to pass an exam / test*

a **Personal Assistant** (n) *pers* 4.3 /ˌpɜːsənl ə'sɪstənt/ the secretary of a manager in a company. (*abbrev* = PA)

**pessimistic** (adj) 9.2 /ˌpesɪ'mɪstɪk/ believing that the worst possible thing will happen, e.g. *She's pessimistic about the future of the company.*

to **pick up** (1) (vb) 10.2 /pɪk'ʌp/ to take hold of and lift something, e.g. *to pick up the phone when it rings.* (2) (vb) 12.2 to collect a person from a place in your car, e.g. *I picked up my wife at the station.*

a **pie chart** (n) 5.2 /'paɪ tʃɑːt/ a circle divided into sections showing the percentage of different activities, figures, etc.

a **pioneer** (n) *pers* 8.1 /ˌpaɪə'nɪə(r)/ the first person (or company) to begin a new area of study, invent a new product, etc., e.g. *Alexander Graham Bell was the pioneer of the telephone.*

to **place** (vb) 9.3 /pleɪs/ to make (an order for something), e.g. *I'd like to place an order for 300 machine parts.*

a **plan** (n) 1.3 /plæn/ an idea or arrangement for the future. Also to **plan** (vb)

to **postpone** (vb) 6.3 /pə'spəʊn/ to change to a later date, e.g. *He postponed the meeting from the 13th to the 15th.*

**PR** (*abbrev*) 4.3 /piː 'ɑː(r)/ public relations – official communication between a company and the media / public, in order to present the best image

to **predict** (vb) 9.2 /prɪ'dɪkt/ to say what you think will happen in the future. Also a **prediction** (n)

**premises** (n pl) 10.1 /'premɪsɪz/ the land and buildings occupied by a company

to **present** (vb) 1.1 /prɪ'zent/ to show or talk about something in an organized way, e.g. *They presented their new sales strategy at the sales conference.* Also a **presentation** (n)

the **President** (n) *pers* 1.3 /'prezɪdənt/ (*Am*) the highest position in a company, above the CEO (*Brit* = Chairman)

to **print** (vb) 9.1 /prɪnt/ to make a copy on paper, e.g. *He wrote the letter on the computer, then printed it.* Also a (laser / inkjet) **printer** (n) a **printer** (n) *pers*

to **produce** (vb) 1.1 /prə'djuːs/ to make something (to sell later), e.g. *We produce shirts for the European market.* Also a **product** (n) **production** (n) [U] **producer** (n) *pers*

a **project** (n) 4.3 /'prɒdʒekt/ a plan, e.g. *They have a new construction project in Argentina.*

**punctuality** (n) [U] 10.2 /ˌpʌŋktʃu'æləti/ being on time, e.g. *Punctuality is important at work.* Also **punctual** (adj)

**purchasing** (n) 4.3 /'pɜːtʃɪsɪŋ/ the act of buying goods; the department in a company which does this. Also to **purchase** (vb)

to **put through** (vb) 6.2 /pʊt 'θruː/ (on the telephone) to connect someone to another person in the same company

e.g. *I'll put you through to the sales department.*

a **qualification** (n) 11.1 /ˌkwɒlɪfɪ'keɪʃn/ a certificate, diploma, etc. that you receive as a result of successfully completing a course or passing an exam. Also **qualified** (adj), e.g. *to be well qualified*

**quality** (1) (n) 4.3 /'kwɒləti/ how good something is, e.g. *The quality of our service is improving all the time.* (2) (n) 11.1 something that is special about a person or thing, e.g. *His personal qualities include patience and adaptability.*

a **quotation** (n) 10.3 /kwəʊ'teɪʃn/ an estimate of cost for a product or service. Also a **quote** (n) to **quote** (vb)

a **range** (n) 1.3 /reɪndʒ/ a group of products sold by one company, e.g. *our new product range*

a **rate** (n) 5.2 /reɪt/ the level of something, or how fast something happens, e.g. *bank interest rates, the rate of inflation*

a **raw material** (n) 4.3 /ˌrɔː mə'tɪərɪəl/ the basic products you need to make or manufacture something, e.g. *Rubber is a raw material for tyres.*

a **receipt** (n) 3.3 /rɪ'siːt/ a paper you receive to confirm that you have paid for something

to **recommend** (vb) 3.3 /ˌrekə'mend/ to suggest or give advice, e.g. *Can you recommend a good restaurant?*

to **record** (vb) 7.2 /rɪ'kɔːd/ to make a note of something, e.g. *He recorded the details on the computer.* Also a **record** (n) /'rekɔːd/, e.g. *to keep a record of all transactions*

**recruitment** (n) [U] 4.3 /rɪ'kruːtmənt/ the process of finding new employees. Also to **recruit** (vb)

to **reduce** (vb) 10.1 /rɪ'djuːs/ to make smaller in size or number, e.g. *We have reduced our workforce from 30 to 25 people.* Also a **reduction** (n)

**redundant** (adj) 11.3 /rɪ'dʌndənt/ no longer having a job because there is no more work available, e.g. *The company made him redundant.* Also a **redundancy** (n), e.g. *a redundancy payment*

a **regulation** (n) 10.2 /ˌregjʊ'leɪʃn/ a rule to be followed (for a company or organization)

to **remember** (vb) 6.3 /rɪ'membə(r)/ to keep something in your mind; not forget

to **remind** (vb) 9.1 /rɪ'maɪnd/ to tell somebody not to forget something. Also a **reminder** (n), e.g. *He received a reminder to pay the last month's bill.*

the **rent** (n) 7.1 /rent/ the money paid to use something. Also to

**rent** (*vb*) an office, car, etc.

a **reply** (*n*) 6.2 /rɪˈplaɪ/ a written or spoken answer, e.g. *There's no reply.* (on the phone) *Thank you for your quick reply.* (in a letter) Also to **reply** (*vb*)

a **report** (*n*) 4.2 /rɪˈpɔːt/ a written or spoken statement about an event, meeting, etc.

a **representative** (*n*) *pers* 4.3 /ˌreprɪˈzentətɪv/ a person who promotes an organization or sells its products, e.g. *a sales representative* (abbrev = rep)

a **request** (*n*) 2.1 /rɪˈkwest/ something you ask for, e.g. *a request for information* Also to **request** (*vb*)

**research** (*n*) [U] 4.3 /rɪˈsɜːtʃ/ a careful and detailed study of something, e.g. *the research and development department* (abbrev = R & D ). Also to **research** (*vb*)

to **reserve** (*vb*) 2.1 /rɪˈzɜːv/ to ask (and pay for) a hotel room, travel ticket, etc. Also a **reservation** (*n*), e.g. *to make a reservation*

to **resign** (*vb*) 8.1 /rɪˈzaɪn/ to leave or give up a job or a responsibilty, e.g. *He resigned from the company.* Also a **resignation** (*n*)

to **resolve** (*vb*) 7.2 /rɪˈzɒlv/ to find a solution to a problem

**responsible** (*adj*) 4.3 /rɪˈspɒnsɪbl/ in charge of something, e.g. *She's responsible for sales.* Also a **responsibility** (*n*) [U] e.g. *to have responsibility for something*

**retired** (*adj*) 9.2 /rɪˈtaɪəd/ no longer working because you are old. Also to **retire** (*vb*) **retirement** (*n*), e.g. *to take early retirement*

**return** (*n*) 8.1 act of going and coming back, e.g. *a return ticket / journey.* Also to **return** (*vb*)

to **rise** (*vb*) 5.2 /raɪz/ to go up, e.g. *Our market share rose from 5% to 7% last year.* Also a **rise** (*n*)

to **run** (*vb*) 8.2 /rʌn/ to manage (a company)

**safe** (*adj*) 7.1 /seɪf/ not dangerous, e.g. *Have a safe journey.* Also **safety** (*n*) [U]

a **salary** (*n*) 11.1 /ˈsæləri/ the money you earn from your job

**sales** (*n pl*) 1.2 /ˈseɪlz/ the number of products sold by a company, or the total value of products sold, e.g. *We have sales of £3 million.*

to **save** (1) (*vb*) 8.2 /seɪv/ to keep money (e.g. in a bank) to buy something later, e.g. *I'm saving money for my next holiday.* (2) (*vb*) to find ways not to spend money, e.g. *We save money by travelling Economy Class on flights.*

a **scanner** (*n*) 7.2 /ˈskænə(r)/ a machine which photographs images, text, etc. to be copied on a computer

a **schedule** (*n*) 2.2 /ˈʃedjuːl/ a plan of work, a visit, etc., with times and dates

**self-employed** (*adj*) 12.1 /ˌself ɪmˈplɔɪd/ working for yourself (not for a company or organization)

to **serve** (1) (*vb*) 3.3 /ˈsɜːv/ to put on the table, e.g. *This dish is served with bread.* (2) (*vb*) to help customers in a shop. Also **service** (*n*) [U], e.g. *good / bad service*

a **server** (*n*) 9.3 /ˈsɜːvə(r)/ the central unit of a computer system which links the different PC's in an organization

a **share** (*n*) 5.1 /ʃeə(r)/ part of the capital of a company, e.g. *to buy shares in a company.* Also a **shareholder** (*n*) *pers*

a **shopping centre** (*n*) 9.2 /ˈʃɒpɪŋ ˌsentə(r)/ a group of shops in the same building or area

a **short list** (*n*) 11.1 /ˈʃɔːtlɪst/ a list of candidates for a job selected from a longer list. Also to **shortlist** (*vb*), e.g. *to shortlist candidates*

**sightseeing** (*n*) [U] 2.3 /ˈsaɪtˌsiːɪŋ/ visiting places of interest, e.g. *to go sightseeing in Venice*

**single** (1) (*adj*) 2.1 /ˌsɪŋgl/ for one person, e.g. *a single room.* (2) (*adj*) not married, e.g. *a young, single woman.* (3) (*n*) a one-way ticket for a journey, e.g. *Can I have a single to Boston, please?*

a **skill** (*n*) 12.1 /skɪl/ knowledge or ability in something, e.g. *computer language skills*

a **slide** (*n*) 5.2 /slaɪd/ a film you put in a projector to show an image on a wall or screen

**software** (*n*) [U] 4.3 /ˈsɒftweə(r)/ programmes you use in a computer

to **sort** (*vb*) 11.1 /sɔːt/ to put things in groups

to **spend** (1) (*vb*) 6.3 /spend/ to pay money for something, e.g. *We spent $0.5 m on advertising.* (2) (*vb*) to give time to an activity [U] etc., e.g. *I spent the weekend at my holiday home.*

a **sponsor** (*n*) 1.2 /ˈspɒnsə(r)/ a company which gives money in return for advertising a product. Also to **sponsor** (*vb*)

a **spreadsheet** (*n*) 12.2 /ˈspredʃiːt/ a computer program which organizes and calculates numbers, such as accounts

**stable** (*adj*) 5.2 /ˈsteɪbl/ at the same level, e.g. *Sales remained stable at 3 million.*

a **stake** (*n*) 8.2 /steɪk/ a percentage of the capital of a company, e.g. *They have a 20% stake in YPF.*

a **starter** (*n*) 3.3 /ˈstɑːtə(r)/ the first dish or course of a meal

**stationery** (*n*) [U] 4.3 /ˈsteɪʃənri/ paper, pens, and other things for writing

to **stay** (*vb*) 4.2 /steɪ/ to remain or continue in the same place, e.g. *to stay in a hotel*

a **stock** (*n*) 10.3 /stɒk/ finished goods that you are keeping to sell, e.g. *We keep a large stock.*

a **stock market** (*n*) 8.2 /ˈstɒk mɑːkɪt/ the place where company shares are bought and sold (*Brit* = stock exchange)

a **strike** (*n*) 9.1 /straɪk/ a time when people refuse to work, because they aren't happy with their working conditions, e.g. *to go / be on strike.* Also to **strike** (*vb*)

a **subsidiary** (*n*) 1.3 /səbˈsɪdɪəri/ a company that is owned by another company

**successful** (*adj*) 8.1 /səkˈsesfl/ having good results, e.g. *a successful product / company / person.* Also a **success** (*n*), e.g. *The project was a great success.*

to **suggest** (*vb*) 3.3 /səˈdʒest/ to say what you think can or should be done, e.g. *He suggested going to the new Indian restaurant.* Also a **suggestion** (*n*), e.g. *to make a suggestion*

a **suit** (1) (*n*) 10.2 /suːt/ a jacket with trousers (or a skirt) of the same colour and material. (2) (*vb*) 6.3 to be convenient, e.g. *Does Thursday suit you for the meeting?*

a **supplier** (*n*) 1.2 /səˈplaɪə(r)/ a company which sells goods to another. Also to **supply** (*vb*)

a **table** (*n*) 5.2 /ˈteɪbl/ an organized list of information

to **take off** (*vb*) 2.3 /ˌteɪk ˈɒf/ (of a plane) to leave the ground. Also **take-off** (*n*) /ˈteɪkɒf/, e.g. *Take-off is at 11.30.*

to **take on** (*vb*) 11.3 /teɪk ˈɒn/ to accept responsibility for something, e.g. *to take on a new project*

a **takeover** (*n*) 4.3 /ˈteɪkəʊvə(r)/ the buying of one company by another. Also to **take over** (*vb*) /ˌteɪk ˈəʊvə(r)/

**terms** (*n pl*) 12.3 /tɜːmz/ conditions (of payment, of a contract, etc.)

a **timetable** (*n*) 2.2 /ˈtaɪmteɪbl/ a list of times for trains, planes, etc.

a **tour** (*n*) 4.1 /tʊər/, /tɔː(r)/ a visit - usually guided - to a company, town, etc., e.g. *to go on a tour of New York*

**training** (*n*) [U] 4.3 /ˈtreɪnɪŋ/ learning / teaching of new skills at work, e.g. *a training manager / course.* Also to **train** (*vb*)

to **transfer** (*vb*) 6.2 /trænsˈfɜː(r)/ (on the phone) to connect the caller to another number

a **translator** (*n*) *pers* 10.1 /trænsˈleɪtə(r)/ a person who gives the meaning of words in another language, spoken or written. Also to **translate** (*vb*) a **translation** (*n*)

a **transporter** (*n*) 9.3 /trænsˈpɔːtə(r)/ a company which takes goods by road, air, or boat from one place to another

a **trend** (*n*) 5.2 /trend/ a general direction or tendency, e.g. *The trend in prices is upward.*

a **trip** (*n*) 1.2 /trɪp/ a journey from one place to another, usually including the return, e.g. *How was your business trip to Paris?*

a **turnover** (*n*) 1.3 /ˈtɜːnəʊvə(r)/ the total sales of a company, e.g. *Our annual turnover is $70 million.*

**unemployed** (*adj*) 12.1 /ˌʌnɪmˈplɔɪd/ not having a job, e.g. *He's unemployed.* Also **unemployment** (*n*) [U]

a **union** (*n*) 9.2 /ˈjuːnɪən/ short for trade union – organization which represents the interests of employees

to **update** (*vb*) 7.2 /ʌpˈdeɪt/ to add the most recent information, e.g. *We have updated our address list with this year's new customers.*

a **view** (*n*) 7.3 /vjuː/ an opinion about something, e.g. *What's your view on this? In my view, it's ...*

**waste** (*n*) [U] 9.2 /weɪst/ things that you throw away because they are not useful, e.g. *toxic / nuclear / industrial waste*

**wide** (1) (*adj*) 7.3 /waɪd/ measurement from side to side, e.g. *The road is about 4 m wide.* (2) (*adj*) big, e.g. *a wide range of products*

**word processing** (*n*) [U] 12.2 /ˌwɜːd ˈprəʊsesɪŋ/ the writing of text on a computer, e.g. *a word-processing program*

a **workshop** (*n*) 1.1 /ˈwɜːkʃɒp/ a place where you make things, usually by hand

a **work-station** (*n*) 10.2 /ˈwɜːkˌsteɪʃn/ a desk with a computer in a company office

**worth** (*adj*) 8.2 /wɜːθ/ to have a value of, e.g. *This painting is worth £2m.*

# OXFORD

UNIVERSITY PRESS

Great Clarendon Street, Oxford OX2 6DP

Oxford University Press is a department of the
University of Oxford. It furthers the University's
objective of excellence in research, scholarship,
and education by publishing worldwide in

Oxford  New York

Auckland  Cape Town  Dar es Salaam  Hong Kong
Karachi  Kuala Lumpur  Madrid  Melbourne
Mexico City  Nairobi  New Delhi  Shanghai  Taipei
Toronto

With offices in

Argentina  Austria  Brazil  Chile  Czech Republic
France  Greece  Guatemala  Hungary  Italy  Japan
South Korea  Poland  Portugal  Singapore
Switzerland  Thailand  Turkey  Ukraine  Vietnam

OXFORD and OXFORD ENGLISH are registered
trade marks of Oxford University Press in the UK
and in certain other countries

ACKNOWLEDGEMENTS

*The authors and publisher are grateful to those who
have given permission to reproduce the following
extracts and adaptations of copyright material:* pp 6,7
Information about Dielle S.r.l. & Lorella Braglia.
Reproduced by permission of Lorella Braglia. p 10
Extracts from www.nokia.com. Reproduced by
permission of Nokia. p 14 'Pizza hut to create
3,500 jobs' by Dominic Rush. Appeared in *The
Sunday Times* 17 January 1999. © Times
Newspapers Ltd 1999. Reproduced by permission
of Times Newspapers Ltd. p 16 Extracts from
www.swatchgroup.com. Reproduced by permission of Swatch S.A. p 19 Information about The
Century Park Hotel, Thailand. Reproduced by permission of The Century Park Hotel. p 37 'The
Loire Valley: A taste of the chateau lifestyle' from
www.headline-vents.co.uk/chateau_life_style.htm.
Reproduced by permission of Headline Event
Management Ltd. pp 56,57 Extracts from
www.Repsol.com. Reproduced by permission of

Repsol YPF. pp 84,85 'Scanner prices vegetables'
by Mark Prigg. Appeared in *The Sunday Times* 3
October 1999. © Times Newspapers Ltd.
Reproduced by permission of Times Newspapers
Ltd. p 90 'Pilot of the jet age' by Juan Trippe.
Appeared in *Time* 7 December 1998. © Time Inc
1998. Reproduced by permission of Time Life
Syndication. p 92 'BA's brightest star' by Tom
Rubython. Appeared in *Eurobusiness Magazine* June
1999. Reproduced by permission of Eurobusiness
Magazine. p 96 'The prince who saves Europe's
capitalist monuments' by Oliver Edwards and
Vernon Silver. Appeared in *Eurobusiness Magazine*
June 1999. Reproduced by permission of
Eurobusiness Magazine. p 98 Information about
McDonald's. Reproduced by permission of
McDonald's Restaurants Ltd. p 107 Extracts from
www.casio.com/timepieces. Reproduced by per-
mission of Casio Electronics Co. Ltd. p 118 'Real
men work part time – that includes the ref.' by
Widget Finn. Appeared in *The Sunday Telegraph* 13
June 1999. Reproduced by permission of
Telegraph Syndication. pp 122,124 Information
about Laporta. Reproduced by permission of
Antonio Laporta.

*Sources:* p 51 Information about Perrier from
'Perrier Vittel S.A. A worldwide leader' Brochure
2000. p 58 Motorola statistics from www.mot.com.
pp 59,60 Social trends statistics from www.statis-
tics.gov.uk. pp 60,61 Statistics on Internet connection from Strategies Group. pp 60,61 Statistics
on Internet use in Asia-Pacific Market from Ernst
and Young Asia-Pacific Economic Outlook 1999-
2009. p 95 Money facts from The Guinness Book
of Records, The Oxford Children's Encyclopaedia
& The Top Ten of Everything 1999 (Dorling
Kindersley). p 97 IKEA from www.bbc.co.uk. p 97
AGF/Alliance from www.agf.fr. p 151 Estée Lauder
history from www.elcompanies.com. p 100 Sony
history from www.sony.com. p 101 Ford Motor
Company history from www.ford.com. p 109
Statistics from 'What future predictions are there
towards teleworking' from www.nbs.ntu.ac.uk. p
109 Climate change statistics from
www.unfccc.de. pp 136,137 Statistics on male and
female bosses from www.gallup.com. p 150
Information about Royal Princess Larn hotel. From
www.hotelguide.com.

*Illustrations by:* Adrian Barclay pp 26, 83, 84. Stefan
Chabluk pp 18, 28, 30, 31, 32, 88, 89, 144. Sarah
Jones/Début Art pp 22, 34, 91, 109. Nigel Paige pp
20, 40, 63, 65, 76, 110, 117, 125, 134, 142. Mike
Stones/Illustration Ltd p 148,149. Technical
Graphics Dept, OUP p 10.

*Commissioned photography by:* Gareth Boden pp 62,
70, 139, 140. Mark Mason pp 38, 49, 75, 92, 103,
122, 140 (notepad), 141.

*The authors and publisher are grateful to the following
for their permission to reproduce photographs and illus-
trative material:* Barker-Evans p 124; Lorella
Braglia/Dielle pp 6, 7; Casio p 107; Century Park
Hotel p 19; Corbis pp 50 (Michael Pole/ Marianna
Tardelli), 78 (Brian Leng/businessman in a car), 106
(Kevin R. Morris/ Dept. Store); Eye Ubiquitous pp
43 (David Forman/ street music), 80 (Michael
George/New York apartment); Getty One Stone pp
9 (Terry Vine/Akiko Takajima), 9 (Tim Brown/
Simon Hastings), 44 (Dan Bosler), 50 (Christopher
Bissel/Daniel Jones), 50 (David Roth/Erica Chang),
50 (Joe Polillio/ Frank Jensch), 50 (Pierre
Shoiniere/Gianni Baresi), 54 (Bob Schatz/ lecturer),
54 (Chad Ehlers/Car production workers), 54 (Jon
Riley/Architect), 54 (Vince Streano/construction
workers), 59 (Jerome Tisne), 66 (John Lund/train),

66 (Ken Biggs/motorway), 72 (Jed and Kaoru Share),
80 (Paul Chesley/ Tokyo apartment), 94 (Laurence
Monneret), 101 (Fred George/Empire State
Building, Hirojuki Matsumoto/ Guggenheim, Lois
and Bob Schlowsky/jeans, Paul Dance/American
Express Card), 102 (Klaus Lahnstein/ Tony Ralph)
106 (Hugh Sitton/ advertising hoarding), 115
(Catherine Ledner/ Dr Biz, Roy Botterell/ Home
office), 120 (Bob Thomas/journalist, Iain
Shaw/teacher, Jon Riley/architect, Klehr Churchill
/receptionist, Stewart Cohen/pilot, Sylvain
Grandadan/ waiter), 126 ( David Joel/accountant,
Timothy Shonnard/ salesperson), 146 (Ken
Fisher/end of meeting/end of interview) 150 (Paul
Chesley/ Bangkok temple); Sally and Richard
Greenhill p 146 (end of social occasion); Hulton
Getty p 69 (Amelia Earhart, Hilary and Tensing);
Hutchison p 78 (Nick Haslam/subway); Image Bank
pp 12(Piecework Products), 54 (Bokelberg, market
researchers), 74 (David Paul Prod), 128 (Jeff
Hunter), 133, 155 (Ulf E. Wallin), 135 (Morrel /
Infoc); James Davies p 80 (Paris apartment); Nokia
pp 10, 11 (Red Consultancy); RGK Penn p 118;
Perrier-Vittel p 51; Pizza Hut p 14; Popperfoto p 69
(Mark Baker/ New Millennium), 101 (Henry Ford);
Repsol pp 56, 57; Rex Features p 96 (Niviere/Abd
Rabbo); Robert Harding Picture Library pp 13 (Nik
Wheeler), 24 (Warsaw Old Town market), 27 (Jeff
Greenberg), 30 (Nigel Francis/taxis), 37 (Roy
Rainford/ château), 66 (Jay Thomas/conference);
Skyscan p 37 (Nick Hanna/hot air balloon); Sony p
86; Swatch p 16; STONE pp 43 (Neil Beer); 146
(Christopher Bissell); Telegraph Colour Library, 50
(Rag Productions Inc/ Carla Dendena), 90 (Valder-
Tormey/ plane); The Stock Market pp 9 (Jose Luis
Pelaez Inc/Sally Kent), 30 (Richard Berenholtz/
street scene), 50 (Jose Pelaez/William Bernstein), 82
(Anthony Redpath/plumber), 126 (Larry Williams/
receptionist); TimePix p 99; UPPB p 92; View p 115
(Chris Gascoigne/ restaurant); West Light p 131
(Mark Adams)